Georges Bernage

The Panzers
in the Battle
of Normandy

5 June to 20 July 1944

EDITIONS HEIMDAL

– Conceived and written by Georges Bernage.

– Production : Jean-Luc Leleu.

– English translation : Anthony Kemp.

– Maps : Bernard Paich.

– Paintings : Erik Groult.

– Lay-out : Francine Gautier.

– Composition : Marie-Claire Passerieu.

– Photogravure : Dominique Alabarbe, Christian Caïra, Christel Lebret, Franck Richard.

– Illustrations : The archives of the Department of Calvados, Bundesarchiv, French Army Photographic Establishment, Imperial War Museum.

Editions Heimdal - Château de Damigny - BP 320 - 14403 BAYEUX Cedex - Tél. : 02.31.51.68.68 - Fax : 02.31.51.68.60 - E-mail : Editions.Heimdal@wanadoo.fr

ISBN 2 84048 135 9

Introduction

On 6 June 1944, six tanks from the 22nd Panzer Regiment managed to reach the coast near Luc-sur-Mer and were forced to retire almost immediately, thus putting an end to the sole German armoured counter-attack on D-Day. Rommel had said that it would be necessary to destroy the Allies on the landing beaches to deny them the chance to establish themselves ashore. In fact, the three months of bitter fighting that ensued, were nothing but a desperate struggle by the Germans to contain the Allied pressure that became more and more irresistible.

Many books have been published about the Battle of Normandy, which is understandable. After the final halting of the advance in the East, caused by the defeat of the German armour in the Kursk salient, the next stage of the war was to be played out on the beaches of Normandy with the opening of a second front which would roll back the German positions in the West and bring the Allies to the *Westwall*. The intention behind this particular book is to help the reader to understand the reasons for the German defeat, when on the evening of 10 June, they had almost 2,000 tanks in the West, quite sufficient for throwing the Allies back into the sea at a time when the latter had few tanks ashore in Normandy. Why the defeat then? Those German units which on paper at least, formed a considerable force, were dispersed and several of them were undergoing reconstition. In May 1940 the French and British tanks were superior in numbers to the Germans, but they were also dispersed and when the panzers attacked where they were not expected, the effect of surprise nullified the Allies' superiority as they were unable to concentrate their armoured forces in time where they were needed. In June 1944, Operation "Fortitude" was a great success in that the Allied disinformation completely confused the Germans who themselves contributed to the confusion by greatly underestimating their adversaries' strength - they expected a landing in the Pas-de-Calais and insisted in believing for almost six weeks that the operation in Normandy was a diversion. A considerable proportion of the Panzer units available were only released when it was far too late to accomplish the mission expected of them.

As for those that were sent to the front during the first days, the distances they had to travel and the total air superiority enjoyed by the Allies, considerably slowed their progress. The acuteness of the situation, however, resulted in their being thrown into the front line in widely dispersed penny packets. The concentration of force which lay behind the German doctrine for the employment of armour, was never achieved and because of that they never had a realistic chance of ejecting the invaders. As of 10 June, for the Germans the battle was already lost.

Spread out all over the place the panzer units trickled into the front line, where their actions made a great contribution to the defensive conducted by the Germans from hedgerow to hedgerow, slowing the Allied advance for more than a month and a half until the final collapse of their front on 25 July.

This books details the battle on a day by day basis in order to establish the conditions under which it was fought, and with the help of numerous eye-witness accounts, enables the reader to experience the violence and the full horror of the fighting.

Contents

German Armoured Units in the west on 10 june 1944 *

Unit	Marks of tank				Assault guns	Booty tanks	Total
	III	IV	V	VI			
Divisions							
2. Pz.Div.		98	79				**177**
9. Pz.Div.		78	40		5		**123**
11. Pz.Div.	26	89			8		**123**
21. Pz.Div.		112					**112**
116. Pz.Div.	13	86			6		**105**
Pz.Lehr-Div.		98	88				**186**
1. SS-Pz.Div.		45	54		45		**144**
2. SS-Pz.Div.		54	78		42		**174**
12. SS-Pz.Div.		98	66				**164**
17. SS-Pz.Gr.Div.					42		**42**
Regiments							
I./Pz.Rgt. 15			4				**4**
I./Pz.Rgt. 24			9				**9**
I./Pz.Rgt. 25			11				**11**
I./Pz.Rgt. 27			79				**79**
I./Pz.Rgt. 29			8				**8**
I./Pz.Rgt. 36			10				**10**
I./Pz.Rgt. « GD »			79				**79**
I./SS-Pz.Rgt. 3			6				**6**
I./SS-Pz.Rgt. 9			40				**40**
I./SS-Pz.Rgt. 10			4				**4**
Battalions							
s.H.Pz.Abt. 510				6			**6**
s.SS-Pz.Abt. 101				45			**45**
s.SS-Pz.Abt. 102				45			**45**
s.SS-Pz.Abt. 103				6			**6**
Pz.Abt. 205						51	**51**
Pz.Abt. 206						46	**46**
Pz.Abt. 213						36	**36**
Pz.Abt.(Fkl) 302					10		**10**
Pz.Ers.u.Ausb.Abt. 100						46	**46**
Total	**39**	**758**	**655**	**102**	**158**	**179**	**1 891**

* The units figuring in this list were not all engaged in Normandy as certain of them had been stationed in the West during the summer of 1944 to be reformed or re-equipped. As far as the figures quoted are concerned (which were taken from a report by the General Inspector of Armoured Troops), they may not correspond exactly to the actual combat strength of the units concerned, as some of them received extra tanks before moving up to the front.

ORGANISATION AND EFFECTIVE STRENGTH OF THE PANZER UNITS DURING THEIR ENGAGEMENT IN NORMANDY

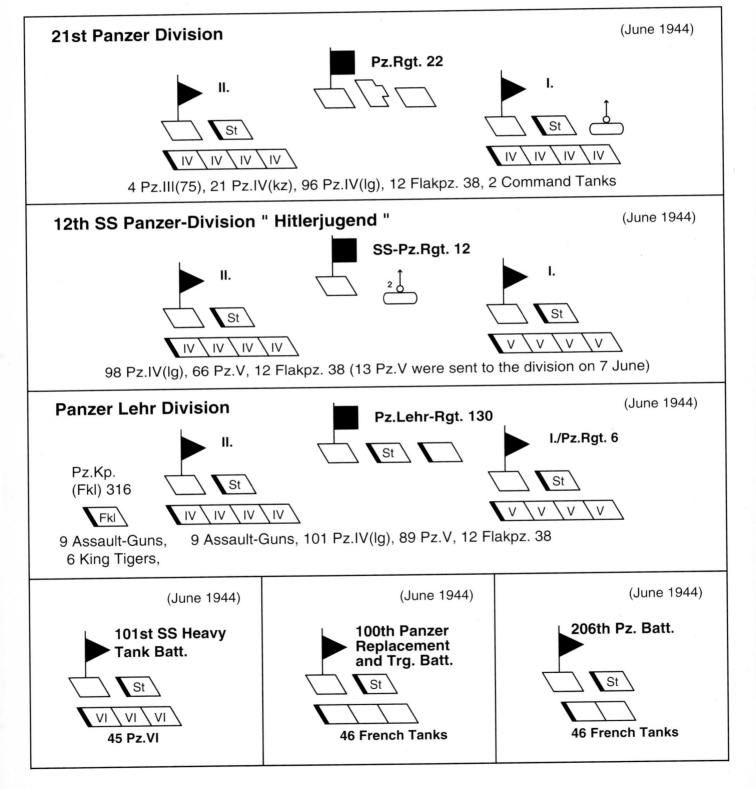

21st Panzer Division (June 1944)

Pz.Rgt. 22

II. I.

4 Pz.III(75), 21 Pz.IV(kz), 96 Pz.IV(lg), 12 Flakpz. 38, 2 Command Tanks

12th SS Panzer-Division " Hitlerjugend " (June 1944)

SS-Pz.Rgt. 12

II. I.

98 Pz.IV(lg), 66 Pz.V, 12 Flakpz. 38 (13 Pz.V were sent to the division on 7 June)

Panzer Lehr Division (June 1944)

Pz.Lehr-Rgt. 130

II. I./Pz.Rgt. 6

Pz.Kp. (Fkl) 316

9 Assault-Guns, 6 King Tigers, 9 Assault-Guns, 101 Pz.IV(lg), 89 Pz.V, 12 Flakpz. 38

(June 1944)

101st SS Heavy Tank Batt.

45 Pz.VI

(June 1944)

100th Panzer Replacement and Trg. Batt.

46 French Tanks

(June 1944)

206th Pz. Batt.

46 French Tanks

17th SS Panzer Grenadier Division " Götz von Berlichingen " (June 1944)

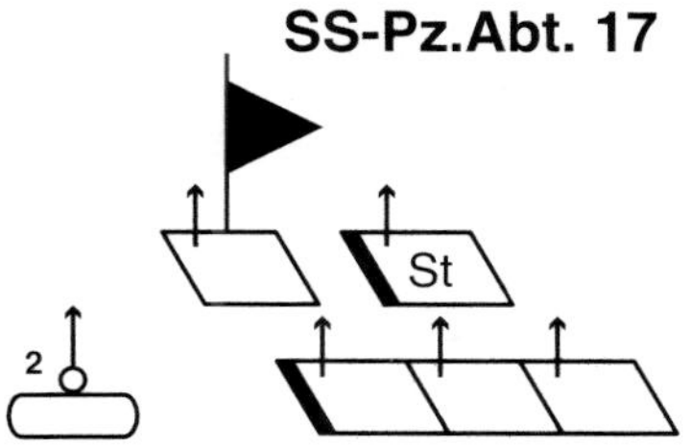

SS-Pz.Abt. 17
St
2

42 Assault-Guns, 3 Command Tanks (12 Flakpz. 38 were sent to the unit on 17 June)

2nd Panzer Division (June 1944)

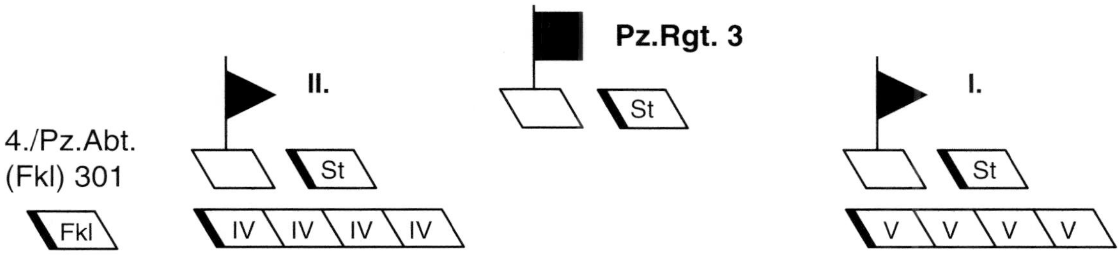

Pz.Rgt. 3
II.
I.
4./Pz.Abt.
(Fkl) 301
St
Fkl
IV IV IV IV
V V V V

10 Assault-Guns, 36 B IV

98 Pz.IV(lg), 79 Pz.V, 12 Flakpz. 38

2nd SS Panzer Division " Das Reich " (June 1944)

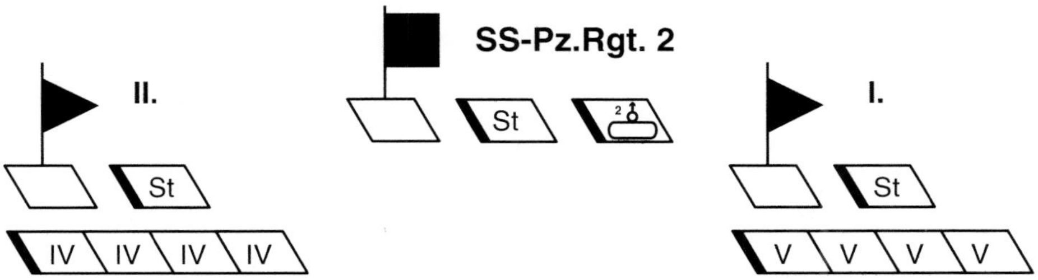

SS-Pz.Rgt. 2
II.
I.
St
2
IV IV IV IV
V V V V

13 Assault-Guns, 78 Pz.IV(lg), 79 Pz.V, 12 Flakpz. 38

9th SS Panzer Division " Hohenstaufen " (June 1944)

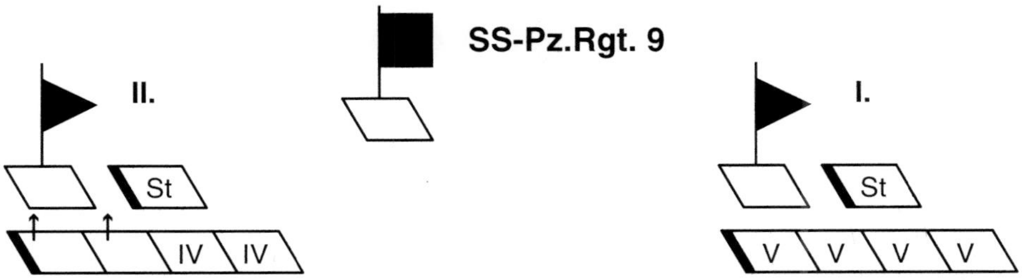

SS-Pz.Rgt. 9
II.
I.
St
IV IV
V V V V

40 Assault-Guns, 46 Pz.IV(lg), 79 Pz. V

10th SS Panzer Division " Frundsberg " (June 1944)

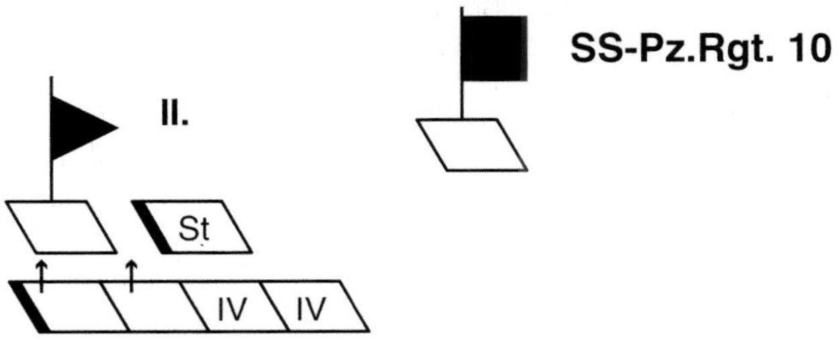

SS-Pz.Rgt. 10
II.
St
IV IV

38 Assault-Guns, 39 Pz.IV(lg), 3 Command-Tanks

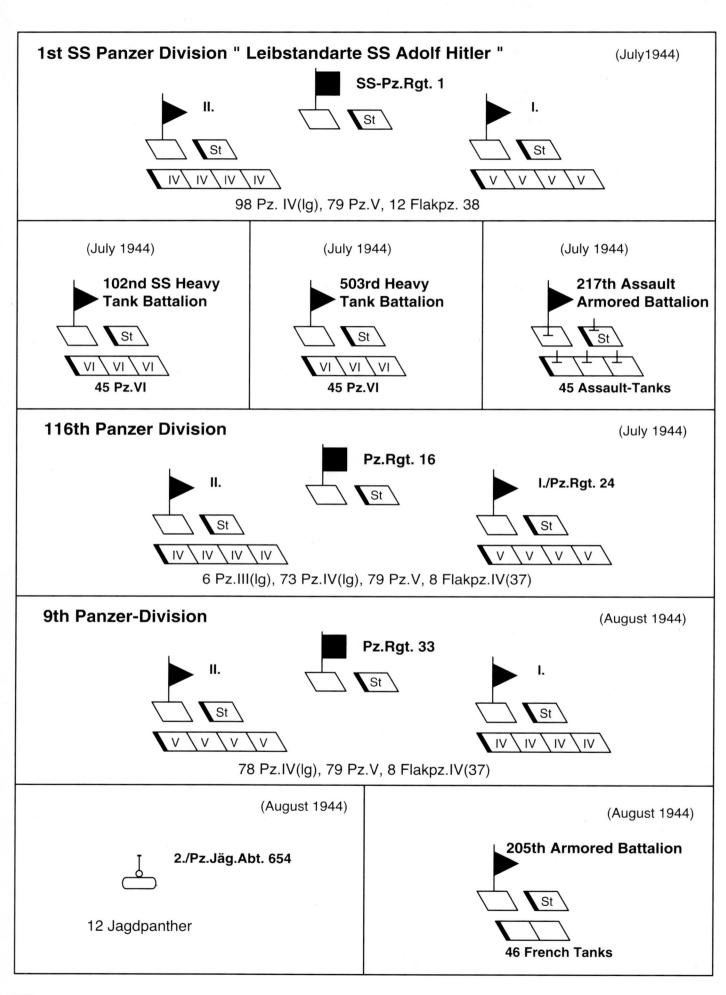

1st SS Panzer Division " Leibstandarte SS Adolf Hitler " (July1944)

II.

SS-Pz.Rgt. 1

St

I.

St

St

IV \ IV \ IV \ IV

V \ V \ V \ V

98 Pz. IV (lg), 79 Pz.V, 12 Flakpz. 38

(July 1944)

102nd SS Heavy Tank Battalion

St

VI \ VI \ VI

45 Pz.VI

(July 1944)

503rd Heavy Tank Battalion

St

VI \ VI \ VI

45 Pz.VI

(July 1944)

217th Assault Armored Battalion

St

45 Assault-Tanks

116th Panzer Division (July 1944)

II.

Pz.Rgt. 16

St

I./Pz.Rgt. 24

St

St

IV \ IV \ IV \ IV

V \ V \ V \ V

6 Pz.III(lg), 73 Pz.IV(lg), 79 Pz.V, 8 Flakpz.IV(37)

9th Panzer-Division (August 1944)

II.

Pz.Rgt. 33

St

I.

St

St

V \ V \ V \ V

IV \ IV \ IV \ IV

78 Pz.IV(lg), 79 Pz.V, 8 Flakpz.IV(37)

(August 1944)

2./Pz.Jäg.Abt. 654

12 Jagdpanther

(August 1944)

205th Armored Battalion

St

46 French Tanks

THE PANZERS
facing D-Landing

6 to 12 June 1944

by Georges Bernage

The dawn of battle
Monday 5 June 1944

That Monday, clouds covered the skies whipped up by a strong wind that gave few breaks. All was quiet in Normandy and that day there was no chance the Allies would land. Heavy clouds will cover the sky the coming night, yet...

To cope with an eventual landing in Normandy there was not much: a few static infantry divisions often incomplete and ill-trained, and a sole armoured division, the 21st Panzer Division, positioned between Caen and Falaise, as well as a battalion of obsolete tanks in position in the Cotentin. Stronger forces were concentrated in the Pas-de-Calais.

An armoured division reformed

Originally the 5th Light Division, the 21st Panzer Division had been created in North Africa in August 1941. It gained fame during the retaking of the Gazala Line, against Tobruk and during the advance into Egypt. It was completely annihilated in Tunisia in May 1943. Some of the members of the division were able to be evacuated from North Africa in time and these men were to form the core of a new unit. Lieutenant General Edgar Feuchtinger commanded it from the beginning of June, having already overseen the reformation (June 1943 to January 1944) ; he succeeded Major General Oswin Grolig (January to March 1944) and Franz Westhoven (March and May). The division had received various units during its reconstruction.

Thus the *Sturmgeschuetz Abteilung 200* which was to form the anti-tank battalion of the division. It had been formed at the beginning of 1943 by transforming sixty odd French Hotchkiss H-39 and Somua tanks into self-propelled assault guns. The chassis of these tanks had been recovered and by installing a 105 mm gun, (*10.5 cm Feldhaubitze 18/40*) a very powerful weapon protected by an armoured open-topped turret was created. This unexpected machine performed well and proved its point. Sent immediately to the eastern front at the beginning of 1943 in the Leningrad sector, the battalion achieved remarkable results and OKW decided to withdraw it from the front at the end of that year and to position it in the west to face the threat of an Allied landing ; thus it was integrated into the new 21st Panzer Division. Commanded by Major Becker, this unit was one of the most effective armoured components of the division.

The divisional tank regiment was also a hybrid unit. The Panzer Regiment 100 had in fact been created at Versailles in January 1943 as an integral unit of Panzer Brigade 100. Placed in general reserve that regiment was composed of local defence tanks, outmoded French models. It was assigned to 21st Panzer Division in July 1943, where for a long time remained entirely equipped with French material. This the 1st battalion fielded 70 Hotchkiss tanks which had been hardly modified and the 2nd battalion 54 Somua tanks more or less modified and fitted with a 47 mm gun. In March 1944 the regiment changed its number and in becoming Panzer Regiment 22 was to a large part re-equipped. The 1st battalion was to finally receive its Panzer IV's but it only got three quarters of its planned complement

Colonel Hermann von Oppeln Bronikowski, commander of the *Panzer Regiment 22*. (Bundesarchiv.)

of vehicles. The 2nd battalion was due to be re-equipped with Panther tanks but it only received 21 Panzer IV's and retained 23 Somuas. The first Panthers did not arrive until several weeks after the landings. The regiment was commanded by Colonel Hermann von Oppeln-Bronikowski who was born on 2 January 1899 in Berlin, the son of a regular officer. During the First World War he served as a second lieutenant in the 10th Uhlan Regiment. An excellent horseman he took part on the 1936 Olympic Games where he won a gold medal. During the campaign in Poland he commanded the 24th Reconnaissance group, where, for an audacious surprise attack he was awarded the 1939 clasp to his 1914 Iron Cross First Class. In 1941, during Operation *Barbarossa,* he fought with Panzer Regiment 35 (4th Pz.Div.) and in January 1942 he succeeded Colonel Eberbach in command of the regiment being promoted to colonel. In the autumn of 1942 he fought at the head of Panzer Regiment 204 where his action brought him the Knight's Cross which was awarded on 1 January 1941. After that he took command of Panzer Regiment 11 (6th Pz.Div) and was wounded during the Battle of Kursk. After convalescence he was appointed to command Panzer Regiment 100. An excellent officer, he received the oak leaves to his Knight's Cross on 28 July 1944 and finished the war as a Major General in command of the 20th Panzer Division (from November 1944 to May 1945).

Spring 1944 at Saint-Martin-de-Fresnay, half way between Lisieux and Saint-Pierre-sur-Dives. One of Panzer Regiment 22's Panzer IV's has stopped in front of Madame Leroy's café-restaurant-grocery shop to organise the resupply of .... Camemberts! Madame Leroy watched the scene from her window on the first floor while her amused employee handed out the precious supplies - which were not going to be much good at throwing the Allies back into the sea. Neither were they going to be able to do that with their obsolete tank which was a short gunned Panzer IV Model C which came into service in 1940. It was covered by the standard yellow sand paint without any markings, except for the name of the driver's girlfriend - Hedi - painted on the steel cover over the vision slit. The name of the radio-operator's lass - Elfriede - is less visible, seemingly written with white chalk.

In the upper photo, while the young tankers were sampling the camemberts, a few of their comrades from the infantry were coming out of the café ; as the pictures show they had been drinking copious amounts of cider which was served from large jugs. As in the German saying, these young soldiers had been living "like God in France", but they were soon to face the hurricane of fire of the landings when the happiness would be replaced by fear. (Bundesarchiv.)

Thus the tank park of the 21st Panzer Division was a mixed-bag of mainly modified French models, although on the eve of the landings an effort of standardisation was undertaken, necessary for facing up to an Allied assault. *Panzer Regiment 22* received almost a hundred Panzer IV's (too late for training the young crews), but no Panthers and it still retained 23 French Somua tanks. It was in fact an armoured regiment which only had available about half its potential force and its crews were inexperienced, which was the heart of the problem. As far as the Sturmgeschuetz-Abteilung 200 was concerned, its home-made devices were to prove a success and very effective in the battles to come.

The 21st Panzer Division was positioned between Caen and Falaise with its command post at Saint-Pierre-sur Dives, facing the future British landing sector of Sword Beach. The infantry components were stationed near to the coast while the armoured units were further inland. The *Sturmgeschuetz-Abteilung 200* was in the broken countryside of the Swiss Normandy, the most southerly element of the division. The two tank battalions were hardly better placed : the second was to the east of Falaise and the first was near Vendeuvre (to the south east of Saint-Pierre-sur-Dives) and these were the only offensive elements at the disposal of the German command in the entire sector !

A battalion of French tanks in the Cotentin

If the *Panzer Regiment 22* was the only unit available for an effective counter-attack against the beaches in the Calvados department, the Manche department and more particularly the Cotentin peninsular was even worse off, although near the beaches was a battalion of obsolete French tanks, the *Panzer-Ersatz-und-Ausbildung-Abteilung 100* (Armoured Replacement and Training Battalion 100).

A Panzer IV, type H or J of *Panzer Regiment 22* crossing the railway line between Troan and Caen on the RN175 road. (Bundesarchiv.)

This unit had been formed in April 1941 at Schwetzingen in the Rhineland and had been sent a year later to the camp at Satory near Versailles where it and its depot was placed at the disposal of the commander of "Greater Paris". Its mission was to provide training for future young tankists: driving skills, firing the integral weapons, using the radio. A veteran of the unit, speaking in 1977, remarked that nevertheless that training could not provide crews for Panthers or Tigers. After leaving that basic training unit it was necessary for them to progress onto an advanced course of instruction. The battalion was equipped with booty French tanks some of which ran on gas and were not even fitted with turrets, but at least the crews could be taught to drive tanks. In fact the formation was severely limited and the crews spent a good part of their time guarding the railway lines in the Paris region against sabotage, more and more frequent at the time and a detachment was even sent to the Vercors. Most of the officers had been wounded and were finishing their convalescence and the nco's were veterans who had been away from the front for a long time. In spite of not being an operational unit, it was still sent at the beginning of May to Normandy, to the base of the Cotentin peninsular to the west of Carentan with its command post in the chateau at Franquetot. The companies were spread out around Carentan, Baupte and Saint-Mère-Eglise. Battalion 100 was under the command of Major Bardenschlager and was attached tactically to the 91st Infantry Division which was stationed in the area.

The men of the battalion spent the long waiting period in planting poles, known as "Rommel's Asparagus" in the meadows of the region as an anti-glider precaution. During the evening of 4 June the sky over Carentan was lit up by explosions and thousands of rounds of tracer streaked into the air with a thunderous noise. The following day it was the same again, and Lieutenant Weber, who commanded the 1st company, reassured his men by saying that it was only "circus - nothing to do with us" *("Zirkus ! Nicht für uns bestimmt")*.

... and more

Two more tank battalions also poorly equipped and non-operational were to be found in Normandy, but were too far away and too ineffective to be able to intervene.

– The Panzer Battalion 205 had been formed at Satory in November 1941. At the beginning of June (1944) it was a reserve unit of Fifteenth Army and stationed around Yvetot, north of the Seine.

– The Panzer Battalion 206 had been created at the same time as the one above, at the Satory camp. In early June the unit was part of the Seventh Army reserve and positioned around La Hague at the extreme north-east of the Cotentin peninsular with the command post at Beaumont-Hague. It took part in and was destroyed during the fighting for the Cherbourg pocket at the end of June 1944. It was equipped with French vehicles - Headquarters company had available 2 S-35's, two R-35's, 4 B1-bis tanks and three B1-bis flame throwers - while the two companies each had 4 S-35's and 10 H-39's. The total effectives on 1 April 1944 were 385 men.

– For the record the Panzer Battalion 213 must also be mentioned. This unit, formed in November 1941 at Kessel was attached tactically to the 319th Infantry Division stationed in the Channel Islands. Its headquarters was at St. Peters Port, but the battalion remained blocked there in the archipelago until the end of the war without being able to intervene.

Where would they land ?

The German command was inadequately prepared to confront the imminent landings, and first of all there was an argument about where the "invasion" would take place. The Pas-de-Calais was considered the most probable on account of its proximity to the heart of the Reich. Nevertheless, with his habitual intuition, Hitler regarded a landing in either Brittany or Normandy a distinct possibility. The latter area had thus been reinforced, in particular by the arrival of additional troops including two infantry divisions (the 91st and the 352nd). Six infantry divisions and two armoured (21st and 12th SS) had been positioned between the Bay of Mont-Saint-Michel and the Seine, as opposed to eight infantry divisions between the Somme and the Belgian frontier on terrain more confined. Between the Somme and the Seine there were five additional infantry divisions and two other armoured ones (2nd and 116th) in process of being reconstituted.

The greatest confusion reigned within the German high command regarding the strategy to be adopted. Field Marshal Rommel (in command of Army Group B) was inclined to position the armoured units close to the coast like a "pearl necklace" because he was sure that it was on the beaches that the Allies could be destroyed before they could reinforce their beachhead. He was also convinced that the superior allied air power would not permit reinforcements to arrive at the front in time - he was proved right in the future.

General Geyr von Schweppenburg (commander of the Panzer Group West) had a totally different point of view. He recommended the concentration of the entire armoured force in the forests around Paris, ready to launch a counter-attack once the Allies had built up a bridgehead based on a front line beyond the range of support from naval artillery. Hitler had not decided in favour of either of the two concepts, but rather had decided on a compromise whereby the armoured divisions were to be dispersed but without being too close to the beaches. Finally the intelligence service *Fremde Heere West* (Foreign Armies West) was ordered to provide an estimate of the allied forces available in Britain for a landing. On 6 June 1944, General Eisenhower had at his disposal thirty six divisions in England whereas the above service had knowingly more of less doubled the figures in order to obtain more resources in the West. These figures were taken seriously and the good intention became a formidable trap which encouraged the German high command to regard the landings in Normandy as a diversion, believing that the considerable remaining resources would be available for a second landing in the Pas-de-Calais.

Thus on the evening of 5 June 1944 there were only the feeble resources of the *Panzer Regiment 22* available to confront a landing in Normandy, and reinforcements would not be able to arrive until much later, in spite of the precautions taken by Rommel, who on that evening was absent from the front in the west.

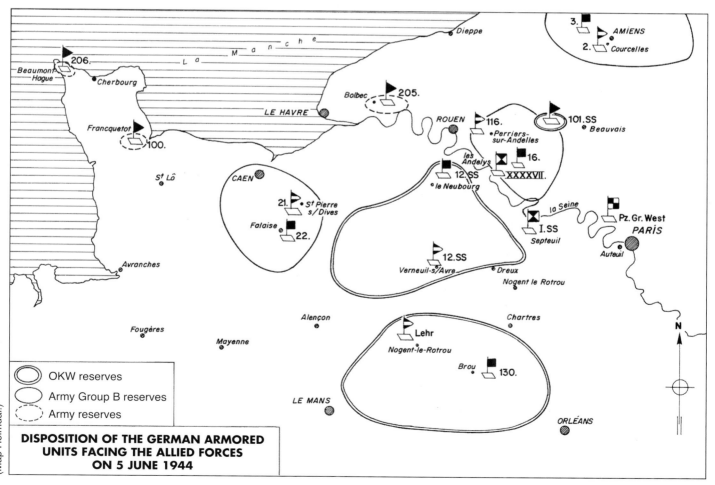

(Map Heimdal.)

OKW reserves
Army Group B reserves
Army reserves

DISPOSITION OF THE GERMAN ARMORED UNITS FACING THE ALLIED FORCES ON 5 JUNE 1944

22nd Panzer-Regiment

1 & 2. A Panzer IV type H in a village in the Caen sector. The two photos show the two sides of the same tank. The turret hatch is fitted with a type 34 machine-gun on an anti-aircraft mounting. The "skirts" are of the first type, more solidly fixed. One of two of the plates are missing on the one side and are completely absent from the other. The front upper plate is bolted on which indicates that it was an very early type H. The crew members are army personnel and according to the evidence the tank would appear to belong to the Panzer Regiment 22 (21st Panzer Division), because on the same roll of film shot by the war correspondent, one can see (Photo 5) a typical tank of that division. On the right one can see BMW R-12, (750 cc) with side-car. 16 motor-cycles of that type were provided for the battalion of Panzer IV's.

3

3 & **4**. The same reel shows two Panzer IV's of the regiment moving up to the front in the Caen sector. They are fitted with their "skirts" and are partially covered with foliage for camouflage. In the foreground of the first photo (no.3) a war correspondent can be seen filming the same scene for the newsreels. Photographers and cameramen often worked together.

5. In this report showing the tanks moving up to the front, you can see here a unique assault gun. The chassis of a French Hotchkiss H-39 has here been used to create an astonishing tank destroyer. A 10,5 cm howitzer *(10,5 cm Feldhaubitze 18/40)* has been mounted on a chassis, a powerful piece with a range of 7,50 miles, a rate of fire of 6-8 rounds per minute and a muzzle velocity of 540 metres (per second). The platform is protected by an armoured cockpit. This assault gun *(abbrev. StuG)* was called a *Panzer-Feldhaubitze 18 auf Sfl. 39H(f)* and 38 of them were produced to equip Major Becker's Assault-gun Battalion 200 which provided the tank destroyer capability of the 21st Panzer Division.

(Bundesarchiv.)

4

5

Tuesday 6 June 1944

A little after midnight - 0015 hrs for the pathfinders of Captain Lilleymann in the Cotentin and at 0020 hrs for Major Howard's men at Benouville - the first Airborne Troops dropped in on Normandy, to be reinforced by further waves of parachute drops.

At **0030 hrs** information concerning the Allied drops was communicated to the headquarters of the 125th Panzer Grenadier Regiment at Vimont (Major Hans von Luck). The information was passed on to the divisional headquarters at Saint-Pierre-sur-Dives. At 0035 hrs the division was put on a state of maximum alert

Up until **0130 hrs** further information came in concerning the parachute drops from the seventh company of the 125th Regiment, around Ranville, and from the sixth, to the north of Sannerville. First landings. The second battalion collected up the first prisoners, men of the 6th Airborne Division.

But, at **0350 hrs** the Supreme Commander West (OB West) signalled the staff of Army Group B that in view of the extent of the sector (from the Cotentin to the Orne estuary), this indicated that this was only an operation of a local nature.

At **0535 hrs** Naval Group West signalled that torpedo boats were engaging Allied naval forces to the west of Le Havre. At that time those forces were moving into position facing the Normandy beaches. The first landings took place at **0640 hrs** ; on Utah Beach, 0630 hrs at Omaha, 0735 hrs at Gold, 0800 hrs at Juno and 0720 at Sword.

The Supreme Command West finally announced the start of the "invasion" at **0624 hrs** They demanded that the OKW reserves be placed at their disposition and had already taken the 12th SS Panzer Division under their command at 0500 hrs without waiting for permission from OKW ; this armoured division had already been placed under Army Group B. At the same time, Army Group B had placed the 21st Panzer Division at the disposal of Seventh Army at 0645 hrs to destroy the airborne troops who had landed to the east of the Orne.

At **0700 hrs** 21st Panzer Division was reattached to LXXXIV Army Corps (commanded by General Marcks). At **1035 hrs** it wanted to attack to the west of Caen where the situation was becoming critical for the German high command. But although it found itself close to the landing beaches in the Caen sector, the sole armoured division available to disturb the Allied operations remained immobilised the entire morning, only to be engaged in a counter-attack during the afternoon. Why ?

With hindsight and having studied the situation, it seems evident that the loss of those decisive hours was a stupid waste , but matters were not that simple and it is easy to judge events after the passage of time. Up until roughly 0700 hrs the German commanders were still unsure. There had been the parachute landings during the night but those could have been a diversionary operation ; there had been another such drop during the night around Saint-Marcel in Brittany: obviously a diversion, without taking into account the dummy parachutists which among other units, kept the 12th SS Panzer Division pinned down in the Pays d'Auge. The ac-

tual "invasion" was only announced by the Supreme Command West at 0624 hrs but it was necessary to wait for at least another hour until the first Allied units had arrived at all of the five landing sectors. And what if there was to be a sixth sector for example, at Deauville in the Pays d'Auge ? The situation only became clear to the German command at around 1000 hrs, when the first counter attacks by 21st Panzer Division had been decided upon. At that time, except for Omaha beach, the Allies had already established beachheads everywhere, although it was necessary to wait until midday until they could be regarded as established: at Utah beach the infantry had to link up with the airborne troops dropped inland, the exits from Omaha beach had to be secured, and the various sectors of Juno had to be cleaned up. A determined counter-attack launched at around 10 o'clock would have stood some chance of success, although there were only the 124 tanks of the 21st Panzer Division available. The Hitler Jugend division was still too far away and as far as the Panzer Lehr Division was concerned, it had still not received orders to move. It should be born in mind though, that an attacker always has the benefit of surprise and it always takes time for the defender to get a clear view of his adversary's intentions, even though the German command still believed in a second landing in the Pas-de-Calais.

The 21st Panzer Division counter-attack

Three tactical formations of the division had already been formed to attack on one side or the other of the Orne - The *Kampfgruppe* (battle group) *Rauch,* (Colonel Rauch was the commander of the 192nd Panzer grenadier Regiment) comprising his regiment minus its second battalion, the Armoured Engineer Regiment 220 and the second battalion of the 155th Armoured Artillery Regiment (10.5 cm guns on self propelled Hotchkiss chassis) - the *Kampfgruppe Oppeln* (Colonel Hermann von Oppeln-Bronikowski, commander of the 22nd Panzer Regiment, comprised of the first battalion of that regiment (minus its fourth company) under the command of Major von Gottberg, which could field roughly fifty Panzer IV's, the second battalion under Major Vierzig with twenty Panzer IV's (the rest of its tanks were captured French Somua S-35's armed with 4.7 cm guns), the first battalion of the 125th Panzer grenadier Regiment (minus the first company), the first battalion of the 220th Armoured Engineer Regiment and the third battalion of the 155th Armoured Artillery Regiment (10.5 cm guns on Hotchkiss self propelled chassis) - the *Kampfgruppe Luck* (Major Hans von Luck) which was already engaged to the east of the Orne.

The *Kampfgruppe Rauch* had the task of reaching the coast near Lion-sur-Mer. The task of *Kampfgruppe Oppeln* was to reach the coast between the eastern edge of Lion-sur-Mer and the Orne estuary, thus hindering a junction between the Canadians on Juno Beach and the British on Sword beach and preventing them moving south.

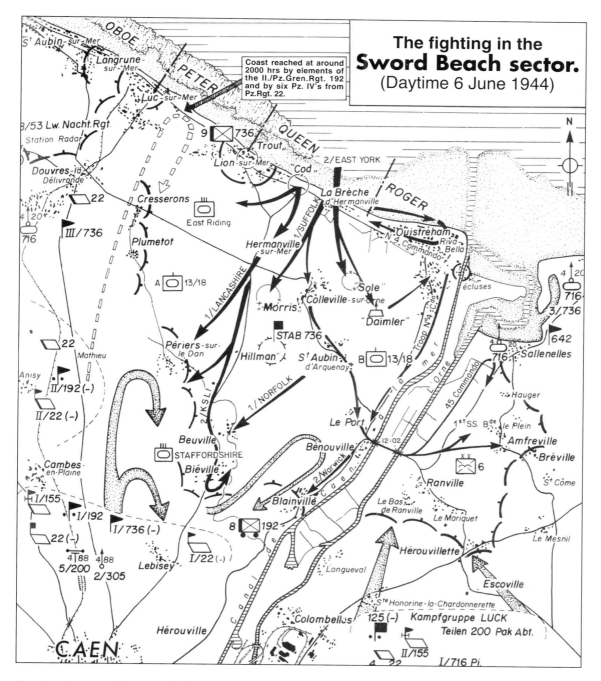

The fighting in the
Swordˑ Beach sector.
(Daytime 6 June 1944)

Coast reached at around 2000 hrs by elements of the II./Pz.Gren.Rgt. 192 and by six Pz. IV's from Pz.Rgt. 22.

The counter-attack by 22nd Panzer Regiment on the 6th June between the Juno Beach sector (Canadian) and the Sword Beach sector (British). The first battalion suffered heavy losses in front of Biéville and a further ten Panzer IV's were destroyed near Périers. The second battalion advanced towards Mathieu and six of its Panzer IV's reached the coast between Luc and Lion around 2000 hrs, but retired because of the arrival of British airborne reinforcements. (Map, Heimdal.)

The forming up of the two battle groups was not achieved until **1600 hrs** But, to get to the front, the two tactical groups coming from the area of Saint-Pierre-sur-Dives had to cross the Orne, knowing that the town of Caen had been bombed by Allied squadrons at 1330 hrs, partly blocking the streets with rubble. Although the majority of the troops crossed the Orne by the road bridge on the national highway 158, elements of the 22nd Panzer Regiment used the bridge at Colombelles, 4,5 km north of the former. Thus the *Kampfgruppe Oppeln* formed up to the west of Hérouville, a kilometre to the north of Calix. *Kampfgruppe Rauch* reassembled around Saint-Contest, and the two battle groups at last mounted their counter-attack at about **1620 hrs**.

We will deal first with the attack by the armoured battle group Oppeln. Major Vierzig with the 2nd battalion of Pz.Regt. 22 was at Lebisey. From there he could distinctly see the tanks of the 1st battalion (Major von Gottberg) and aligned his tanks to the left of that unit. In complete radio silence, Major

Vierzig formed up near Major von Gottberg and together, they reached the hill where Colonel von Oppeln Bronikowski had installed his headquarters ; The corps commander, General Marcks was also there. The attackers had suffered near Lebisey from the fire of British tanks and anti-tank artillery coming from the area of Biéville, where they found themselves engaged with the Kings Shropshire Light Infantry (KSLI). Two Panzer IV's were hit at around **16.45 hrs** to the west of Biéville by the tanks of the Staffordshire Yeomanry. The lead Panzer IV brewed up before von Oppeln's regiment had fired its first shot in anger. Von Gottberg lost ten Panzer IV's in front of Périers and that attack was broken off. The counter-attack then developed more to the west with Major Vierzig's battalion moving via Epron and Cambes to the area of Mathieu, slanting westwards. Fourteen Panzer IV's formed up near Douvres-la-Delivrande where they were joined by elements of the 2nd battalion of the 192nd Panzer Grenadiers from the Rauch battle group. The combined forces thus passed between the Juno Beach and Sword Beach landing areas and arrived at Luc-sur-Mer at around 2000 hrs with six Panzer IV's, reaching the sea at last. But about an hour later, around 250 aircraft towing gliders as part of Operation Mallard, passed overhead, bringing in the 6th Airlanding brigade to reinforce the bridgehead east of the Orne. The staff of 21st Panzer Division imagined that the Allies were going to land in the rear of the two exposed battle groups and ordered them to suspend their counter-attacks. In addition, British tanks coming from Cresserons were attacking them. The Rauch battle group withdrew to Anguerny and then on corps orders, to Epron. The Oppeln battle group retired to the start line and maintained contact on its left flank with Rauch. Their anti-tank resources were insufficient to oppose the advance of the British armour, and with bitterness, von Oppeln, the cavalryman, had to order his tanks to dig in and spread out into fixed positions from which they were able to repel the British 27th Armoured Brigade. On that day the 22nd Panzer Regiment lost sixteen tanks and its attempts to mount a counter-attack had been completely stymied.

To the east of the Orne, the regiment had detached its fourth company to hunt down the British airborne troops. The tanks rolled on to Hérouvillette which they reached as night fell, but only encountered friendly positions, and spent the night there.

Alert for the *Panzer Battalion 100*

In the Cotentin, the American troops only had the thirty odd obsolete French tanks to contend with, hardly capable of throwing them back into the sea. At dawn the men of the battalion saw with surprise the parachutes dangling from the trees and the wreckage of gliders in the hedgerows. Worried, they scrutinised the countryside but did not see a living soul. Major Bardenschlager sent some of his men to collect milk ; just like every morning ; their comrades only later found their dead bodies. They did not get into fighting order until 0900 hrs as a result of a radio message. Motor cycle dispatch riders brought the first information about what was happening and Major Bardenschlager left the chateau at Franquetot for Hautteville, the headquarters of the 91st Infantry Division ; nobody ever saw him again. At around 2000 hrs his deputy collected together the first and second companies at Baupte where they spent the night ; their task was to block the D903 road leading to Carentan. The elderly French tanks opened fire at anything that moved, but at the least sound of an engine, they camouflaged themselves and broke off the contact. On the morning of 7 June the first company was ordered to St. Lo and the second to Carentan. A veteran of the battalion who was interviewed by the author in 1977 about his experiences, (transcribed for the book, *The Panzers in Normandy,* by E Lefèvre), finished by saying with a grin that finally the battalion was reduced to the level of one anti-tank company "of which the heaviest weapon was the *panzerfaust*, and that the tanks had been replaced by bicycles". One can recall the counter-attack by two tanks of the battalion against the causeway at La Fière at midday on 6 June. The 57 mm gun used by the American paras' from the 505th Airborne Infantry Regiment was destroyed by two shells but the first tank was disabled by bazooka rounds and the other one was set on fire. C Fitt, a soldier from C Company even threw a hand grenade into the turret of one of the tanks. The Germans retreated along the west bank of the Merderet to Cauquigny. The only real counter-attack by the French "panzers" in the Cotentin had been defeated.

The advance to the front by *SS Panzer Regiment 12*

While *Panzer Regiment 22* and *Panzer Abteilung 100* attempted to block the Allied attack under difficult conditions (no *Panther* tanks and many obsolete French models), the tank regiment of the Hitler Youth Division, *SS Panzer Regiment 12*, finally moved up to the front.

At 0130 hrs, Fritw Witt, the divisional commander woke up his chief-of-staff, *Sturmbannfuehrer* Hubert Meyer, and said to him "Meyer, its the invasion, that's good" ! The alert was given at 0300 hrs with the code word "Blucher" and an hour later all the units of the division were ready to move off. But the division was a part of the OKW (Wehrmacht high command) reserve, and this last operational reserve could not generally be engaged until the situation had been sufficiently clarified and the forces already engaged in battle were insufficient. The reserves of *Army Group B*, 2nd and 116th Panzer Divisions should have been engaged first but they were further away from the battle zone that the 12th *SS Hitler Youth Division*. That was why the latter division was freed at 1430 hours while the 2nd and 116th were retained in reserve. Thus at **1432 hrs** Supreme Command West informed Army Group B that OKW had freed the 12th SS at five o'clock that morning, to intervene in support of Seventh Army. Shortly afterwards, Army Group B also discovered that the *Panzer Lehr Division* had been released by OKW. Supreme Command West advised that it be transferred to the area of Flers. At **1507 hrs** the latter informed *Army Group B* that the two divisions would be placed under the command of *I. SS Panzer-Korps* which would have at its disposal all their organic units.. The following order was written into the war diary of Seventh Army at 1500 hrs "12 SS PD *and the Pz Lehr Div. have been placed immediately under the orders of Seventh Army command to be engaged against the bridgehead in the 716th Infantry Division sector. The army command issued the following order via the Panzer Group Command West: 1). 12th SS Pz. Div. is to immediately take up positions to the north of a line from Alencon (excluded) - Carrouges (included) - Flers (excluded) in the area on both sides of Evrécy (author's note - 8.5 km south west of Caen) and is placed under the orders of LXXXIV. Corps. Its mission is to place itself to the west of 21st Pz.Div. and destroy and throw back into the sea, the enemy that has penetrated to the west of the Orne. 2). Pz. Lehr Div. is to position itself to the south of the line described above and assemble in the area of Flers-Vire."* Immediately after this, Seventh Army sent orders to *SS-Brigadeführer* Fritz Kraemer, chief of staff of Ist SS Panzer Corps, informing him of the attachment to his armoured corps of 21st Panzer Division, 12th SS Panzer Division, Panzer Lehr Division and what remained of the 716th Infantry Division, in order to reunite them on the right flank of LXXXIV Corps. Thus all the German forces so far involved in the fighting in Normandy were to be in one armoured corps on a limited sector of the front, concentrating all the assets as a single spearhead. The first job, though, was to collect together these three armoured divisions as rapidly as possible.

The movement was going to have to take place in full daylight and when the orders to march were transmitted the weather conditions were favourable (overcast), but by 1800 hrs the sun broke through and the clouds cleared. On the part of the tank regiment of the division, according to the testimony of *SS Sturmmann* Hellmuth Pock, there was great enthusiasm when the Allied landings were announced. *"There was then an intense coming and going in our holding area. The soldiers were preparing the equipment while the officers and liaison staff were arriving continually arriving. Each time one or more of our officers arrived they shouted out a loud 'hooray'. Some of them hugged us and slapped us on the back ; others took off their caps and threw them in the air. Morale was very high and we were caught up in this atmosphere which engulfed us in our turn. The noise of an engine from the sky and they were already there. 'Take cover' yelled the officers and as fast as possible everyone tried to make himself invisible. On lifting my head I saw the German cross on the aircraft. They were ours, our Me 109's, between 30 and 40 machines that flew over us at low-level. We shot out of our shelters and greeted our pilots with all our might, shouting 'Hooray', 'Heil' and 'Bravo' to demonstrate our enthusiasm at seeing our fighter aircraft. Would they see us ? Yes, they waggled their wings in salute and roared over our heads. They were so low we could see the pilots in their cockpits. It was that which made our 'soldiers' hearts rejoice, an image of power and strength, and energy ready to engage with determination. Enthusiasm reigned everywhere and phrases like 'we're going to give it to the Tommies', recurred time and time again in our conversations. The order to be ready to move off was issued and we went back to our vehicles. The drivers tested their engines once again to see if everything was in order, but that was more a sign of nervousness than dictated by technical necessity. We were ready for the order to move off as we though we should not stay any longer there. Time was pressing and we believed we would arrive too late for the battles that awaited us. One could feel the tension that gripped the men. Even those gifted with a sense of humour found it difficult to make their usual jokes. After the first wave of enthusiasm we were seized than by fear of the unknown although we knew that to wait about would be the worst thing for the troops. It was best to get on with it right away! 'Is it that they don't want to leave or that they don't need us ?' asked one of our comrades."* Then after the hanging around, the departure, hours on the dusty roads protected by the bad weather, the vehicles giving an impression of strength, but during the afternoon, the sun appeared. Let us return to *Sturmmann* Pock : *"On a hill we made contact again with our company and learned that they had suffered the first losses. The supply truck had been hit by aircraft ; the driver and his passenger had been killed. We would go on ! The number of vehicles destroyed increased ; burned out they took on the typical rusty red colour."* The tanks of the Hitler Youth division were not going to be able to counter-attack that day.

12th SS Panzer Regiment which was moving up to the front had been created at the Mailly-le-Camp exercise area in November 1943. It was placed under the command of *SS Obersturmbannführer* Max Wünsche, who had previously commanded the 2nd Battalion of the 1st SS Panzer Regiment (the tank regiment of the *Leibstandarte* (LAH) Division.

Born on 20 April 1914 at Kittlitz in Saxony, Max Wünsche joined up in 1934 at the age of twenty, into the new *SS Verfügungstruppe*. He was sent as an orderly officer to Hitler in 1938, staying in that post until 1940 when he took command of a company in the *Leibstandarte*. He was wounded during the offensive in the west and during the Balkan campaign he served on the staff of the LAH. Before *Barbarossa* he took command of a new assault-gun unit and in 1942 he commanded the 1st

---

Order of battle of the 12th SS-Panzer-Regiment. 12 June 1944

Headquarters

Rgt.Kommandeur (Regimental commander): *Ostubaf.* M. Wünsche
Adjutant (Deputy commander) : *Hstuf.* G. Isecke
Ord.Offz. (Adjutant) : *Ustuf.* Nerlich
Nach.Offz. (Signals Officer) : *Hstuf.* Schlauss
Verw.Offz. (Admin. Officer) : *Hstuf.* Lütgert
Rgt.Arzt. (Regimental doctor) : *Hstuf.Dr.* Stiawa
TFK, Stabskompanie, Chef (HQ company commander) : *Ostuf.* Sammann
Versorgungskompanie, Chef (Quartermaster) : *Ostuf.* Donaubaner

I. Abteilung *(1st Battalion)*

Abt.Kdr. (Battalion commander) : *Stubaf.* Jürgensen
Adjutant (Deputy battalion commander) : *Ustuf.* Schröder
Ord.Offz. (Adjutant) : *Ustuf.* Hogrefe
Nach.Offz. (Signals officer) : *Ustuf.* Jauch
Verw.Offz. (Admin. officer) : *Ustuf.* Hoffmann
Tr.Arzt. (Doctor) : *Ostuf. Dr* Daniel
TFK : *Ostuf.* Surkow
TFW, Stabskompanie, chef (HQ Company): *Lt.* Schulenburg
1. Kompanie (1. Company) : *Hstuf.* Berlin
2. Kompanie (2. Company) : *Ostuf.* Gaede
3. Kompanie (3. Company) : *Ostuf.* R. von Ribbentrop
4. Kompanie (4. Company) : *Hstuf.* H. Pfeiffer († 11.6.44)
Werkstatt-Kp. (Workshop Company) : *Ustuf.* R. Maier

II. Abteilung *(2nd Battalion)*

Abt.Kdr. (Commander) : *Stubaf.* K.H. Prinz († 14.8.44)
Adjutant (Deputy) : *Ostuf.* Hartmann
Ord.Offz. (Adjutant) : *Ustuf.* H. Walther
Nach.Offz. (Signals officer) : *Ustuf.* Kommadina
Verw.Offz. (Admin. Officer) : *Ustuf.* Schwaiger
Tr.Arzt. (Doctor) : *Hstuf.Dr.* Jordan
Tr.Zahnarzt (Dentist) : *Hstuf.* Hofner
Stabskompanie, chef (HS Company) : *Hstuf.* Pezdeuscheg
TFK : *Ostuf.* Breitenberger
TFW : *Lt.* Pfannkuch
5. Kompanie, Chef (5. Company) : *Ostuf.* Bando († 27.6.44)
6. Kompanie, Chef (6. Company) : *Hstuf.* Ruckdeschel
7. Kompanie, Chef (7. Company) : *Hstuf.* Bräcker
8. Kompanie, Chef (8. Company) : *Ostuf.* Siegel
9. Kompanie, Chef (9. Company) : *Hstuf.* Buettner
Werkstatt-Zug (Workshop platoon) : *Ostuf.* D. Müller

SS-Obersturmbannführer Max Wünsche, commander of the 12th Panzer Regiment since his creation in July 1943. (Bundesarchiv.)

Battalion of the tank regiment of the LAH, being decorated with the Knights' Cross on 28 February 1943 after the battle of Kharkov. In July 1943 he returned to Germany before taking up his new command at the head of the tank regiment of the Hitler Youth Division. He was then 28 years old and was promoted to *SS Obersturmbannführer* (Lt. Colonel). A pure product of the Nazi regime, his career had progressed rapidly.

12th SS Panzer Regiment - 2nd Company, Ist Battalion *(2./SS-Pz.Rgt. 12)*

1. *SS Hauptsturmführer* (wearing here the rank of *SS Obersturmführer)* Wilhelm Beck in the company of his wife. Born on 22 December 1918 he joined up in the regiment *Deutschland* in 1938. He participated with great dash in all its battles and then joined the armoured forces. During the Battle of Kharkov he achieved brilliant success, in command of the 2nd company of the LAH tank regiment; in 19 days of combat, with his crews, he destroyed more than 120 artillery pieces and nine T-34 tanks. During the fighting he lost two tanks in succession. In the suburbs of Kharkov he destroyed another two T-34's with his own tank. He was decorated with the Knights' Cross on 28 March 1943.

2, 3 and **4.** These three photos of SS-PK Woscidlo taken in Normandy prior to the landings at which time Wilhelm Beck was still commanding his company of Panther tanks. He was later transferred as liaison officer to Ist SS Panzer Corps attached to Panzer Group West and was killed during the bombardment of La Caine on 10 June 1944.

5. *SS Standartenoberjunker* Paul Dienemann was a section commander in the 2nd Company of 12th SS Panzer Regiment. In this photo he is still wearing the insignia of a *SS Oberscharführer* and the standard cap with rigid peak and without the chinstrap.

6. *SS Untersturmführer* Helmut Gaede who took command of the 2nd Company following the transfer of Wilhelm Beck to the staff of Panzer Group West.

(Heimdal's collection.)

12th SS Panzer Regiment - 2nd Company *(2./SS-Pz.Rgt. 12)*

1. Lunch break during manoeuvres at the beginning of 1944. These men from the 2nd Company are wearing the camouflaged jacket which was in process of becoming official issue and black forage caps. From left to right: *Untersturmführer* Bogensperger who was transferred to the 3rd company and was killed on 7 August 1944 ; *Standartenoberjunker* Dienemann ; Hans Helmle (tank commander) ; Richard Heinz.

2. Tank crewmen from the 2nd Company. From left to right: *Sturmmann* Hans Ulrich Dietrich (gun layer) ; *Sturmmann* Horst Bootz ; *Sturmmann* Erich Hicker ; Crew member Erich Siebe ; *Rottenführer* Hans Helmle.

3. One of the company's Panthers loaded for transport from Belgium to Normandy in April 1944.

14

4. Training at the camp at Mailly during the winter of 1943-44.

5. Fred Lehmann and *Unterscharführer* Rudi Knoche. The latter was a tank commander in the 2nd Company and was killed in action.

6. Jochen Dedow, Werner Ehrsam and Theo Stahl on their Panther ; all three were killed.

(Heimdal's collection.)

12th SS Panzer Regiment - 3rd Company *(3./SS-Pz.Rgt. 12)*

The 3rd Company posing for the lens of a war photographer at Harcourt in April 1944. The first on the left is *Unterscharführer* Hermani, the third is *Uscha.* Krahl, followed by *Untersturmführer* Jungbluth, then Wilhelm Post, the company adjutant, *Obersturmführer* von Ribbentrop (with his Knights' Cross at his neck), *Oberjunker* Bogensperger, *Oberjunker* Alban and *Untersturmführer* Stagge.

The nco's of the company posing in front of the Hotel de Commerce (transfomed into an SS canteen) at Harcourt in April 1944. **1.** *Uscha.* Hermani (tank commander) ; **2.** *Uscha* . März (tank commander) ; **3.** *Oscha.* Post (adjutant) ; **4.** *Uscha.* Eismann (tank commander) ; **5.** *Gruppenführer* Hetzel ; **6.** *Uscha.* Krahl (tank commander) ; **7.** Fischer (armourer) ; **8.** *Uscha.* Gose (medical orderly) ; **9.** *Uscha.* Freier (tank commander).

Above : Alban's section at Harcourt in April 1944, the 2nd. Section. **1.** Trapnik ; **2.** *Uscha.* Krahl (tank commander) ; **3.** *Oscha.* Alban (tank and section commander) ; **4.** Werner Uhr ; **5.** *Uscha.* Eismann (tank commander) ; **6.** Gerd Krieger (gun-layer) ; **7.** Gemassner.

Below : Bogensperger's section ; **1.** Hansen ; **2.** Sokoliss (?) ; **3.** *Uscha.* März (tank commander) ; **4.** *Uscha.* Bogensperger (tank and section commander) ; **5.** Schiemann (driver) ; **6.** Porochnowitz (gun-loader) ; **7.** Fischer (gun-layer) ; **8.** Niebisch (driver) ; **9.** Pastor. The make-up of sections was later altered.

(Photos : Kam. 3 Pz.Kp./Author's collection.)

12th SS Panzer Regiment - 3rd Company *(3./SS-Pz.Rgt. 12)*

1. *Obersturmführer* Rudolf von Ribbentrop, the company commander. He was the son of the Minister of Foreign Affairs of the Reich, who fought with great courage, in spite of having extremely poor vision (in this photo he is not wearing his usual thick glasses). (Theffo's collection.)

2. *Untersturmführer* Jauch in the turret of his tank. At the time of the attack on Norrey, 9 June 1944, he was not a member of 3 Company. He is wearing a garment made of Italian camouflage cloth like a lot of the men of the Hitler Youth Division. The 3rd Company used such camouflaged jackets as well as the uniforms in black cloth, sailcloth jackets and uniforms camouflaged with green dots. Note the large numbers painted on the back of the turret of "338". (Photo SS-PK Woscidlo/Heimdal's collection.)

4. "313", this tank has an odd number for one of the 3rd Company's machines. On 9 June 1944 it was commander by *Uscha.* März, known as "handsome März" who always wore black leather gloves and the gun-layer was Günther Gotha who can be seen in this photograph beside the turret. Note the tank's camouflage. (Coll. Gotha/Bernage.)

5. In Normandy, Hermann Lammers who had just been decorated with the Iron Cross second class on 20 July 1944. He was the driver and the gun-layer was Gerd Krieger, easily recognised by his mop of blonde hair. They were in "326" on 9 June when *Uscha.* Eismann was cut in two by a shell, just above them. (Coll. Lammers/Bernage.)

7. During a pause between battles, three young crewmen (left to right : Lammers, Korte and Krieger) playing cards. (Coll. Lammers/Bernage.)

3. The company's tanks were painted sand colour with camouflage effect sprayed on top in green and reddish colours, as was usual in the 12th SS Panzer Regiment. Here, the tank "304" during training in Flanders, actually the company commander's tank, *Ostuf.* von Ribbentrop. Note that the identification numbers have been hand painted without a stencil. According to the testimony of veterans they were red with a white outline. On the left in black sailcloth and forage cap, Fritz Freiberg, the gun-layer of "304". (Coll. Stephan/Bernage.)

12th SS Panzer Regiment - 4th Company *(4./SS-Pz.Rgt. 12)*

1. *Hauptsturmführer* Hans Pfeiffer, photographed here when he was an *Ostuf.* at Hitler's headquarters. He took command of the 4th Company and was killed in action at Rots on 11 June 1944. (Author's collection.)

2. Left. *Ustuf.* Hillig, in command of the 1st Section of the company. (Mrs Pfeiffer's collection.)

3. *Rottenführer* Helmut Lange, half brother of Hans Pfeiffer, who also served in the 4th Company. (Mrs Pfeiffer's collection.)

6

4. *Uscha.* Ekkehard Stuhldreher. On 11 June 1944, during the fighting at Rots, he was the gun-layer of the tank situated near the church which destroyed four or five Canadian tanks in ten minutes. (Stuhldreher/Author's collection.)

5. The Panther "415" of the commander of the 1st Section, *Ustuf.* Hillig. (Stephan/Author's collection.)

6. Crewmen from the 4th Company. Note the variegated nature of the uniforms worn. A black cloth blouse surrounded by green sailcloth. The two men on the left are Eberhard Wenzl and H Rohrbach, the two on the right are G Mahlke and Probst, nicknamed the "crow" (*Rabe).* (Wenzel/Author's collection.)

7. A 4th Company Panther destroyed on 11 June 1944 near the school (now the *Mairie)* in the Rue Haute-Bony at Rots. The turret is turned towards the church and in front is the edge of the RN13 highway, that is to say facing south. In this photo, taken in 1945, Therese Doublet, an inhabitant of Rots, wearing a British or Canadian cap is posing in the Panther. *Hstuf.* Pfeiffer's tank, the turret covered in blood, was recovered and taken to the rear. (Godin's collection.)

7

21

2nd Battalion of the 12th SS Panzer Regiment *(II./SS-Pz.Rgt. 12)*

1. The battalion was commanded by *Sturmbannführer* Karl-Heinz Prinz who can be seen here on the right during the move to the front on 6 June 1944. He was born on 28 February 1914 at Marburg an der Lahn in Hessen. An officer of the "LAH", he commanded the *Marder* self-propelled anti-tank guns during the battle of Kharkov in 1943. He then took command of the 2nd battalion of the 12th SS Panzer regiment, was awarded the Knights' Cross and was killed north-east of Falaise on 14 August 1944. (Walther/Author's collection.)

2. Well camouflaged, the Panzer IV's of the 2nd Battalion await the order to move up to the front. (Kretzschmar's collection.)

3. A Panzer IV from the 5th Company. "536" was the section commander's tank, *Ustuf.* Willi Kandler, en route for the front. (Kändler's collection.)

4. A 2nd Battalion Panzer IV (note the Hitler Youth Division marking on the left) near Bernay during the advance to the front. (Bundesarchiv.)

5. Another Panzer IV of the battalion on the march. You can see the divisional marking on the wing of the pick-up. (Bundesarchiv.)

2nd Battalion of the 12th SS Panzer Regiment *(II./SS-Pz.Rgt. 12)*

1. An example of a "Whirlwind" (*Wirbelwind*) a quadruple 2 cm anti-aircraft guns mounted on a Panzer IV chassis, developed by Karl-Wilhelm Krause for the 2nd Battalion. (Photo W. Krause.)

2. Four subalterns on the staff of the battalion, from left to right : *Ustuf.* Komadina (battalion signals officer) ; *Ustuf.* Porsch (who took over the 5th Company after the death of *Ostuf.* Bando on 27 June) ; *Ustuf.* Herbert Walther (adjutant) ; and *Ostuf.* Freitag. All four are wearing different uniforms. (Walther/Author's collection.)

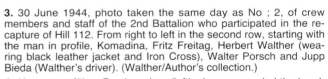

3. 30 June 1944, photo taken the same day as No ; 2, of crew members and staff of the 2nd Battalion who participated in the re-capture of Hill 112. From right to left in the second row, starting with the man in profile, Komadina, Fritz Freitag, Herbert Walther (wea-ring black leather jacket and Iron Cross), Walter Porsch and Jupp Bieda (Walther's driver). (Walther/Author's collection.)

4. *Hauptsturmführer* Pezdeuscheg (left) who commanded the head-quarters company. (Stephan/Author's collection.)

5. *Obersturmführer* Hartmann and his driver. He was deputy to *Sturmbannführer* K-H Prinz. (Stephan/Author's collection.)

6. Medical orderly Manfred Stephan (right) with one of his comrades from the reconnaissance section of the headquarters company of the 2nd Battalion. (Stephan/Author's collection.)

12th SS Panzer Regiment - 5th Company *(5./SS-Pz.Rgt. 12)*

1. March 1944 in Belgium during an inspection by Field Marshal von Rundstedt, the Panzer IV's of the 5th Company lined up. The camouflage consisted of green and reddish splodges on the base of sand coloured *Zimmerit*. At that time the identification numbers were only represented by a black painted outline. (Bundesarchiv.)

2. Part of the crew of the commander of the 3rd Section (*Ustuf.* Kändler) on the Panzer IV "535". From left to right : Kändler, (section and tank commander) - ? - *Sturmmann* Willi Schnittfinke (gun-layer) - an *Uscha.* (probably from the workshop section - a replacement driver. (Coll. W. Kändler.)

3. *Sturmmann* Willi Schnittfinke, the company commander's gun-layer who achieved several victories near Cheux and on Hill 112. (Author's collection.)

4. Panzer IV "526" camouflaged in a cornfield in the Caen area. (Photo coll. W. Kretzschmar.)

5. *Ustuf.* Willy Kändler (left) commander of the 3rd section and *Uscha.* Kretschmar, one of his tank commanders. Note the mixture of uniform clothing : standard officers' jacket left and sailcloth camouflage blouse on the right. Both are wearing leather trousers. (Author's coll.)

6. The first rest days for the 5th Company between 1 and 3 July near Etavaux in the Caen area. From left to right, Corporals (*Sturmmaenner*) Schreiner, Stefan and Gaude.

7. *Ustuf.* Helmut Kunze, (wearing here the insignia of a *Standartenoberjunker*) , section commander in the 5th Company who was killed on the 28th June 1944. (Coll. W. Kändler.)

12th SS Panzer Regiment - 5th Company (5./SS-Pz.Rgt. 12)

1. The Panzer IV of *Uscha*. Willy Kretschmar, the "536" at Esquay-Notre-Dame on 28 June 1944. Wearing a motorcyclist's coat is the section commander, *Untersturmführer* Willi Kändler. On his right is *Uscha*. Kretschmar in leather uniform, which was good protection against burns. "536" has lost one of its side protection plates.

2. *Uscha*. Kretschmar with his tank crew after their success defending Hill 112. From left to right : *Strm. (Sturmmann)* Schreiner (driver), *Strm.* Stefan (radio operator); *Uscha*. Kretschmar (commander) ; *Strm.* Schweinfest (gun-layer) ; *Strm.* Gaude (loader). Note the white rings around the barrel of the *KwK 40 L/48* gun indicating the number of victories.

3. Panzer IV "538" received a hit between the engine and the crew compartment during the first attack on Hill 112, south-west of Caen. *Uscha*. Kretschmar (cap), and the *Sturmmaenner* Schweinfest (left) and Stefan inspect the damage.

4. 7 June 1944, during the first engagement of the 12th SS Panzer Regiment, the tank "536" was hit by an artillery shell near Buron (north-west of Caen), damaging the track bogies. The crew managed to repair the damage in a day and a half, near to the *I-Trupp* (company workshop) which was situated at the time near the crossroads where the Caen-Bayeux and the Caen to Villers-Bocage routes cross (south of Tilly). You can see *Uscha.* W. Kretzschmar with his back turned.

5. This photo shows the damage sustained by "536" on 7 June 1944 and was taken the following day when the tank was still immobilised. Note the large numbers hand painted without stencil on the turret. For this company they would appear to be black with a white surrounding. (Photos : Kretzschmar's collection.)

12th SS Panzer Regiment - 6th Company (6./SS-Pz.Rgt. 12)

1. The 6th Company took part in an exercise in the Ostend area of Belgium in the winter of 1943-44. This is tank "604" of the deputy company commander.

2. The company commander, *Obersturmführer* Ruckdeschel, looking out of the turret of his tank "604". He was a member of the Nazi parliament and deputy *Gauleiter* of Bayreuth.

3. "625" crossing a bascule bridge to test its solidity, guided over by a man.

4. A halt in a typical village in Flanders. The girlfriend of the commander of "615", also in charge of the 1st section, was called Wilma and her name was painted on the turret hatch. The driver's girlfriend was Paula .

5. *Oscha* Terdenge was the commander of the 3rd Section. He was a veteran in comparison with the majority of young crew members. He was cold and had folded down his fur-lined cap.

6. Here we see *Oscha*. Terdenge in the turret of his "635". The numbers appear to have been roughly hand painted in black without a stencil and outlined in white. (Bundesarchiv.)

12th SS Panzer-Regiment - 6th Company *(6./SS-Pz.Rgt. 12)*

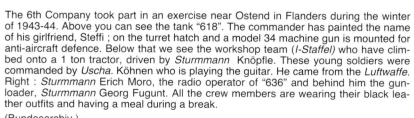

The 6th Company took part in an exercise near Ostend in Flanders during the winter of 1943-44. Above you can see the tank "618". The commander has painted the name of his girlfriend, Steffi ; on the turret hatch and a model 34 machine gun is mounted for anti-aircraft defence. Below that we see the workshop team (*I-Staffel*) who have climbed onto a 1 ton tractor, driven by *Sturmmann* Knöpfle. These young soldiers were commanded by *Uscha.* Köhnen who is playing the guitar. He came from the *Luftwaffe.* Right : *Sturmmann* Erich Moro, the radio operator of "636" and behind him the gunloader, *Sturmmann* Georg Fugunt. All the crew members are wearing their black leather outfits and having a meal during a break.

(Bundesarchiv.)

12th SS-Panzer-Regiment - 8th Company *(8./SS-Pz.Rgt. 12)*

1. *Hauptsturmführer* Hans Siegel commanded the 8th Company. He was awarded the Knight' Cross of the iron Cross on 23 August 1944. (Siegel's collection.)

2. *Obersturmführer* Herbert Höfler commanded the Ist Section ; he is seen here during the fighting at the beginning of August 1944, wearing a blouse made of Italian camouflage material. The soldier standing to attention in the background has a standard camouflage blouse. (Höfler's collection.)

3. Three members of the company before the Battle of Normandy. From left to right : *Oscha.* Rudolph Polzin who was the adjutant of the company. He has the regulation notebook tucked into his jacket. ; *Ustuf.* Jeran, commander of the 3rd. Section ; and *Hscha.* Drebert who was killed on 7 June 1944. (Polzin's collection.)

4. Panzer IV "837" (numbers painted in black, outlined in white) during the inspection by Field Marshal von Rundstedt in Belgium. In the turret is *Ustuf.* Jeran who commanded the 3rd. Section. The tank is an "H" type. (Author's collection.)

5. Here we see the same tank a few months later. This photo was taken by Sergeant Hardy on 6 July and shows tank "837" being towed by a Cromwell armoured recovery vehicle from 11th Armoured Division, after it had been knocked out near Cheux. The turret is trained to the rear and one can see the divisional insignia on the back of the engine compartment. (IWM.)

Half success for the tanks of the Hitler Youth Division

A little before midnight on 6 June, during the final minutes of that fateful day, *Standartenführer* Kurt Meyer, commander of the 25th SS Panzergrenadier Regiment, one of the two motorised infantry regiments in the 12th SS-Panzer-Division *Hitlerjugend*, arrived at the headquarters of the 716th Infantry Division to inform himself of the progress of the battle in the sector and to discuss coordination with other units. The headquarters was installed in a bunker dug into a quarry with the entrance facing south, protecting it from the view and fire of the enemy. It was at a place called La Folie to the north of Caen and today the Mémorial Museum is built on top of the bunker. There, Kurt Meyer met Lieutenant-General Wilhem Richter, the commander of 716th Infantry-Div. and Lieutenant-General Edgar Feuchtinger, the commander of 21st Panzer-Div. Meyer encountered the wounded in the underground corridor, spread out in the middle of the frantic coming and goings of the stretcher-bearers - the front was close by. General Richter confirmed to him that the situation was serious and explained that his division had ceased to exist at the end of that day. He no longer was in communication with his battalions reduced to company strength and engaged with the attackers as more and more isolated battle groups. General Feuchtinger listened to this report in silence. He was fed up with having engaged more than a third of his armoured division to *"block up the holes in the defence instead of being able to mount a solid blow against the British 6th Airborne Division, 24 hours had passed before they were able to consolidate".* He confided to Kurt Meyer that he did not intend to let his infantry and artillery be sacrificed in small unit counter-attacks for a disorganised and panic stricken command. Then Richter carried on with his report : Carpiquet had been evacuated by its *Luftwaffe* defenders at 1400 hrs and the solid network of underground bunkers was empty. Three companies of the 736th Infantry Regiment (part of 716th Infantry Division) were at Buron, La Folie and Epron with a few tanks from the 22nd Panzer Regiment. Richter finished his report by revealing that the radar station at Douvres with its bunkers was surrounded but had all that was necessary to hold out for several days. Thus with the exception of the Douvres radar station which remained on the Allied flank and gave precious information about their movements to the German command, the front in that sector had more or less ceased to exist. Carpiquet and its airfield had been ceded without resistance to the advancing Canadian 3rd Infantry Division and the road leading to Caen was open as well. When Kurt Meyer was leaving General Richter's headquarters he received a telephone call from his divisional commander, *Brigadeführer* Fritz Witt, who passed on the orders from I SS-Panzer-Corps : 12th SS-Panzer-Division was to attack on 7 June at 1600 hrs to the left of the railway from Caen to Luc-sur-Mer with 21st Panzer-Division on its right flank, and the two divisions were to drive the enemy back into the sea. After that, Kurt Meyer went off to set up his headquarters in a small café at Saint-Germain-la-Blanche-Herbe.

On that 7 June at **0300 hrs** *Standartenführer* Kurt Meyer issued oral orders to his reinforced regiment for the attack. Two battalion of the 25th SS-Panzer-Grenadier Regiment - the 1st on the right and the 2nd ; on the left - plus the 3rd also to the left but echelonned to the rear. The 1st Battalion was to maintain contact on the right flank with 21st Panzer-Division and the tanks of 22nd Panzer-Regiment between Epron and La Folie. But the left flank remained wide open and there was nothing other than Meyer's regiment to the left of 21st Panzer-Division although he had been reinforced by the 15 cm guns of the 3rd Battalion of the divisional artillery whose fire could guard the open flank, and the 2nd Battalion of the tank regiment (12th SS-Panzer-Regiment) with its Panzer IVs which were due to arrive at the front. At **0900 hrs,** Meyer reached his new headquarters at the Abbaye d'Ardenne where *Sturmbannführer* Bartling informed him that the 15 cm howitzers of his artillery battalion were ready to open fire, but that the tanks had still not arrived; the first of them did not appear until **1000 hrs** The battalion commander, *Sturmbannfuhrer* Karl-Heinz Prinz, announced that he had fifty Panzer IV's available but that the remainder would arrive during the course of the day and the following night.

Karl-Heinz Prinz had sent his aide de camp, *Untersturmführer* Herbert Walther with an advance party to prepare the battalion's arrival at the front.

Preparing the attack on 7 June 1944 in the courtyard of the Abbaye d'Ardenne. From left to right : *Sturmbannführer* Karl-Heinz Prinz , commander of the 2nd battalion of the 12th SS-Pz.-Regt. and *Sturmbannführer* Karl Bartling who commanded the 3rd Battalion of the 12th SS Panzer Artillery Regiment, equipped with 15 cm howitzers. Prinz is wearing a leather jacket and Bartling, a jacket made of Italian camouflage material. In a superb affectation, his map case is covered in the identical cloth. (Photo PK Woscidlo/ Author's colleciton.)

Second-Lieutenant Herbert Walther was a particularly remarkable figure of the battalion. He had taken part in the Battle of Kharkov at the end of the winter of 1943 with his assault gun *Lausbub,* which can be translated as « little mischief ». That brought him to the notice of his company commander Karl-Heinz Prinz. The latter was a great tank commander, had no sense of direction, but he sensed that Herbet Walther, whose style of fighting he found pleasing, also had a sense of terrain sufficient for two.Thus when the 2nd battalion of the tank regiment of the Hitler Youth division was formed, its commander, Prinz, took Herbert Walther with him as his aide de camp. The latter had a surly and choleric temperament, well known for his plain speaking. He had a habit of dividing those whom he knew into two categories : his comrades to whom he vowed a sincere and unbreakable friendship and those who he dismissed as « arse-holes » (*Aschloch*). He was a sort of Captain Haddock type (from the Tintin comics) - a great heart but with a terrible temper. He had a tense relationship with the commander of the headquarters company of the battalion, *Hauptsturmführer* Pezdeuscheg, but on the other hand he got on extremely well with *Obersturmführer* Hartmann, Prinz's deputy, who dealt with all the staff work in the battalion. As far as Herbert Walther was concerned, he a job to do which was way above that of an aide de camp, driving up to the front and positioning the companies according to the terrain and in line with the plans of his boss.

He went everywhere in his *Schwimmwagen* (a light amphibious vehicle based on a Volkswagen chassis). One of his comrades described his thus : « when you heard shots and explosions, when you saw smoke and a S*chwimmwagen* appeared, it was bound to be *Ustuf. Walther* arriving. » He was a forceful personality who know how to handle his responsibilities towards his men, and things were bound to be dangerous during his trips around the front, yet he took no heed of his own life (or that of his driver). He said : "my comrades needed me. *Ustuf.* Walther counted for nothing in the face of his responsibilities towards others".

At dawn on 7 June he went to the underground headquarters of the 716th Infantry Division at La Folie to get some information from the chief-of-staff of 21st Panzer-Division who had his office there. Herbert Walther drove into the entrance tunnel of the headquarters on a BMW motorcycle, right up to the office of the intelligence officer of the division and was surprised that nobody checked his identity. « I could have been an enemy and got in there with hand grenades. » He asked the staff officer for maps of the sector and the latter replied that « he did not have any at that moment ». Thus it was that *Ustuf.* Walther was unaware of the anti-tank ditch that had been dug during the preceding months by men of the 716th Infantry Division and civilian forced labourers, in advance of the sector over which the Hitler Youth division was going to have to attack. He then rejoined Kurt Meyer at his headquarters at the Abbaye d'Ardenne where together, from the gallery that ran around under the roof of the abbey church, they observed the arrival of the advance guard of the 9th Canadian Brigade (commanded by Brigadier D.G.Cunningham) : a battle group commanded by Major Learment comprising the Stuart light tanks of the reconnaissance section of the Sherbrooke Fusiliers Regiment (Lieutenant Kraus) followed by C Company (Captain Fraser) of the North Nova Scotia Highlanders riding on carriers and then a section of machine-gunners from the Cameron Highlanders of Ottawa also mounted on carriers and a section of the 3rd Antitank Regi-

ment equipped with M10 Tank destroyers. That battle group was followed by the main body of the advance guard which consisted of the bulk of the North Nova Scotia Highlanders (Lt.Col. Petch) and the bulk of the Sherbrooke Fusiliers Regiment (Lt.Col. Gordon). The 320 infantrymen of companies A, B and D of the NNSH were mounted on 45 Sherman tanks of the Sherbrooke Fusiliers. This advance guard of the 3rd Canadian Division invested the village of Buron towards the end of the morning and the battle group Learment forced on towards Authie with the Stuart tanks of Lt. Kraus in the lead, destination Carpiquet. Behind him Captain Fraser occupied Authie with C Company of the NNSH and at roughly **1330 hrs** his men spread out under the apple trees to eat their rations. It was at **1400 hrs** that Kurt Meyer noticed the Canadian advance towards Carpiquet from his vantage point below the abbey roof, studying the landscape through his binoculars as if it was a sand table exercise.

Having received his orders, *Ustuf.* Walther went off to position the fifty tanks of the 2nd Battalion. He posted them on a reverse slope to hide them from enemy view and to achieve surprise. But suddenly he saw a vehicle arriving with an officer senior to himself (it was in fact *Ostubaf.* Milius who commanded the 3rd Battalion of the 25th Panzer-Grenadiers). That officer walked on foot up to the crest of the ridge with his maps and gave a commentary on the situation to those accompanying him. Once again, Walther gave an example of his fiery temper. Although only a second lieutenant he addressed the lieutenant colonel : "bugger off, you'll get us spotted by the enemy". Milius did not appreciated being spoken to in such a manner by a second lieutenant and that evening he encountered him again together with his boss. He complained to *Stubaf.* Prinz about his behaviour, who retorted that he had confidence in *Ustuf.* Walther : "what he said I would have said myself" and there the matter rested.

Kurt Meyer noticed that the Canadians were about to cross the main Caen-Bayeux road (RN 13) and that Carpiquet and its airfield would be taken in their stride. But he held his fire/the counter-attack was planned for the afternoon and it was necessary to maintain the effect of surprise. Already *Untersturmführer* Porsch with four Panzer IV's from the 5th Company had reconnoitred the road between Franqueville and Authie, just north of the RN 13 and had to his surprise encountered the Shermans of A Squadron of the Sherbrooke Fusiliers. In quick succession he lost three of his tanks (those of *Hscha.* Muller, *Oscha.* Auinger and *Uscha.* Klempt). That skirmish had put the Canadians on their guard and Kurt Meyer could not wait for the attack due to start at 1600 hrs ; it was necessary to hammer the enemy immediately. Right away he ordered the commander of the 12th SS Panzer-Regiment, *Ostubaf.* Max Wunsche to engage with his Panzer IV's on the left and *Ostubaf.* Milnius yo join the attack with his 3rd Battalion of the 25th Panzer Grenadiers. Wunsche received the order by telephone in his command tank and passed it on to his companies by radio : *"Achtung, Panzer marsch !"* That was at **1420 hrs** The 5th and 6th companies of tanks rushed off ahead and took the Canadian advance guard in the flank ; Rapidly, at a cost of four Panzer IV's destroyed, the 6th Company knocked out more than ten Canadian armoured vehicles. Explosions, crewmen baling out, screaming and burned, from the tanks engulfed in flames ; black plumes of smoke rose above the plain. The tanks rolled on towards Authie accompanied by the 9th Company of grenadiers.

Ustuf. Herbert Walther was the aide de camp to the commander of the 2nd Battalion of the 12th SS Panzer Regiment, *Stubaf.* K.-H. Prinz. He was one of the most remarkable and picturesque personalities in the regiment. (Author's collection.)

Ustuf. Karl-Heinz Porsch was a section commander in the 5th Company of the 12th SS Panzer Regiment on 7 June and before the attack had been out on reconnaissance. He subsequently became the company commander but was killed on 8 August to the south of Saint-Aignan. (Photo W. Kändler/Author's collection.)

37

The Canadian attack and the counter attack by the 12th SS-Panzer-Div. on 7 June 1944. The NNSH had sent its advance guard through Buron to Authie and Franqueville. The german counter-attack was carried out in the west by the 3rd Batt. of the 25th Pz.-Grenadiers and two companies of Panzer IV's (5th and 6th), in the centre by the 2nd Batt. of grenadiers and the 7th Company's Panzer IV's and in the east by the remaining battalion of grenadiers plus the five Panzer IV's available to 8th Company. (Heimdal.)

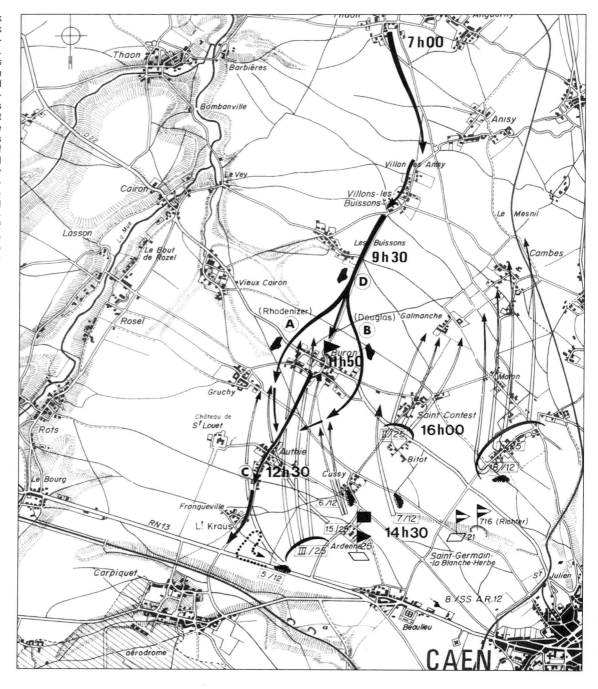

They rapidly reached Authie and from there, the 6th Company carried on towards Buron. But, when they approached the latter village, the Canadian artillery put down a heavy barrage on the company, causing significant losses among the tanks and the grenadiers accompanying them. Several tanks collected up the wounded and withdrew back to the Abbaye d'Ardenne, where *Standartenführer* Meyer ordered them to reinforce the grenadiers who were fighting it out in the streets of Buron.

Any tanks that remained were to support the infantry.

Thus the 5th Company whose tanks were the first to be engaged attacked to the south of Authie and then on the left flank as far as Gruchy where they were to cover the northern border, while the 6th Company took Authie and then entered Buron to support the 3rd Battalion of grenadiers.

As far as the 7th Company was concerned, it sup-

ported the attacks on Saint-Contest and then Galmanche by the 2nd Battalion of grenadiers. Under the command of *Hauptsturmführer* Bracker, the tanks followed three companies of grenadiers into the attack, spread out in a fan-shaped formation. Saint-Contest was taken without major difficulty and then the tanks forced three enemy ones to retreat. Malon and Galmanche were also taken without encountering serious opposition.

On the right - and to the left of the front of the 21st Panzer-Division - the tanks of the 8th Company commanded by *Ostuf.* Hans Siegel, were to support the attack in the direction of Cambes by the Ist Battalion of grenadiers. But Hans Siegel only had five Panzer IV's available. The grenadiers took Cambes in the face of stiff opposition. The tanks went into action but one broke down. The remaining four passed to the west of Malon. Hans Siegel led the advance but while attacking a copse to the north of Cambes, a shell took off a tree branch which landed on his tank, blocking the turret. Two of his tanks rejoined him ; both had been hit and one had lost a track. The fourth tank, further to the rear, had driven into a shell crater and was stuck. The attack stopped dead before anyone had had a chance to fire a single shot. Thus while the Ist Battalion of grenadiers had progressed north of Cambes, pushing back the British Royal Ulster Rifles, the attack could not be continued because of the defection of the tanks. To the right, some of the tanks of 21st Panzer-Division had failed to arrive and the grenadiers found themselves without protection on their right flank which forced them to withdraw. "The order to retire was greeted with incredulity and was obeyed with some reluctance." Every where the attack was broken off and the Hitler Youth division was unable to reach the sea as had been envisaged : it was a half success. The only tangible result was that the enemy advance in the sector had been stopped and some territory had been regained.

The companies of 12th SS Pz.-Regt. which had attacked on the left flank (5th and 6th) had lost 9 Panzer IV's and suffered 13 killed and 11 wounded. The 7th Company had lost three tanks and two soldiers killed, plus two officers, one nco and two soldiers wounded. The 8th Company had four tanks damaged and counted four dead with one nco and a soldier wounded. The 9th Company in reserve had one tank damaged. The tank losses of the enemy were far higher : the Sherbrooke Fusiliers lost fifteen according to their war diary, and the North Nova Scotias had 21 Cruiser tanks destroyed and seven others damaged.

At the end of that second day the 21st Panzer-Division had not attacked and the elements of the Hitler Youth (a little less than half the division's effectives) had not been able to push their assault through to the coast. On the other hand, on the left wing, the German flank was wide open with only the reconnaissance section of the 12th SS maintaining a level of patrol activity. The Panzer-Lehr-Division had still not arrived. There had not been a decisive or coherent German attack and there was still not a continuous front line.

Two Sherman tanks destroyed between Buron and the Abbaye d'Ardenne on 7 June 1944 by the Panzer IV's of the 2nd. Battalion of the 12th SS Pz.-Regt. They are being examined by crew members of the latter unit. (Author's collection.)

Panzer-Lehr-Division

These nine previously unpublished photos are of an exercise carried out by Panzer-Lehr-Division at Amboise in May 1944. Three Type "A" Panthers from the 3rd Company (we can see "322" and "325") from the 1st battalion of the divisional tank regiment, *Panzer-Lehr-Regiment 130,* were moving along the Quai Charles Guinot. The battalion rejoined its original unit, 3rd Pz.-Div. in October 1944. The numbers painted on the turrets are very large and appear to be red with a white outline. The divisional engineer battalion, the *Panzer-Pionier-Bataillon 130,* had assembled a pontoon bridge over the Loire, joining the roadway on the left bank with the so-called Ile d'or (golden isle). (Coll. E. Santin.)

Thursday 8 June

That day a third armoured division finally reached the front : the Panzer-Lehr-Division. That elite formation, partly made up of demonstration and instructional units, has been habitually presented as the best armoured and the most powerful. But what was it exactly ?

On 26 January 1944, Colonel-General Heinz Guderian, said to the man who was about to become its commander a few days later, Major-General Fritz Bayerlein : "with this single division you can throw the Anglo-Americans back into the sea. Your objective is the coast, no, not the coast, the sea !"

Its tank regiment, *Panzer-Lehr-Regiment 130,* was commanded by Colonel Rudolf Gerhardt. His staff had available a signals section made up of three Panther command tanks (*Befehlspanzer V*), a strong reconnaissance section of five Panzer IV's and an armoured flak section (12 2 cm Flak 38 guns - Sd.Kfz. 140).

The 1st Battalion (*I/Pz. Lehr-Rgt. 6*) was commanded by Major Markowksi and equipped with Panther tanks. His staff had a signals section with three command Panthers, a reconnaissance section (five Panthers), a motorcycle reconnaissance section, an engineer section mounted on armoured cars, and a section of armoured anti-aircraft artillery (two Type « H » Flakpanzer IV's each mounting a four barrelled 20 mm canon). The four companies were each equipped with 17 Panzer V's (Panthers) to which should be added a workshop and a quartermaster supply company.

The 2nd battalion (*II/Pz.Lehr-Rgt. 130*) was commanded by Lieutenant-Colonel Prince von Schönburg-Waldenburg. Born on 3 April 1913 at Guteborn (40 kilometres north of Dresden), Prince Wilhelm came from an ancient princely line and he made his impression on his battalion : the tanks all had his personal coat of arms painted on their turrets. They were Panzer IV's, mostly "H" Types. His staff consisted of a command company identical to that of the 1st Battalion except that the Panthers were replaced here by Panzer IV's. The four fighting companies were each allotted 22 Panzer IV's , and the battalion also had a workshop company, a company of remote-controlled tanks and a quartermaster service company.

As far as the company of remote-controlled tanks was concerned *(Funklenk-Kompanie 316),* it was equipped with devices made by Messrs. Borgward *(Sd.Kfz 301)* which carried an explosive charge. It had originally been intended to guide them from ten "E" Type Tigers but they were replaced in February 1944 by nine assault guns and then by five "B" Type Tigers *(Sd.Kfz. 182)* of which the chassis numbers ran from 28001 to 28005. In May these heavy tanks remained at Chateaudun on account of mechanical problems. No Tiger tanks were ever brought into action by the divisional tank regiment which remained a classical unit and in spite of the legends it was never an over-equipped one.

The Advance to the front

Lt. Gen. Bayerlein was alerted on 6 June by General Warlimont at 0230 hrs. He had to stop the transfer to Poland of the 1st Battalion of his tank regiment, although the first train of Panther tanks was already in Germany, near Magdeburg, while the rest of the battalion was waiting to load in the Paris region. Thus Major Markowski's battalion was unable to take part in the early battles and only rejoined Tilly-sur-Seulles sector on 15 June. The Panzer-Lehr-Division was only able to advance to the front line with half the strength of its tank regiment.

Apart from that unit, all the others were put in a state of alert on 6 June at 0415 hrs with the code-word *Blücher.* The 2nd Battalion of the tank regiment only had 1,400 rounds of 7.5 cm KWK L/48 with which to go into action. At 0900 hrs the division was ready to take to the road, but at midday was still awaiting orders to march. Finally, Colonel-General Dollmann, commander of Seventh Army, give the necessary order to move at 1700 hrs. But it was still daylight and the divison was vulnerable to attack by the Allied aviation. In June the nights were short and during the period of darkness, the vehicles could only move at a maximum speed of 10 to 12 km/h which meant that they could only cover between 60 and 70 kilometres in a night. To reach the coast the distance to be covered was 140 km, and if the unit was to get into combat on 7 June, it would have to drive by night and day.

The division moves along three axes : B1, B2 and B3. The tank regiment followed the B2 axis in the centre via Brou, Nogent-le-Rotrou, Alencon, Flers, Condé-sur-Noireau and Villers-Bocage. With only the 2nd. Battalion, the unit was placed under the command of Colonel Gerhardt. Franz Kurowski recounted the story of the advance to the front on the late afternoon of 6 June : *"with a screeching of metal the tanks took to the road and headed north. With relaxing the crews scanned the skies. Suddenly 'they' were there and nobody know where they had come from. The 'jabos' (fighter-bombers) approached with their engines screaming and flew by hedge-hopping below the trees. A quadruple flak gun from the escort opened up and thanks to its concentrated firepower, the aircraft withdrew. The first explosion echoed down from the front of the column and those who heard it asked each other 'is it one of ours ?' It was this thought that was imprinted on all faces. The tank crews, appearing again from the hatches passed a fighter bomber shot down beside the road, the petrol pouring from its burst tanks flaming and its ammunition exploding. A staff car was a victim of the low-level attack which killed three men including the gun-layer of the Flak piece. The first in the division to be dead."* (from F Kurowski, *Die Panzer Lehr Division,* pages 35-36). The battalion of Major von Schönburg would suffer three more attacks before nightfall.

In the early hours of 7 June the advanced elements of the division were 55 km south-west of Caen on a line from Argentan to Domfront. Shortly after four in the morning, having thus only covered about

80 km, roughly half the distance that separated them from the front, the battalion of the tank regiment was spotted by Allied aerial reconnaissance in the Foret d'Ecouves north of Alencon. The tanks had been well camouflaged in the dense forest but were spotted just at the moment when the crews were refuelling their tanks with petrol. Two Panzer IV's and several other vehicles were destroyed as a result of that attack, but in spite of the threat, General Dollmann ordered the division to continue its march. Lt. Gen. Bayerlein drew up a balance of his losses since the march began. Prince von Schönburg-Waldenburg's battalion had already lost five Panzer IV's before even arriving at the front and the losses of other units in the division were even heavier : 23 tractor units, 85 or 86 light armoured vehicles and 123 lorries, 60 of which were fuel tankers. According to Ritgen, those figures were exaggerated and apart from the five Panzer IV's, the losses came to 84 armoured cars and tractor units plus 90 wheeled vehicles of which most were fuel tankers.

From his headquarters at Cheux, General Bayerlein acting on orders received from I SS-Panzer-Corps, prepared his counter-attack for 8 June : *"The I SS-Panzer-Corps, together with 21st Panzer-Division, 12th SS-Panzer-Division and Panzer-Lehr-Division which have been placed under its orders, will push into the bridgehead from the area of Caen - Saint-Croix (Grand Tonne) and will gain the line St. Aubin (sur Mer) - Vauvres (Douvres) - Creully. To achieve that the left flank on the line Carcagny - Ellon - Trungy will be covered by reconnaissance units. Panzer-Lehr-Division will take up positions during the night of 7/8 June in the area of Bretteville (Orgueilleuse) - Sainte-Croix-Grand-Tonne by 0300 hrs ready to attack towards Courseulles."* (Divisional attack order 8.06.44). But although it should attack towards Courseulles, General Bayerlein was unaware that Maj.-Gen. Graham's 50th Infantry-Division had already taken Bayeux.

In fact, the attack did not get underway until the beginning of the afternoon of 8 June. And Prince von Schönburg-Waldenburg's battalion of tanks did not even participate; they were still well to the rear. The orders from I SS-Panzer-Corps had created a certain amount of confusion : in effect the PLD had to take up positions on the left flank which were also assigned to one of the two grenadier regiments of the Hitler Youth division, the 26th SS Panzer-Grenadier-Regiment. Apart from that the start lines were already in the hands of British and Canadian troops. Thus the attack on the 8 June could not take place in the way that was intended. 21st Pz.-Div. was already on the defensive to the north of Caen and PLD could only insert its advance elements into a confused situation which would not permit it to launch an effective counter-attack. As far as 12th SS-Pz.-Div. was concerned, it intended to attack to the west of Caen at the end of the day.

The Hitler Youth Division night attack

As we have seen, the 26th SS-Panzer-Grenadier-Regiment was to position itself on the left flank of the "HY" Division which completely negated the orders given to install some of its units in the same sector. The 1st Batt. of the 26th according to its orders had attacked at 0300 hrs on 8 June towards Norrey-en-Bessin and the 2nd. in the direction of Putot-en-Bessin, while the 3rd. covered the open left flank. But Canadian troops were already installed in those two locations to the south of RN13 and

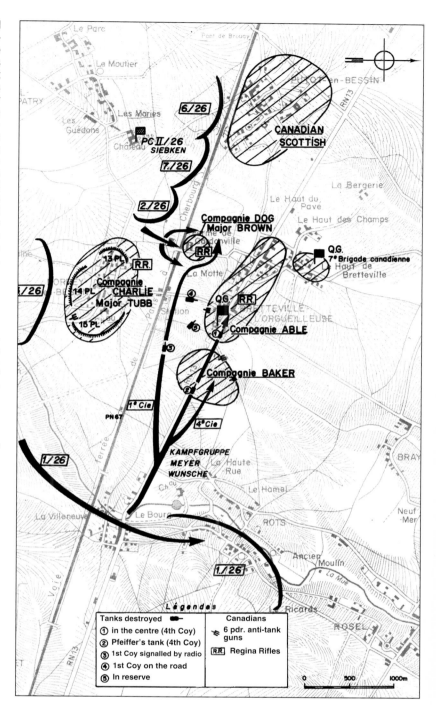

Légendes

Tanks destroyed		Canadians	
① in the centre (4th Coy)		6 pdr. anti-tank guns	
② Pfeiffer's tank (4th Coy)		RR Regina Rifles	
③ 1st Coy signalled by radio			
④ 1st Coy on the road			
⑤ In reserve			

0   500   1000m

the 26th Regiment did not have the support for its 1st Battalion (*SS-Sturmbannführer* Jürgensen) from 12th SS-Panzer-Regiment which had been promised.

By the end of the day on 8 June the situation was hardly brilliant. 21st Panzer and the right wing of 12th SS (25th Panzer-Grenadier-Regiment and the 2nd Battalion of the tank regiment) were blocked on the defensive to the north of Caen. On the left, Panzer-Lehr was preparing to attack towards Bayeux, but only the 26th SS-Panzer-Grenadiers were carrying out a limited offensive in the centre. It was necessary for several reasons : - the radar station at Douvres was still holding out with determination and needed to be relieved ; - a successful attack would separate the British 50th Infantry Division from the Canadian 3rd Infantry Division. For the attack to succeed it was necessary to take Rots, Bretteville-l'Orgueilleuse and Norrey-en-Bes-

The attack by the Meyer-Wünsche battle group during the night of 8/9 June was carried out from Rots in the direction of Bretteville-l'Orgueilleuse , a village solidly held by Canadian anti-tank defences. On the map north is to the right and west on top. (Heimdal.)

sin, then proceed north along the valley of the Mue and that of the Seulles to its estuary at Courseulles. In other respects that would facilitate liaison between the two grenadier regiments of the 12th SS.

To support that attack, two companies of 12th SS Pz.-Regt. finally arrived at the end of the day : the Ist. Commanded by *Hauptsturmführer* Berlin and the 4th by *Hauptsturmführer* Hans Pfeiffer. The accompanying infantry was furnished by a company of the *15./26* Grenadiers (*Hstuf.* von Büttner) and the reconnaissance company of the 25th Grenadiers. The self-propelled 10,5 cm guns of the 2nd Battery provided fire support. The attack was to be directed by *Standartenführer* Kurt Meyer, accompanied by the commander of the tank regiment, *Ostubaf.* Max Wünsche with his command tank, although the staff of the Ist battalion had not then arrived.

General Fritz Witt had visited the positions of the 25th Grenadiers during the afternoon, accompanied by Kurt Meyer, to prepare the attack which was to be launched from the west into the flank of the Canadians of the Regina Rifles Regiment, thus allowing the 26th Grenadiers to move north along the RN13. The Meyer-Wünsche battle group could call on 25 Panthers, a hundred grenadiers and six 10,5 cm self-propelled guns, which was not a lot for the scale of attack envisaged. But on top of that there was the other battalion of grenadiers, the 1st of the 26th. The success of the plan rested on securing a surprise, and Meyer had often mounted such attacks against a superior enemy force on the Eastern Front.

The preliminary phase of the attack was to be the capture of Rots, an operation that was achieved by the 1st Company (commander *Hstuf.* Eggert) of the 1st Batt. of the 26th Grenadiers, but before retiring from the village, the Canadians of the Regina Rifles were able to observe the preparations of the battle group and the arrival of the Panthers to the east of Rots. The effect of surprise was lost but the Germans were not yet aware of that. In fact the Canadians did not put up a strong resistance to the attack on Rots and regrouped at Bretteville-l'Orgueilleuse where they awaited the

Meyer-Wünsche battle group from behind solid positions.

Just before 2000 hrs on the north side of the RN13 and to the east of Rots, Kurt Meyer spoke to the men of the 25th Grenadiers : *"We will attack and tomorrow at dawn we will meet again on the Channel coast. Good luck comrades."* Then the rumbling mass of the Panthers arrived and the grenadiers scrambled up onto the rear deck plates. It was raining slightly and the mens' clothes were wet through. The 4th Company of tanks was to attack straight on following the RN 13 into the centre of Bretteville while the 4th Company was to turn the position from the south on the left flank. The Panthers which had been travelling in a spread out formation, formed into file to get through Rots and its hamlet of Villeneuve which were separated from each other by the RN13. Stopped just in front of the park of the chateau, "Panzer" Meyer who was in the side-car of a motorcycle made a last speech before the two tank companies continued their advance. It was **2120 hrs** and night was falling.

The 1st Company (Berlin) then deployed to the left of the road in the middle of a cornfield that was already high. The 4th company (Pfeiffer) followed suit and drove towards Bretteville travelling partly on the RN13 road. Pfeiffer's Panther was the third in line on the road which was bordered by ditches and plane trees (cut down after the war). Suddenly a well camouflaged Canadian tank lurking beside the road, appeared right in front of the first Panther, which stopped. Both turrets traversed slowly and the two guns lined up. The Canadian fired first and its shell exploded with a mighty blast as it skidded off the front plate of the Panther without doing any damage. Then the Panther fired in turn and its shell too ricocheted off the Canadian tank, which fired again without effect. Finally the Panther scored a direct hit and the Canadian exploded, its turret flying through the air and burning furiously. That Panther from the 1st Company intended to follow the road towards Bretteville and then turn to the left cross-country to encircle the village from the south. The two Panthers from the 4th Company which were following would thus move up into first and second (Pfeiffer's tank) positions on the road.

The Canadian infantry (from "B" Company of the Reginas) withdrew to the left through the corn towards the village after having engaged the grenadiers accompanying the tanks. The plain separating Rots and Bretteville is slightly elevated in the middle and at that moment the two 4th Company Panthers were protected by the reverse slope, and when they reached the crest, Pfeiffer stopped them to survey the situation, receiving in the process machine-gun fire and anti-tank shells. They came from the northern edge of Bretteville where the Canadians had carefully prepared their defensive positions with at least four anti-tank guns. Pfeiffer turned his guns in their direction, but the incoming rounds impacted on the armour plating of the tanks, causing the *Zimmerit* (a cement-based coating on the tanks to protect them against magnetic charges) to splinter off, stinging the faces of the grenadiers. *Hstuf.* Pfeiffer looked out of the cupola of his tank and gave orders to fire at the houses of Bretteville to set them alight so that he could see what was happening. *Sturmmann* Hans Kesper, driver of one of the 4th Company tanks remembered : *"We were receiving violent anti-tank fire and a few houses were burning. I heard our commander, Pfeiffer, shouting ; 'spray the houses with fire so that they light up the scene for us'. The tank in front of me received a hit."* Suddenly Pfeiffer's tank was hit by an anti-tank round and the crew had to bale

The battle group Meyer-Wünsche had 25 Panther tanks available. *Ostubaf. Max* Wünsche directed the battle from the turret of his command tank. He was wearing a jacket made of Italian camouflage material. He was lightly wounded in the head by a shell burst at the beginning of the attack.

The main view of Bretteville after the attack by the Panthers of the 4th Company.

1. In this photo taken around 20 June, the church tower had tumbled down after having been damaged by fire from *Uscha.* März's "313". Canadian soldiers are examining the Panther Type "G" destroyed by Joe Lapointe in the main street - the first one destroyed by the Allies in close combat in Normandy. Behind the railings on the left was the Canadian headquarters.

2. Detail of the rear of the turret of the same tank showing the hole made by a shell fired in error by the Panther following it, penetrating the 45 mm thick steel.

3. View taken from the other direction towards the east, showing a wrecked German half-track and the Panther already seen, which when it burned spewed flames as high as the church tower.
(IWM.)

out - Pfeiffer himself was OK but the tank went up in flames. Around the tanks the grenadiers went to ground, many of them wounded. The first tank on the road, the one in front of Pfeiffers wreck drove on into Bretteville on the main road and advanced towards the church. The Canadians had placed strings of grenades joined together with cords. The tracks bit into the asphalt and the Panther got half way to the church which could be seen at the main cross-roads and just after the farm which was the headquarters of Lt. Col. Foster Matheson who commanded the Regina Rifles Regiment. The men of the Reginas, hidden by the darkness saw the steel colossus approaching. For the first time in Normandy, Allied troops were confronted by a Panther tank at close quarters. Among them the soldier Joe Lapointe had loaded his PIAT, a by then outclassed personal anti-tank weapon, which was fired by pulling a piano wire. "B" Company which was guarding the edges of Bretteville had gone to ground - the situation was serious for the Canadians with that Panther approaching their regimental headquarters. It was **midnight** and Joe Lapointe was behind a wall about fifteen metres away. A hit ! The Panther rolled on another thirty metres and suddenly a string of grenades was in front of it. Someone pulled a cord and they exploded shattering the right track. The tank swerved and mounted the pavement. Lapointe fired again and missed but was successful with his third shot. The crew baled out and were killed immediately. A second Panther was following the first, saw the attack and opened fire with its machine-gun and main turret weapon, but the street was not wide enough and it hit the first Panther in the rear of the turret. It was probably that which caused the major damage and blew apart the rear hatch. The first Panther was burning and according to eye-witnesses the flames reached as high as the church tower. The second Panther disengaged and withdrew in reverse gear.

While the tanks of the 4th Company and the grenadiers from the 25th attempted to enter Bretteville from the east, those of the first company were moving round to the south to encircle the village and attack from the west. Max Wünsche had given his orders : "encircle the village from the left and penetrate to the centre of the place from the south-west". *Ustuf.* Jürgen Chemnitz who commanded the 1st section of the 1st Company, gave his account of the action : *"Hauptsturmführer Berlin ordered me by radio to circle around the village from the south and to enter it from the west. A few houses as well as the station were burning on the southern edge. To avoid being a target for too long while passing in front of the burning buildings, I ordered the section to move into line and told them to drive as fast as possible towards the protective darkness. Meanwhile the three tanks received hits from anti-tank rounds from the right as they traversed the danger zone, that is to say from the edge of the village. The vehicle on the right brewed up like a torch having probably received a direct hit in the engine compartment ; the crew baled out. Then my tank received a hit on the turret seriously wounding the gun-loader, blinded, with various bones broken and the electrical system was knocked out. The vehicle on the left, that of Unterscharführer Rust had also received a hit but was still manoeuvrable. From the latter vehicle I managed to contact Hauptsturmführer Berlin by radio who gave me the order to retreat. We got my loader out and laid him on the rear deck and returned to the road with the two remaining tanks. I saw to it that my loader was taken to hospital and then repaired the electrics of my tank before reporting to Hauptsturmführer Berlin, who ordered me to go to the village and report on the situation."*

Now let us follow the progress of the 3rd section of the 1st Company. *Sturmmann* Leopold Lengheim was the gun-layer of the second tank of that section who was firing continuously. As regards the 2nd Section, commanded by *Untersturmführer* Teichert, it was advancing to attack Bretteville from the south, while the 3rd section tank in which Lengheim was travelling was more to the west. Suddenly Dietrich, his section commander (tank "135") called up on the radio and told them to follow his Pan-

ther. Teichert was immobilised in Bretteville and surrounded by Canadian infantry. It was necessary to follow "135" and try to rescue him. From a hedgerow about 100 metres away, "135" received a hit and the crew evacuated , leaving the radio operator behind. He fired at the hedge. Then Dietrich came running up with the three other members of his crew, clambered up onto the tank and made a sign to effect an about turn to avoid the Canadian fire. After about 500 metres the Panther took shelter behind some trees and continued to fire back at its targets. Suddenly, through his visor, Leopold Lengheim saw about 900 metres away, a ball of fire coming towards him. No time for reflection : load, fire load, fire, just as fast as possible. A shell on the glacis plate and one on the gun. The enemy fire was too short, but then another round just at the base of the turret. The turret and the head of the tank commander, Hohnecker, were ripped off. Binder, the driver, realised what had happened and put his foot down to get into cover. Then over the radio calm the order to withdraw to the workshop detachment "assuming the vehicle is no longer operational". Their nerves shattered and with their dead comrades inside the tank, the survivors crept back to Martinville where Hohnecker was buried. The tanks retired beyond the farm at Cardonville where Max Wünsche gave the order to retreat.

In fact the infantry from the 1st Battalion of the 26th Grenadiers (I./26) had not been able to take Norrey and thus support the tanks of the 1st Company (1./12) from the south, which explains their defeat to the south of Bretteville, exposed to the Canadian anti-tank guns and without infantry support. To assess the situation, Maw Wünsche departed in his command tank towards Norrey : there he was fired on heavily, but did not lose anyone and with a heavy heart he turned round, suspended the attack and withdrew behind the Mue. *Ustuf.* Chemnitz reported thus on what happened : *"The tanks returned from the attack. As the road there was elevated, one had to show them where to get on to it. A tank had reached the road and I was guiding the driver. Behind me on the right was Wünsche and on the left, Nehrlich (liaison officer from the regimental staff). At that moment a Canadian tank fired at our leading vehicle and Wünsche was slightly wounded in the head by a shell burst. I received a shower of splinters around my feet, but Nehrlich was seriously injured, and in spite of being put into a side-car to take him to the field hospital, was dead on arrival."*

The attack on Bretteville proved to be a costly defeat. The 1st Company of the 26th Grenadiers was unable to attain its objectives and the tanks were degraded by a determined and well organised anti-tank defence, in spite of some success at the beginning which could not be exploited because of the lack of infantry support. Only Rots was captured and held onto which was a meagre result from such an ambitious plan. From the men of the tank regiment, two officers, three nco's and seven men were killed/four officers, three nco's and twenty three men were wounded - a total of twelve killed and thirty wounded.

1. One of the Panther tanks from the 1st Company destroyed to the south of Bretteville, probably by an anti-tank gun situated in the garden of Almir to the south of the church. In the background the barn of Mr Lemanissier can be seen, on the southern edge of the village. (IWM.)

2. The same tank seen in profile. Its position would appear to be strange which has led to claims that it was destroyed by an Allied fighter-bomber. In fact it was wrecked by an anti-tank gun and because it was blocking the road between Bretteville and Norrey, it was rolled over into the neighbouring field by engineer vehicles. The holes in the bottom of the body were simply caused by trials with explosives tried out a few days later. (RR.)

5

Friday 9 June

As dawn broke on a new day, General von Geyr arrived in the Caen area to examine his now sector of command and went to the Abbaye d'Ardenne to study the terrain from the towers of the church there. He estimated that the Allies would undertake a wide ranging attack when they were ready. There was no question of simply waiting for this to happen, he thought, but rather to confront it by mounting an attack northwards from Caen. He ordered that his three available panzer divisions should be ready to undertake an attack by the evening of 10 June, northwards along and on either side of the light railway line that ran from Caen to Luc-sur-Mer. From the Abbey he observed the movement of tanks from the 12th SS which while leaving the suburbs to the west of Caen were attacked by Allied fighter-bombers. That only served to reinforce his conviction that without support from the *Luftwaffe*, such an attack could only be undertaken at night.

The tanks that General von Geyr had observed were in fact from the 3rd Company of the divisional tank regiment. That company was commanded by *Obersturmführer* Rudolf von Ribbentrop who had fought courageously in Russia with the tanks of *Leibstandarte* division. On 15 July 1943 he had been decorated with the Knights' Cross of the Iron Cross, having three days earlier confronted 150 T-34 tanks when he was only at the head of seven panzers. He himself had destroyed fourteen of the enemy. He had accomplished more than his duty but it was true what his father (the Nazi foreign mi-

313

Kommandant :
Uscha. März

Gun-layer :
Günther Gotha

nister) had said to one of his instructors : "if my son should benefit by being given any sort of preferential treatment, you are finished". He was an officer with a human touch, greatly appreciated by his men. On the 3 June 1944 while driving near Bernay, he was machine-gunned from the air by a Spitfire causing his left lung to be ruptured. At the hospital in Bernay, he was told that he would be repatriated to Germany for convalescence, but as soon as he realised that his company was going to the front on 6 June, he escaped from the hospital. His replacement as company commander was an

army officer, Captain Lüdemann and it was he who led the unit into battle.

Towards the end of the morning on 9 June, the 3rd Company only had thirteen tanks fit for action. One of them, the "313" had been posted as an observer to the north of the RN13 between Rots and Bretteville.

The "313" carried a peculiar number, because in theory there were no numbers ending in a "3" on a tank of the Hitler Youth Division (see following page). It was commanded by *Uscha.* März, who on account of a breakdown could not take part in the attack on Norrey which was being prepared by the remaining twelve tanks of the company. He had been sent to give them cover to the west of Rots in a stationary position, accompanied by another Panther (commander *Uscha.* Eiter) and a *Flakpanzer,* a Panzer IV chassis mounting a quadruple barrel 20 mm anti-aircraft piece. The three vehicles positioned themselves on the lane to the north of the RN13 between Rots and Bretteville, near the level-crossing known as PN 67, which will be mentioned later. But they soon became a target for Canadian artillery. To the east of the lane was a bank crowned by a hedge. There was a gap through the bank so they retreated behind it, whereupon the enemy artillery stopped firing. They went back out again to reposition themselves on the lane, and shortly afterwards the guns opened up again. Once again, they took cover behind the hedge, and without warning, the other tank and the *Flakpanzer* departed leaving "313" alone. März repeated the same manoeuvre three times, but each time he reinstalled his tank on the lane, he was fired upon. It was quite obvious that enemy artillery observers could pinpoint the tank's movements with precision, and equally obviously their observation post was in the church tower of Bretteville. *Uscha.* März, who was nicknamed *der schöne März,* "handsome März", by his men on account of his elegant appearance and leather gloves, ordered his gun-layer, *Sturmmann* Günther Gotha, to fire at the tower. He took a high explosive round. Distance 3,000 metres. Fire. After they had done this the crew noticed with satisfaction that "313" was no longer a target for the Canadian gunners . In wrecking the tower they may well have wounded one of their own men who had been holed up in Bretteville, Wolfgang Ziermann, a grenadier from the 26th Regiment, who was captured shortly afterwards and posted definitively as missing (executed ?).

Defeat in front of Norrey

From 7 June onwards, the elements of 12th SS Panzer Division had been arriving at the front in small groups, which had to be avoided at all costs oif they were to mount an effective counter-attack. The 2nd Battalion (Panzer IV's) had been engaged on 7 June and the 1st and 4th Companies (Panthers) at Bretteville during the night of 8/9. It was thus the turn of the 3rd Company that morning, and as we have already seen, only twelve tanks were ready for action. Under the temporary command of Capt. Lüdemann, the section commanders were

The tank markings of 12th SS-Panzer-Regiment

In the German army between 1939 and 1945, most tanks had three numbers painted on their turrets. The first indicated the company, the second the number of the section within the company and the third, the number of the individual tank within the section. Thus "121" was the first tank (generally that of the section commander) in the 2nd. Section of the 1st. Company. "333" was the third tank in the 3rd. Section of the 3rd. Company. Normally a section consisted of five tanks, thus the numbers ran from 1 to 5. Sometimes, however, there were only four sections in a company, thus bearing the second number from 1 to 4. But, just before the Battle of Normandy, tank companies which normally were equipped with 22 tanks, had the numbers reduced to 17. Companies had to slim down to three or four sections and the surplus crews were sent to the reserves. Lack of sufficient material was the cause of this reorganisation of armoured divisions in 1944 - *Panzerdivision 44*.

But in Russia, the officers of the 1st SS-Panzer-Division, the *Leibstandarte Adolf Hitler,* noticed that Soviet tank gunners aimed first at the tanks carrying a number ending with "1", hoping thus to eliminate the officers and hamper the enemy attack. Fur purposes of camouflage a new system was adopted. The number of the first tank in each section was displaced by five digits and thus the "1" became a "5". Thus when the tank regiment of the *Hitler Jugend* division was formed from cadres of the *Leibstandarte,* it adopted the same system. The following is the theoretical numbering of the 3rd. Company of the 12. SS Panzer-Regiment, commanded by *Obersturmführer* von Ribbentrop :

1st Section : 315, 316, 317, 318, 319.

2nd Section : 325, 326, 327, 328, 329.

3rd Section : 335, 336, 337, 338, 339.

HQ Section : 304 instead of 301 (von Ribbentrop's command tank which was passed on to Captain Lüdemann for the 9 June attack), 305 instead of 302 (the tank of the commander of the HQ section - *Kompanietruppführer*).

Thus 315 was *Ustuf.* Bogensperger's tank, in command of the 1st. Section; 325 belonged to *Ustuf.* Alban of the 2nd. Section and 335 was *Ustuf.* Stagge's. The above was theoretic because there was a tank with an odd number, the 313. As a result of losses and breakdowns, a section commander could use any other tank from his section. (Information supplied to the author by Rudolf von Ribbentrop.)

---

instructed about their mission at the hamlet of Villeneuve at Rots : - the 3rd Section (five tanks) commanded by *Ustuf.* Stagge, was to attack on the right flank to the south of the railway line, while the 2nd Section *(Ustuf.* Alban, Panther "325") was to advance on the left. Behind them the Ist Section, commanded by *Ustuf.* Bogensperger in his "315" was in reserve. Their objective was the village of Norrey which formed a salient in the Canadian lines and blocked the way to Bretteville. Taking Norrey was a prerequisite to reopening the attack to the north and was to be carried out to the south of the railway line from the valley of the Mue. Max Wünsche was still in hospital and the order for the attack was given directly by *Standartenführer* Kurt Meyer. General von Geyr's plan, foreseen for 10 & 11 June, which he had discussed with Meyer, would be greatly aided by the capture of Norrey. The 3rd Company had arrived at the front on 8 June, via Thury-Harcourt and then Carpiquet, and Franqueville to Authie. The Panthers spent the night there before being relieved at around 0900 hrs on the 9 June by the Panzer IV's of the 2nd Battalion, and then drove to Rots for the final briefing. Their action was to be coordinated with an attack by the Ist Battalion of the 26th Panzergrenadiers which was to start at 1300 hrs von Ribbentrop, his arm bandaged, had rejoined his company. Unable to participate in the attck he was able to follow from a distance the movements of his twelve operational Panther tanks.

The tanks passed underneath the railway bridge heading south and then turned immediately right (to the west) to take the lane running parallel to the railway and crossed the Mue which was little more than a large stream before forming up into battle order at the foot of the slope. The accompanying infantry was provided by the 3rd Section *(Hscha.* Wilhelm Boigk) with twenty odd grenadiers. The tank crews were very young, except for the tank commanders (who had mostly come from the *Leibstandarte),* and had no combat experience. They were about to risk their lives without knowing what awaited them. The company song was *Das Leben ist ein Würfelspiel* - "life is just a game of di-

ce" - a mercenaries' song *Panzer Marsch.* And at Villeneuve they had the pleasure of seeing again their "boss", von Ribbentrop, who was going to follow the attack from a distance together with Max Wünsche who had left hospital with his head bandaged, to arrive for the beginning of the advance.

On the right, in the 3rd Section, was the tank of *Uscha.* Hermani, heavily loaded with ammunition. He was carrying a hundred rounds instead of the normal eighty. Hermani was not a very experienced tank commander; a veteran tank driver he had been retrained for that new job. But, he had been with the *Leibstandarte,* had experienced the Russian front, had been wounded and burned. His gun-layer was Willi Fischer, a young man of 19, small, very lively, energetic and an "idealist". Rushing between the body and the turret, Werner Sokoliss, the loader was an 18 year old Prussian. Driver of the tank, Hirschmann with his rather sombre air, was a direct contrast to the radio operator sitting to his right : Werner Geukler, the life and soul of the party with a permanently merry expression. He could play the piano and the accordion and it was he who enlivened the evenings in camp. When their commander wanted to create a musical atmosphere, all he had to say was *Geukler, los!* (Geukler, let's go !). The merry songster of the company would pick up his accordion and sing a Spanish song which would not have pleased Dr. Goebbels - *Barcelona.* Fischer and Geukler were an incredible team of joyous lads, energetic, dynamic and enthusiastic. That incredible team, loaded with ammunition, departed for their objective without a care, believing themselves invincible and having the best tanks in the world. Victory was just around the corner. Geukler gave a thunderous rendering of *Barcelona* that reverberated through the headphones, as the Führer's black hussars charged singing into battle ; young lives thrown without concern towards the Canadians, waiting for them in fixed positions. It was **1230 hrs** and everything was quiet. As usual at midday there were few fighter bombers in the sky.

To the right of Hermani's tank, another one, and then on the right flank, the last tank which was that

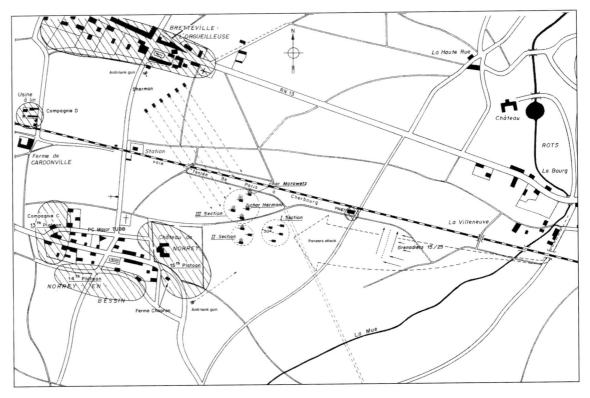

On the morning of 9 June, the 3rd Company of 12th SS Pz.-Regt. attacked with twelve Panther tanks in the direction of Norry-en-Bessin, but they were taken in the flank by nine Sherman Fireflies from the Elgin Regiment. Seven Panthers were destroyed including those of the 3rd. Section. (Heimdal.)

of the commander of the half-troop, *Uscha.* Alois Morawetz, 19 years old, who advanced close to the railway line. That tank was loaded with 12,000 Austrian cigarettes and a bottle of Cognac "acquired" from the German stores in Paris ! The terrain climbed and then flattened out. In front of them a wood, the park of the chateau of Norrey which masked a good part of the village and the railway on the right. The latter formed an embankment which protected the right flank of the advance, but then it ran into a cutting before emerging on the same level as the plain at PN67 (level crossing with the gate keeper's cottage). The tanks advanced speedily and the accompanying infantry fell behind, unable to keep up. Morawetz's driver, Hans Schiemann, a lad of 20 with a serious face, remembered von Ribbentrop's advaice - « *drive fast, stop, fire and drive on again* ». Schiemann thought that the tracks of 45 tons of Panther tank at full speed would soon be biting into the enemy front line. Then suddenly in his earphones crackled the order of Captain Lüdemann - "advance slowly and open fire on the edge of the village". Schiemann was gripped by fear as this went totally against the recommendations of the "boss". He could not resist taking the microphone and saying to *Uscha.* Morawetz : *"watch out Louis, we are going to cop one in a minute"* ("Pass auf Louis, Bald haben wir einen Sitzen !"). Morawetz heard a second order directed at the left wing of the company approaching Norrey : *Wartesaal, links schwenken (Literally, "waiting room", the company code word, "swing left")*. Morawetz ordered Schiemann to put his foot down and effect a gentle turn left. Still no opposition, but about 1,000 metres in front of them, near the station, something moved. Morawetz's tank was about 30 metres ahead of the rest of the company and angled slightly to the left so as not to be left behind. The tank stopped and Morawetz thought they had hit a mine. He looked out to the left through the prism of his visor and saw the turret of a tank blown off. A second explosion, and fire. The machine-gun ammunition started to burn, crackling like dry wood , going off without having been detonated. Morawetz could not

get the rear turret hatch open and exited through the top one. He remained unconscious for a moment before falling onto the ground beside the tank, safe but burned. Inside the hull, Schiemann had seen the radio operator exiting to his right. As the flames flickered all around him, he too tried to get out but was caught up by the cable of his microphone which he had to cut in order to escape. His left leg was outside, bent against the hull when a fourth shell arrived from the right. The explosion slammed his left leg against the escape hatch aperture and broke it. He managed to throw himself out into the corn and he ran to the rear as fast as he could with a broken leg and severe burns. The wreck of the tank was stuck five metres from the railway line.

On the left in Hermani's tank, Willi Fischer was in the process of setting his sights onto the church tower of Norrey and open fire, when he saw a flame. He thought it was a shell going over, but in fact it was an impact on the right. A second shell arrived from the same direction, penetrated the turret and went under Fischer's seat. A violent fire broke out in the tank, consuming the oxygen and the crew members sensed a red veil before loosing consciousness almost instantaneously. Hermani's experience saved his life : that veteran of the *Leibstandarte* had not bolted the turret hatch and it blew open with the second explosion, allowing him to scramble out. Willi Fischer was afraid but he had an enormous will to live. The heat had pulled his forage-cap off but in two leaps he was out of the turret and through a curtain of flames. He snapped the microphone cable on the edge of the turret and jumped off to the left, only to land on Geukler who cried out that he had received a bit of the tank in his back. The « old fox » Hermani had got out without burns and it was the same with Hirschmann, but Sokoliss was slightly burned. Fischer and Geukler had severe burns. The former was wearing a tanker's uniform of camouflaged sailcloth, but he had probably had some phosphorous on his trousers, which forced him to drop his pants to avoid being burned on the buttocks. Thus he departed for

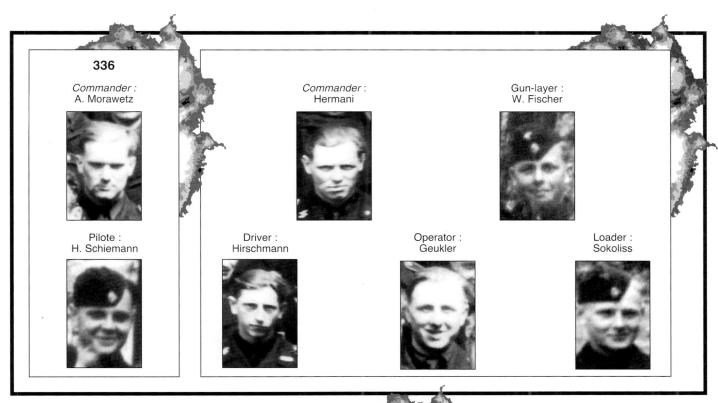

336

Commander :
A. Morawetz

Pilote :
H. Schiemann

Commander :
Hermani

Driver :
Hirschmann

Gun-layer :
W. Fischer

Operator :
Geukler

Loader :
Sokoliss

the rear with his pants around his ankles and his face burned, presenting an amazing spectacle.

All five tanks from the 3rd Troop were destroyed by shells from the right, while on the left, the 1st Troop lost two. The section commander, Alban's, was hit and brewed up, while that of *Uscha.* Willi Krahl, was blown apart by the explosions of the shells in the hull which ripped the turret off. The third tank of the troop was intact, but its commander, Friedrich Eismann had stuck the upper part of his body out of the turret of his "326". That escapade did not last for long and he was cut in two by a shell, emptying his blood onto his gun-layer, Gerd Krieger, a lad known for his very blond hair. The lower part of the tank commander's body fell onto Krieger who was terrified. The troop in reserve was intact, but the "315" of Bogensperger had received hits in the bogeys and had lost most of its track links. In "315", the gun-layer, (Ernst Sammet), the loader (Fritz Porochnowitz), the radio operator (Leopold Heindl, known as "Poldi", an Austrian), and the driver (Ferdinand Stange, a Bavarian), counted themselves lucky to have escaped a massacre and retreated on what was left of the tracks. (In 1991, Sammet, Porochnowitz and Heindl were still alive and their statements permitted the reconstruction of this engagement). In "304", Captain Lüdemann's tank which was intact, the gun-layer, Heinz Freiberg, did not see all that much of the drama, as the prism of his visor gave him a much reduced field of vision.

The 3rd Company lost seven tanks and only five managed to retreat in reverse gear and by zig-zagging. Behind the railway embankment, Maw Wünsche and Rudolf von Ribbentrop had observed the scene. The latter noticed that the tanks had driven on exposing their flanks. Weighed down by sadness he had watched the massacre of his tank crews who he considered to be like his children. Beside him, Max Wünsche had to content himself by not shouting out in his rage and despair. Seven of his tanks had been destroyed in the space of a few minutes. The accompanying infantry found themselves well to the rear when the action happened near the PN67. Boigk ordered his

335

Troop commander :
Ustuf. Stagge

The tanks commanded by Alois Morawetz and *Uscha.* Hermani were destroyed near the railway line. The "335" of the section commander of the 3rd Section was also destroyed and *Ustuf.* Stagge was killed. In the 2nd Section two were destroyed : the "325" of the section commander and that of *Uscha.* Krahl who was killed. The "326" returned intact but its commander, *Uscha.* Eismann was cut in two by a shell. (Photos : Author's collection.)

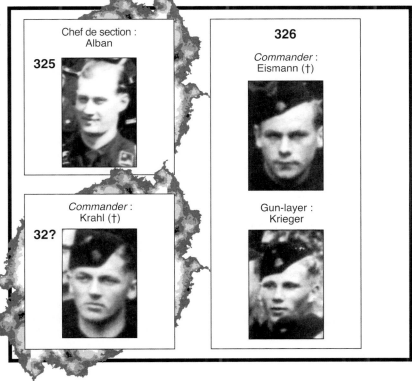

Chef de section :
Alban

325

Commander :
Krahl (†)

32?

326

Commander :
Eismann (†)

Gun-layer :
Krieger

"304" was the tank of the temporary company commander, Captain Lüdemann, whose gun-layer was Heinz Freiberg. "315", the tank of the commander of the 1st Troop got back to base with a damaged track mechanism.

304

Company commander :
Hptm. Lüdemann

Gun-layer :
Heinz Freiberg

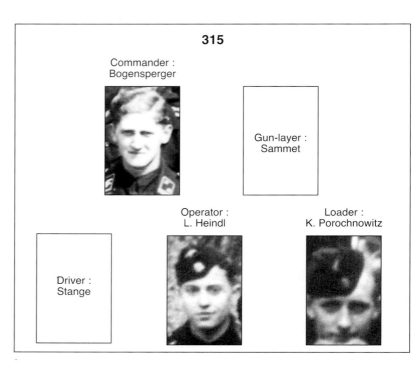

315

Commander :
Bogensperger

Gun-layer :
Sammet

Operator :
L. Heindl

Loader :
K. Porochnowitz

Driver :
Stange

Werner Uhr

Siegfried Gose

Willi Schwarz
(Author's coll.)

troop to withdraw : *"quick, get behind the railway embankment"*. There were killed and wounded among the 25th Grenadiers. Suddenly the firing stopped, and the medical orderly of the 3rd Company, *Uscha.* Gose, looking thin and delicate with his blond hair and large glasses went off in the side-car of a motor cycle driven by *Uscha.* Harting to see what he could do for the wounded. Like ghosts the long column of the wounded reached the rear area along the railway embankment. The burned crewmen passed in front of their comrades, some strangely silent while others were screaming hysterically. The faces burned, black and red, were unrecognisable. One of them held out his hands, the skin of his arms hanging in tatters. Siegfried Gose who had gone out to help the wounded, examined Morawetz who appeared to be badly hit and the three of them returned to the rear. Suddenly there was a burst of machine-gun fire from the direction of PN67and Gose, who was sitting behind Harting, collapsed, hit in the stomach. *Uscha.* Hermani cleaned out the position with grenades, leaving a dead Canadian in front of the level crossing, where Gose died as well. The five tanks that had survived the battle finished their withdrawal firing furiously , and when the wounded reached Villeneuve, they were grouped together in a café before being transported to hospital. At the café there were several men from the company workshop train (*I-Gruppe*) including Willi Schwartz with his one ton tractor unit for the eventual recovery of a tank. They saw the arrival of the horribly burned crewmen unable to recognise them. They set about coating their wounds with engine oil, an unusual but effective remedy. Willi Fischer's wounds healed and in 1991 the scars had almost disappeared which he attributed to the miraculous engine oil.

The losses were severe and the state of shock was immense. The young crewmen had believed that their tanks would not burn, but nevertheless had gone up like torches. Because of the lack of fuel the petrol tanks had been only half filled, thus rendering them more explosive on account of the vapour that collected inside. Only two of the bodies of the killed could be taken back to the rear for burial. Most of the others were irrecoverable and had been incinerated in their steel coffins

where, much later, scrap-metal merchants found their shrivelled remains reduced to the "size of a doll". One of those missing, Werner Uhr, was wounded and remained left behind between the lines, where he was finally taken prisoner by the Canadians, who amputated one of his legs. It was long after the war that his comrades discovered that he had not been killed, but had returned much later to Germany in an exchange of prisoners and been awarded the wounded medal. One officer had been killed, *Ustuf.* Erich Stagge and one nco, Friedrich Eismann. One of those severely burned, Kurt Petersen, died in hospital on 11 June, while the other wounded were healed and rejoined the battle. At the hospital in Alençon, Werner Geukler, never lost his morale. His face and arms covered in bandages, he called out in Russian to a Ukrainian nurse, "Julitta, I love you", so frightening the poor girl that she ran away.

Hubert Meyer, the historian and once chief-of-staff of the division remarked : *"right from the beginning, this attack had been a disastrous cock-up, without a shadow of doubt. Once again, it had demonstrated that surprise attacks had no chance of success"*. Captain Lüdemann lost his nerve and was hospitalised. He rejoined the front later only to be killed near Fontenay-le-Pesnel on 14 June. Even though still wounded, von Ribbentrop retook command of his company.

As late as 1991, the way in which those seven tanks had been destroyed remained somewhat of a mystery. There were two Canadian anti-tank guns positioned to the south-east of the park of the chateau of Norrey, and those at Bretteville could also intervene. On the other hand, while the Panthers were approaching Norrey, Major Tweedale of the tank replacement unit of the 2nd Canadian Brigade, (The Elgin Regiment) was delivering nine Shermans for the 10th Armoured Regiment (The Fort Garry Horse). He disembarked the infantry reinforcements at the headquarters of the Regina Rifles in Bretteville, when he suddenly saw the Panthers approaching through the cornfield, while his nine Shermans were to the north of the station at Norrey. *"The one in the lead* (Morawetz's) *turned towards us at high speed, the first section fired from 900 metres and scored a bullseye. Six others* appeared over the crest of the ridge at ranges of between 800 and 1,100 metres, and the two sections of Shermans opened up, destroying the Panthers without giving them time to reply. (...) *Our nine Shermans with the 17 pounder Firefly of Lieutenant Henry destroyed seven Panthers in four minutes at an average range of 1,000 metres* (translator's note : the 'Firefly' version of the standard Sherman tank was fitted with a British 17 pdr. anti-tank gun instead of the normal 75 mm gun). *My own gun-layer, Private Bennett, destroyed a Panther at 850 metres with his first shot. His second missed the target aimed at but hit another which exploded, blowing off the turret"* (Krahl's). Then the infantry of a company of the Regina Rifles, commanded by Major Tubb, who were positioned in Norrey, joined in the hunt. The section stationed around the chateau had a PIAT available, and Ma-

1. Four of those wounded from the 3rd Company on 9 June at Norrey, in hospital. From left to right : Willi Fischer, Braje, Müller and Geukler, still managing to look cheerful. (Coll. Kam. 3. Kp.)

2. One of the Panther tanks destroyed at Norrey. (R. Hervieu/Author.)

3. One of the Panthers from the 3rd Company of the 12th SS-Pz.-Regt. wrecked near the railway line (Hermani's ?). It had been perforated by multiple PIAT bomb impacts, as these wrecks were used for training Canadian soliders. Note the violence of the fire. (R. Hervieu/Authors.)

jor Tubb recalled that Sergeant Wilson came to ask for the two PIAT's held in reserve ; Private Ross Hill recalled that he took the PIATs and their bombs. At least one of the Panthers was hit by a PIAT bomb, the "315" of Bogensperger. As we have seen, his track mechanism was severely damaged by projectiles fired at ground level. In all cases the Germans were sure that the impacts came from the right, that is to say from the direction of the Shermans. At least three of the Panthers remained where they were (those situated more to the north). Debris from those tanks has since been found ; fragments of glass from the visors and undetonated shells where Morawetz's tank lay which corroborates his story. The three tanks were used as targets for training Canadian troops and numerous fragments of PIAT bombs have been found in the vicinity : remains of battle but also of training sessions. The four other Panthers were taken away elsewhere for training Allied troops. Thus the Battle of Norrey marked the first success by the Allied armour against the Panthers in Normandy : the Sherman Firefly proved its worth with the effective 17 pdr. gun.

1. On 9 June at the end of the morning, that attack on Norrey had been defeated and the Panthers of the 3rd Company of the 12th SS had been withdrawn to Villeneuve, a hamlet of Rots. Here can be seen two Panther tanks in position towards the west, facing the Canadians as well as light vehicles from the divisional escort company. (BA.)

2. Panther "326" parked in front of a barn, already seen in the photo above. The gun-layer, Gerd Krieger, was cleaning the blood of his commander, *Uscha.* Eismann, who had been sliced in two by a shell, from the interior of the turret. This photo was published in the press at the time.

3. Photo published in the first edition of the "Illustrated Observer" (*Illustrierte Beobachter*) on 22 June 1944, showing from left to right : Max Wünsche (head bandaged), *Hscha.* Boigk and von Ribbentrop (in profile).

Wilhelm Post, Squadron Sergeant Major of the 3rd Company of 12th SS-Pz.-Regt.

At roughly **1430 hrs** exhausted by the fighting of the previous night, and the attack they had undertaken, the grenadiers of the 25th SS-Panzergrenadier Regiment rested at Villeneuve (de Rots) : Max Wünsche, Rudolf von Ribbentrop and Bernhard Krause (commander of the Ist Battalion of the 26th Grenadiers) were with them. Two war correspondents seized the opportunity to take some exceptional photographs, before the tension caused by the fighting had subsided and while the horror of it all could still be seen in the eyes of the grenadiers. On the other side of the street, the tank "326" was parked, and up on the turret, the gun-layer, Erich Krieger, appeared to be going about his normal duties with an apparent calm. In fact he was cleaning up the blood of his commander, Friedrich Eismann, from the inside of the turret. The company squadron sergeant major, Wilhelm Post, who had a reputation for being strict and in these dire moments he did not want to let up. He told Krieger *"you are not going to get a new uniform - wash it !"* Shortly afterwards, replacement crews arrived, and in spite of the losses, took up their duties with enthusiasm. Moved by this, Rudolf von Ribbentrop said *"That is the spirit of the* Hitlerjugend".

Heinz-Hugo John killed to the north of Caen

While the 3rd Company mourned its heavy casualties, the other battalion of the regiment, the 2nd with its Panzer IV's had also suffered an important loss. The 7th Company lost its commander, *Ostuf.* Heinz-Hugo John, killed that day. He had held important posts with in the Hitler Youth movement : he had been an *Obergebietsführer* and chief of the *Hauptamt I* at the headquarters of the movement. Aged 40 he had also been a deputy in the *Reichstag (*Nazi parliament) since 1932, and after having fought with the Army he applied for a transfer to the "HJ" division when it was formed. During the attack on 7 June he had been in command of the 1st Section of the 7th Company and, after *Hstuf.* Bräcker

was wounded, he took command of the Company. On 9 June at roughly 2000 hrs John was with his Panzer IV at La Folie, to the north-west of Caen with his company on the defensive. He received a radio message to go to the battalion HQ to receive his orders. But the moment he climbed out of the tank, a shell hit the radio operator's hatch cover. The explosion snapped his spinal column killing him instantly as well as the radio operator *(Sturmmann Mende)* and the loader *(Schütze Noa)*. The driver and the gunner reached the HQ on foot to report the incident. As the area was being drenched with shellfire, the bodies were not collected up until nightfall.

Prince von Schönburg's Panzer IV's take Ellon

To the west of the sector of Panzer Group West, the Panzer-Lehr-Division had also gone onto the offensive, northwards towards Bayeux, as that important road junction had become the objective for the Ist SS-Panzer-Corps. The attack was mounted from the Tilly-sur-Seulles area on either side of the road leading to Bayeux. At the end of the morning, on the western flank, von Schönburg-Waldenburg's armoured battle group, consisting of the Panzer IV's of the 2nd Battalion of the 130th Panzer-Lehr-Regiment and the infantry of the 1st Battalion of the 902nd Panzergrenadier-Regiment, were advancing. But, a little further to the east, the 8th Armoured-Brigade-Group was advancing southwards : a German attack and a British attack were about to collide and we shall shortly read of the consequences. General Bayerlein was in the lead with his reconnaissance battalion and circled around Ellon to reach Arganchy, a small village only five km to the south-west of Bayeux, where he set up his HQ in a small wood. At the same time, von Schönburg-Waldenburg's armoured group was marching on Ellon but their movements were spotted by the British who drenched the whole area with large calibre shells fired from ships anchored at sea ; the accompanying grenadiers were forced to take shelter behind the tanks. Before any direct confrontation had taken place, once again the Allied material superiority was evident. The advance continued amidst explosions and fountains of earth. The church tower of Ellon, a village held by elements of the 56th Infantry brigade, appeared at around midday. The Prince's tanks went onto the offensive over a broad front, their aim being to crush the British defence. An enemy tank appeared from behind the church and it was taken on by a Panzer IV from the headquarters section of the 6th Company, the "602". The first shell ripped off a track and the seond fired by "602" set it alight. A group of British infantry leap-frogged towards "604" but were mown down by the on-board machine gun, although three or four grenades exploded on the engine casing without causing any damage. The British artillery then concentrated its fire on Ellon, exploding among the houses and all around the tanks, while mortar bombs burst on the roadways, damaging the side protection plates of the Panzer IV's. Then the tanks of the 7th and 8th Companies reached the northern border of the village, followed by the grenadiers who collected up the prisoners and marched them away to the rear. The tank battalion suffered its first deaths and the Prince von Schönburg-Waldenburg, lifted his cap as a mark of respect for the bodies of several of his comrades from the 1st Tank Regiment who had been with him in the 1st Company when he was awarded the Knights' Cross. Ellon was taken

and secured, but Bayeux, dominated by the spires of its cathedral was still six kilometres away. Now, the second phase of the attack could start.

In the meanwhile, however, the 8th Armoured Brigade Group had reached the hamlet of Saint-Pierre, a few hundred metres east of Tilly-sur-Seulles, threatening that strategically important place as well as cutting off the German offensive from the rear. An order to suspend the attack, without doubt issued by Ist SS Panzer Corps, was received at **1400 hrs** by Captain Hauck, the divisional signals officer of Panzer-Lehr, and he passed it on to all units, telling them to withdraw back to Tilly. But General Bayerlein decided provisionally to leave the 902nd Grenadiers' battalion in Ellon, supported by the Panzer IV's of the 5th and 6th Companies, while the 7th and 8th Companies were assembled at Fonteney-le-Pesnel to mount an eventual counter-attack against the 8th Armoured Brigade Group.

To find out more, General Bayerlein went to the headquarters of the commander of Ist SS-Panzer-Corps, *Obergruppenführer* Sepp Dietrich. In the face of the Allied advance it was no longer a question of throwing them back into the sea and it was going to be necessary to mount a defensive campaign. Henceforth the Panzer-Lehr-Division would have to occupy a defensive line from Cristot, through Tilly-sur-Seulles to Verrières (a hamlet of Lingèvre). That prudent measure is also explained by the fact that Montgomery who has blocked north of Caen by two armoured divisions, would attempt to turn the position by a swing to the right from Bayeux.

To the east of Tilly, at the hamlet of Saint-Pierre, at a cost of some vicious fighting, the 1st battalion of the 901st Grenadiers succeeded in repelling the 8th Batt. of the Durham Light Infantry (151st Brigade) supported by the tanks of the 24th Lancers (8th Brigade). The bridge over the Seulles leading to the heart of Tilly had been saved and the tanks if the 7th and 8th Companies did not have to intervene. Thus a new attack by the panzers which had started off well was once again forcefully stopped and it was no longer a question of throwing the Allies back into the sea.

Ostubaf. Max Wünsche, his head bandaged as a result of his wound the night before, came to take part in the attack by the 3rd Company of 12th SS-PZ.-Regt. He was forced to restrain himself from shouting our his rage and despair. (Heimdal.)

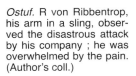

Ostuf. R von Ribbentrop, his arm in a sling, observed the disastrous attack by his company ; he was overwhelmed by the pain. (Author's coll.)

6

Saturday 10 June

The *Panzer-Lehr-Division* confronting the British offensive

At **0500 hrs** a violent British artillery barrage descended for 45 minutes upon the positions of the PLD, and those veterans of the eastern front were dumbfounded by the Allied material might. Around **midday,** after savage fighting the defensive line was broken through when five Cromwell tanks arrived near the headquarters of *Major* Zwierzynski, commander of the 1st Battalion of the 902nd Grenadiers. The 1st Company (*Oberleutnant* Werner) of the 130th *Panzerjäger-Lehr-Abteilung* (tank destroyer instructional battalion) was in position near the headquarters with its new tank destroyers, Panjerjäger IV's armed with Pak 39 75 mm L/48 anti-tank guns. The first Cromwell was rapidly set on fire and a second, immobilised by a damaged track, suffered the same fate, followed by a third. The remaining two attempted to withdraw, but collided with each other and remained stuck and as their crews tried to escape, they were captured by the grenadiers. In spite of this local success, all German resistance was neutralised at Jerusalem (in the commune of Douet-de-Chouain on the Bayeux - Tilly road) and the 22nd Armoured-Brigade continued its advance in the direction of Bucéels. Captain Hartdegen attempted to slow them by bringing up a half hour later, two 88 mm guns and four Panzer IV's which he placed in a favourable position. In front of them the British tanks advanced in complete disorder and the first shells fell among this confused mass, fired at point blank range. Huge pillars of flame shot into the sky, 200 metres high, from the middle of the exploding petrol bowsers, covering the vicinity with black clouds of dense smoke. Three British tanks tried to gain the high ground where the German defence was positioned, but the 88's destroyed them. Then the British artillery which had been alerted, entered the fray. Guns of all calibres including naval artillery concentrated their fire on the high ground, forcing the two guns and the four tanks to withdraw without loss.

Five Panthers from the 1st Battalion had arrived at the front, an advance guard from Major Markowski's unit. They were attached to the divisional reconnaissance group and prepared themselves to counter-attack towards the village of Mondaye, south of the abbey. A war correspondent set out to photograph them but they did not get very far. They had to withdraw in the face of British pressure in the late afternoon and pulled back to the south of Juaye-Mondaye

The suspension of the Panzer attack

Some one hundred hours after the landings, the great German counter-offensive which was to drive the Allies back into the sea, had still not taken place. It should have been mounted during the 48 hours after the landings to have stood any chance of success. It was to have finally been mounted the following night, but destiny and the constraints of available resources were to decide otherwise.

The tactical HQ of Panzer-Group-West was positioned in an orchard at La Caine, a tiny village situated 19 km. south-west of Caen and a few kilometres north-east of Aulnay-sur-Odon. On 10 June, in the evening, Baron Geyr von Schweppenburg was in the process of modifying his plan which would enable his Panzer Group to cut the Allied bridgehead in two by way of a grand offensive to be undertaken during the following hours.

The general of armoured troops who had successfully commanded an armoured corps in the East, still had not understood the need for caution in the face of Allied air superiority. None the less, on the morning of 8 June, during one of his visits to the Abbey d'Ardenne, he had seen how the Allied fighter-bombers had dealt with the Panthers of the 3rd Company who had decided to pre-empt the major offensive planned for the night of 10/11 June, and he did not want to engage his tanks in daylight. But perhaps he thought himself safe at La Caine ; well behind the front line. His headquarters had made no effort at camouflage : four large radio trucks, diverse vehicles serving as offices, and tents could be seen in the orchard, and around them, Geyr and his staff officers strolled with their red-striped trousers in full view of Allied aircraft : even "watching the Royal Air Force at work" as Chester Wilmot commented in his book "The Struggle for Europe". But the radio transmissions from the HQ had been intercepted by British intelligence and decoded by "Ultra". They issued the following information at O439 hrs on the 10 June - "HQ of Panzer Group West at La Caine on the evening of 9 June". Such imprudence could only have serious consequences. At **2030 hrs** the headquarters was attacked by fighter-bombers, wounding General Geyr von Schweppenburg. Among the 17 to be killed were Major-General Edler von Dawans, the chief-of-staff, Major Burgsthaler and *Hauptsturmführer* Wilhelm Beck, liaison officer from Ist SS-Panzer-Corps. The survivors of the staff left the front and command was transferred to the SS-Panzer-Corps.

It had often been said that the destruction of this HQ caused the attack by the panzers for the following night to be aborted, although in fact, nothing changed. The offensive had already been suspended in view of the general situation. Panzer Group West had already noted in its war diary : *"the attack planned by Ist SS Panzer Corps for the night of 10/11 June will not now take place, after discussion with Field Marshal Rommel, because of insufficient own forces and enemy reinforcements"*. The war diary of Army Group B confirms this : *"the situation is such that Panzer Group West has been forced onto the defensive"*, referring to a discussion between Rommel and Colonel-General Jodl, the *Wehrmacht* chief-of-staff. On the other hand, at 2200 hrs almost two hours after the bombardment of the HQ at La Caine, contrary information was issued. Field Marshal Rommel telephone the chief-of-staff of the Supreme Commander West (*OB West*) to state that : *"Pz. Group West is going to attack during the course of the night. That is in agreement with the principle of the attack, but it will not be able to achieve a decisive result because of*

1. One of the Panzer IV's of the 2nd Batt. of the 130th Panzer Lehr Regiment, destroyed near Audrieu. During the British attack on 10 June, supported by large calibre naval guns, firing from ships anchored out at sea, a shell scored a direct hit on the tank, to the amazement of British soldiers who witnessed the violent explosion. The two-stroke engine hanging out of the end of the hull, show that it was a Type "H". (IWM.)

2, 3 and **4.** Another Type "H" from the 5th Company destroyed during the British attack on the PLD front. An anti-tank round from a 6 pdr. gun easily penetrated the side of the hull, blowing off one of the side protection plates in the process. (IWM.)

the involvement of the enemy aviation and their superior artillery". (War Diary, Army group B. p. 115). In fact, in spite of its apparent contradictory nature, that latest statement confirmed the two previous ones : that the attack was necessary but it would not lead to a decisive success.

It is certain that the defeats suffered by the Panthers at Norrey and Bretteville as well as the abortive attack on Ellon, prompted that note of caution. 10 June was the first great turning point in the Battle of Normandy : all the German counter-attacks had been stopped, and faced by only three armoured divisions on a front between Caen and Bayeux (although that sector should have been held by three infantry divisions with the three armoured ones held as an offensive reserve), the Allies had considerably reinforced their bridgehead which by then was continuous from the Cotentin to the estuary of the Orne. The panzers were about to become acquainted with a new type of combat whereby they were to become a pivot of the defence, serving as mobile anti-tank guns. Their cavalcades were to be stopped and they were to have to endure severe defensive combats.

Colonel Rudolf Gerhard who commander the 130th Panzer-Lehr-Regiment was born on 26 March 1896 at Greiz in Thuringia. On 4 August 1914 he joined the 96th Thuringian Infantry Regiment and was promoted to lieutenant on 22 March 1915, being wounded four times during the First World War. He re-entered the service in October 1934 with the rank of captain and became commander of a company in the 1st Panzer-Regiment in October 1935. Promoted Major on 1 January 1939, during the following two years he commanded one of the battalions of the 7th Pz.-Rgt., decorated with the Knights' cross on 22 September 1941. On 1 January 1942 he took command of the latter regiment with the rank of lieutenant-colonel, fought with it in Tunisia and then too charge of 130th Pz.-Lehr-Regt. in mid-November 1943. (RR.)

Opposite. Map of the Allied bridgehead with the positions of the armoured units engaged. (Heimdal.)

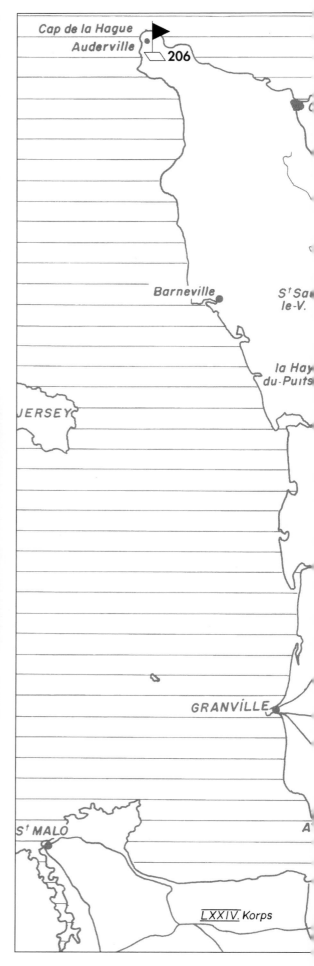

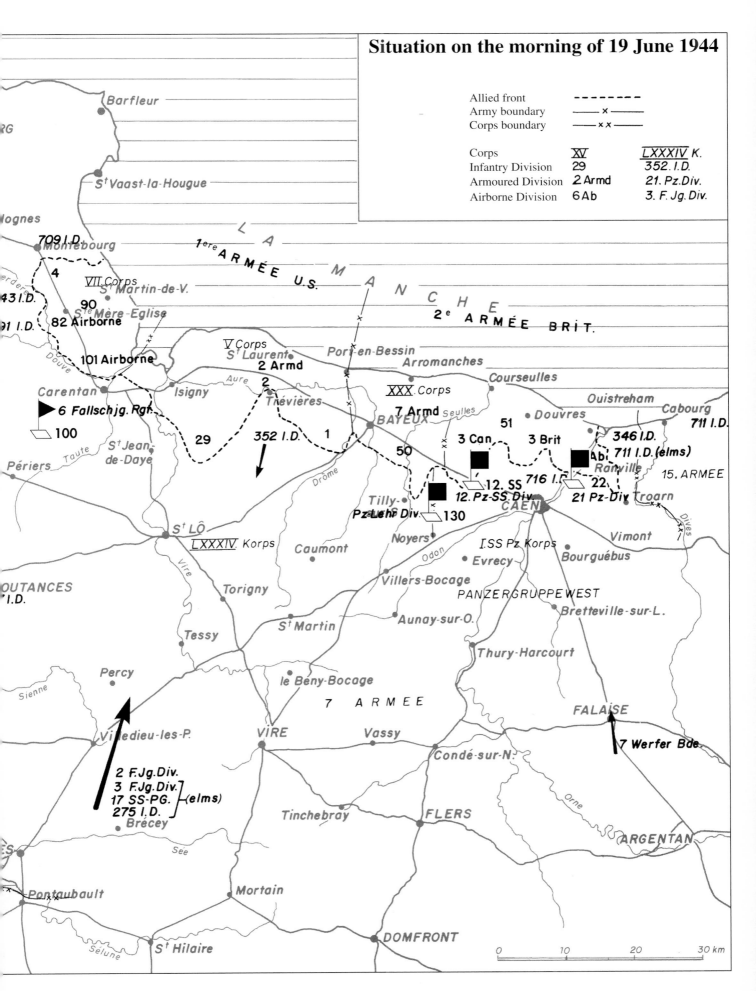

Situation on the morning of 19 June 1944

Allied front	– – – – – –
Army boundary	—— × ——
Corps boundary	—— × × ——

Corps	XV	LXXXIV K.
Infantry Division	29	352. I.D.
Armoured Division	2 Armd	21. Pz. Div.
Airborne Division	6 Ab	3. F. Jg. Div.

Barfleur

St Vaast-la-Hougue

LA MANCHE

Nognes

709 I.D.
Montebourg

1ere ARMÉE U.S.

2e ARMÉE BRIT.

4

VII. Corps
St Martin-de-V.

431.D.

90
Ste Mère-Eglise

91 I.D.

82 Airborne

101 Airborne

V Corps
St Laurent

Port-en-Bessin

Arromanches

Courseulles

Ouistreham

Cabourg

Carentan   Isigny

2 Armd

Aure

2

Thévières

Drôme

BAYEUX

Seulles

Douvres

711 I.D.

XXX. Corps

7 Armd

51

3 Can   3 Brit

346 I.D.

711 I.D. (elms)

6 Fallschjg. Rgt.

100

St Jean-de-Daye

29

352 I.D.

1

50

716 I.F.

12. SS

12. Pz-SS Div.

Ranville

22

21 Pz-Div.

6 Ab

Troarn

15. ARMEE

Périers

Taute

Tilly-

Pz-Lehr Div.   130

Noyers

CAEN

Dives

St LÔ

LXXXIV. Korps

Caumont

Odon

I. SS Pz Korps

Evrecy

Vimont

OUTANCES

I.D.

Torigny

Villers-Bocage

Bourguébus

Bretteville-sur-L.

Tessy

St Martin

PANZERGRUPPE WEST

Aunay-sur-O.

Thury-Harcourt

Sienne

Percy

le Beny-Bocage

7 ARMEE

FALAISE

Villedieu-les-P.

VIRE

Vassy

Condé-sur-N.

7 Werfer Bde.

2 F.Jg.Div.
3 F.Jg.Div.
17 SS-PG. (elms)
275 I.D.

Brécey

Tinchebray

FLERS

Orne

ARGENTAN

Sée

Pontaubault

Mortain

St Hilaire

DOMFRONT

Sélune

| 0 | 10 | 20 | 30 km |

Major von Schönburg-Waldenburg commanded the 2nd Battalion of the 130th Pz.-Lehr.-Regt. He was killed on the 11 June at around 1600 hrs ; during an attack on Hill 103 to the north-east of Tilly-sur-Seulles.

The death of Prince von Schonburg

On that day the Panzer-Lehr Division had a new task. No longer attacking, it was placed on the defensive although it had received a first reinforcement at dawn : five Panthers from the 1st Battalion of the 6th Panzer Regiment.

On the left flank, the commander of the tank regiment, Colonel Gerhardt, took command of all units including the newly arrived Panthers. On the right wing as far as the boundary with the 12th SS-Pz.-Div. all units were under the orders of Colonel Georg Scholze, commander of the 901st Panzergrenadier-Lehr-Regiment. As well as his own regiment and two battalions of artillery he had control of the Panzer IV's of the 2nd Battalion of the 130th Pz.-Lehr.-Regt.

On the other side, the British received orders at 0715 hrs to attack the entire front at Tilly-sur-Seulles. At 1430 hrs they reached their start lines and at **1600 hrs** the 6th Green Howards supported by the tanks of the 4/7 Dragoon Guards passed through Audrieu and attacked Cristot at around **1730 hrs.** They were received by a violent burst of machine-gun fire from the German positions and by the Panthers of the 2nd Battalion of the 12th SS-Pz.-Regt. of *Obersturmführer* Gaede who counter-attacked Hill 102 : with the support of anti-tank guns he destroyed seven of the Dragoon Guards' tanks, forcing a British withdrawal to the high ground at Audrieu.

Meanwhile the 7th Green Howards whose task was to occupy the small wood at Cristot, had withdrawn under the fire of the 3rd Battalion of the 26th Panzergrenadiers. To the west of Cristot, the 5th East Yorkshires advanced on Saint-Pierre and in consequence were directly threatening Tilly. To counter that, at **1400 hrs** the commander of the 2nd. Batta-

lion of the 130th Pz.-Lehr.-Regt. was ordered to counter-attack them with his 5th and 8th Companies, leaving the 6th and 7th in reserve. The terrain over which the attack would take place was wooded and unfavourable, but Major von Schönburg-Waldenburg protested in vain. From the vicinity of Fontenay-le-Pesnel, where they had been held in reserve, the 5th (Captain Lex) and the 8th (Lieutenant Walter replacing Captain Reche who was sick) Companies reached their start lines where they were joined by the Prince who was going to lead the attack in person. In spite of the ground where the view was constantly obscured , just after **1600 hrs** they managed to break into the British positions on Hill 103 in the face of determined resistance. That hill rose to the north-east of Tilly and from its north side the terrain sloped downwards to the coastline, eighteen kms. distant, while the southern slope was covered with sparse trees. At the moment when the Prince's Panzer IV breasted the latter slope, a British anti-tank gun opened fire, its shell piercing the turret of the command tank, killing the Prince and his radio operator, Lieutenant Hermann. A second tank was also knocked out, that of a Troop commander, Lieutenant Finsterwalder. Captain Helmut Ritgen thus took over the battalion, and lacking both artillery and infantry support, he decided to withdraw the tanks : to continue the attack would have been suicidal. The "801" of Lieutenant Stohr covered the retreat and protected the repair crews who were trying to fix the damaged tanks. The Prince was posthumously promoted to lieutenant-colonel and buried in the cemetery of Parfouru-sur-Odon (north-east of Villers-Bocage) together with his batman, Corporal Füssel who was also killed on 11 June and Lieutenant Gerhard Hartmann, his radio operator who also received posthumous promotion to a rank one higher.

Fighting in the *bocage*

The battle for Tilly raged throughout that 11 June and a company of tank-destroyers, the 3rd. of the 130th *Panzerjäger-Lehr-Abteilung* (battalion) equipped with *Panzerjäger 39's* under the command of Captain Oventrop, was positioned in reserve to the south of the village. Captain Phillips of the 901st. Grenadiers called for help and Oventrop sent him six tank-destroyers which he placed on the reverse slope and ordered his crews to : "open fire when you are certain that each shell will eliminate a Cromwell". He directed his crews by radio : the first enemy tank was hit fair and square, flames shot out of the hatch, the ammunition inside exploded and the Cromwell disintegrated, two other tanks were hit, and the British attack was repulsed.

Further to the west, the British reached the wood which stretched to the north of Lingevres, threatening that place. Colonel Gerhardt engaged his 6th and 7th Companies, commanded by Captain Ritgen and his Panzer IV's destroyed the enemy tanks at more or less point blank range.

Lieutenant Ernst was one of the Troop commanders in the 6th Company who moved off in his tank, codenamed *Zitrone* (lemon) at the start of the alert.

"We reached Lingevres and were immediately thrown into the counter-attack. With a deafening racket, the engines and tracks of our steel monsters propelled us into the narrow streets of the village. We swivelled, gratingly in front of the church, took the road and found in front of us the wreck of a British radio tank which had been destroyed. Along a dirt track we steered towards a wood about 300 metres away. 'Take up fighting formation', ordered Captain Ritgen, followed by 'shut hatches'. The prisms in the turret visor only provided a view of a thin strip of countryside : hedges, fields and the edges of trees. The noise of the engine and tracks was then agreeably deadened and inside the hull there reigned a nervous calm. (...) There were three tanks driving in front of us in a column and they moved obliquely to the left (westwards) along the edge of the wood which apart from a dense blanket of foliage, only consisted of a dense thicket of scrub, hedges and apple-trees which had reverted to the wild state. Suddenly the lead tank turned abruptly right into a small clearing, followed by the second and then the third. I had not yet turned when I heard in my headphones, frantic shouts and the orders of several tank commanders : 'Look out, enemy tank ! - Enemy tank 11 o'clock - Fire !' There were several shots from the guns of our tanks. 'Go right', I ordered. On turning into the wood I saw our three tanks in front of me and fifty metres further on the smoking wreck of a Churchill. Behind it was the outline of another enemy tank which was disengaging already under the protection of a smoke grenade and which disappeared behind a hedge. At the same moment I also saw to our right, moving behind the hedge the indistinct silhouettes of tanks which I assumed to be British ones only a few metres distant. At almost the same moment I saw in the thicket on the left, the square outline of a Cromwell tank which was drawn up in front of me and also opened fire. 'Fire !', I ordered the gun-layer. Our first shell skidded over the surfa-ce of the turret and the enemy withdrew behind the hedge. At the same time I received a shot from the left. 'Go left', I shouted. Shudderingly the tank moved. The outline of the enemy tank expanded in the gun-sight. A powerful recoil made the tank jump backwards and the shell sped towards the thicket. Then, a mighty explosion resounded and smoke billowed towards the sky. But nothing moved, and evidently the enemy, just as surprised as we were, had abandoned the tank after the first impact and thus escaped death. The other Cromwells retired pursued by our fire, and the attempt to force a break through had been checked." (Eye-witness account quoted in : F Kurowski. *Die Panzer-Lehr-Division*, pages 71/72.)

On the west flank of the PLD, four Panzer IV's had been sent to form a blocking position on the crossroads at la Belle Epine.

Hans Pfeiffer's Panthers defeated at Rots

After the taking of Rots on 8 June, before the night attack on Bretteville, the village formed a salient, towards the west facing Bretteville-l'Orgueilleuse and to the north facing Thaon. On the other hand it controlled a part of the Mue valley to the north of the main RN 13 highway. It was defended by the 4th Company of the 26th Panzer-Grenadiers who had replaced the 1st Company, a Platoon of engineers from the same regiment, and the Panther tanks of the 4th Company of the 12th SS-Pz.-Regt. The latter were commanded by *Hauptsturmführer* Hans Pfeiffer who had positioned several of his tanks in such a way as to enable them to intervene either to the north or to the north-west. Some were placed at the south-east of the chateau park (side facing La Villeneuve), others near the school crossroads (nowadays the *mairie*)and others near the church at the north of the village.

Crewmembers of the 2nd Batt. of the 12th SS-Pz.-Regt. had camouflaged their Panzer IV in the expectation of an Allied attack, having been forced onto the defensive. The men are wearing camouflaged uniforms. (Photo PK Woscidlo/Author's coll.)

To eliminate this threat to the western flank of the Canadian 3rd Division, it was decided to launch an offensive, to be carried out by the 46th Royal Marine Commando (from the 8th Canadian Infantry Brigade), reinforced by a tank squadron of the 10th Canadian Armoured Regiment. They followed the course of the Mue from the north towards the south and after the attack by the Marines started, two battalions - from the Régiment de la Chaudière and the North Shore Regiments, were sent into the valley as reinforcements.

During the **morning,** the commander of the heavy platoon saw the first Sherman. Then, after a heavy barrage of artillery, a dozen Shermans came into view, followed by a considerable force of infantry. The following account of the battle is recounted by *Sturmmann* Hans Kesper : *"We were in a well camouflaged observation position, near to a farm. After we had been subjected to a violent artillery barrage, our front was attacked by ten to fifteen Sherman tanks. My Panther (of which the gun-layer was Unterscharführer Ecki Stuhldreher), knocked out four or five of them in ten minutes and the others withdrew. In revenge, the enemy subjected us to a most violent barrage and our infantry suffered severe casualties. There was a new attack on the village during the afternoon and our tanks from the 3rd. Troop fought in the streets with the Shermans and the infantry which had infiltrated. The Ist. Troop tanks, including the commander's one, reached a small hill, behind which a Panther with a damaged track had sought shelter. I asked a couple of grenadiers to give me a hand to repair the track which they did in spite of the enemy shell bursts. From the outside I heard the radio operator transmitting urgent orders to Hauptsturmführer Pfeiffer : "hurry up. The pressure is too strong". Our own infantry moved onto the reverse slope of the hill, while I drove up to the top to be beside the troop commander's tank. A group of our grenadiers found themselves exposed without the means of defence, in a ditch, under fire from the explosive shells of the Canadian tanks. We opened fire on the Shermans and the enemy infantry. I took a glance out to my left and saw the boss's tank moving down from the hill and a minute later I heard he was dead. Although the English or the Canadians were in the village, our repair crew recovered the boss's body in a half-track."*

The commander of the 4th Company of tanks had been killed in that attack. During the battle, *Oscha.* Erwin Wohlgemuth followed the fighting from his tank : *"Suddenly a Panther appeared to support us. It was a terrible sight as we saw the tank churning through the dead and wounded. It slipped as far as the crossroads as there was no possibility to turn round in that street lined by houses and walls, and we launched a counter-attack with its support. A little later, someone shouted : 'tank behind you !' Our tank was in a difficult position as it was impossible to turn round in that narrow street. I reversed as far as a place where I could at least traverse the turret though 180° and then I drove slowly as far as the way out of the village. Suddenly a Sherman appeared in front. Our crew (that of Hstuf. Pfeiffer) then realised what was happening, as with roaring engine, I tried to reach the edge of the village to be able to traverse the turret. But I never got there and our Panther was destroyed, whether from the front or the back I am unable to say. I found out later that Hstuf. Pfeiffer had been killed in that tank."* In fact, the 4th company had suffered few casualties : one officer (Pfeiffer) and one other rank had been killed, an nco and two other ranks had been wounded. But, the village of Rots had been lost, submerged under the weight of the Allied offensive.

Defensive struggles at Mesnil-Patry

In the sector of the 12th SS Pz. Div. the 3rd. Canadian Infantry Division was preparing an attack by the 2nd. Canadian Armoured Brigade for the 12th June, the objective of which was the capture of the high ground to the south of Cheux (Hill 107). But as a preliminary, it was necessary to clean up the Mue valley to the south-west of Rots, the scene of the previously mentioned fighting. In supporting an attack to the west by the 50th Infantry Division, around Brouay-Cristot, the preliminary attack was also to take place on 11 June. The 2nd. Canadian Armoured Brigade was under orders to attack at 0800 hrs. Its 6th Armoured Regiment (the First Hussars) had received twenty replacement tanks at dawn that morning, and was to be accompanied by an infantry battalion, The Queens Own Rifles of Canada. This battle group was to move through Norrey, then first of all take Le-Mesnil-Patry before branching left via the Haut du Bosq to attain the high ground south of Cheux, finally arriving in the Odon valley to encircle Caen from the west .

B Squadron of the Hussars was in the lead, carrying the infantry of D Company of the Queens. C Squadron covered the right flank, facing Putot , with A Squadron and HQ *Company* to the rear. This concentration, however, was spotted by German observers, and as they passed the church in Norrey, the Hussars were subjected to German artillery and mortar fire. The actual attack started at **1430 hrs.** The engineers of the 12th SS who were holding the area had been given order to let the tanks pass but fire at the accompanying infantry. That resulted in bitter fighting between the infantry of both sides in the cornfields, and in spite of their orders, the 12th SS engineers attacked the tanks with *Panzerfausts* (hand-held one-man rocket launchers). But in spite of the courage of the young engineers of the division, the Canadian armour swamped them and drove on to reach the meadows of the Odon valley.

At around **1400 hrs** the commander of the 8th Company of the 12th SS Pz.Regt., *Ostuf.* Hans Siegel was on his way to the headquarters of the 2nd. Battalion (to the south of Fontenay-le-Pesnel) with a tank and a group of nco's and other ranks who were to receive decorations, But just before Fontenay, he met his battalion commander, *Stubaf.* Prinz. He said that the commander of the 26th Panzergrenadier Regt., *Ostubaf.* Mohnke, was at his HQ to ask for tank support against an attack directed against Mesnil by Canadian armour and infantry. Siegel received orders to turn back, observe the situation and intervene if necessary. His company was to the rear of the 26th Grenadiers, a kilometre to the south of Mesnil, where the troop commanders were in the process of celebrating the birthday of *Ustuf.* Jeran. The noise of the fighting grew closer and smoke rose from the tanks destroyed in close combat. Siegel went to see what was going on with the three tanks which were on the right of the positon, one of which was Jeran's. This is his recollection of the battle that ensued : *"When we advanced and then stopped to observe, I became aware of where the danger was by noticing the gestures of our own engineers who were indicating where the enemy was by pointing with their entrenching tools. 'Fighting Order !' The hatches of the three tanks slammed shut and the guns were loaded with anti-tank shells. But a hedgerow blocked our view. But suddenly there was a break, the lead tank was in among our own infantry and several Shermans appeared near an orchard. We were driving past their guns and presenting our flanks. 'Enemy tank left - 9 o'clock - 200 metres - fi-*

re !' Hans Siegel was commanding the company from the lead tank, could not do more, although that was not necessary after the months of training and the experience of the crews. The driver turned the tank to the left and took up a good position. Even before the fan could start up, which was necessary to circulate fresh air inside the hull, the nearest enemy tank was knocked out. In the space of a long minute, four or five tanks were burning. Only the last one, the furthest to the left, made the boss sweat, as we saw that it was traversing its turret towards us. 'Enemy tank - extreme left - 10 o'clock - 100 !' The two guns were facing one another and they seemed to be almost touching when seen through the visor. Then, an explosion, the cartridge was ejected and the other tank blew up. It was at that moment that the other two tanks which were behind the hedge, arrived, not having seen what we had seen before our very eyes. Before the infantry could begin to move forward, the three tanks drove past the burning wrecks and among the trees in the orchard towards our front line. Two other Shermans that were attempting to escape about 1,200 metres in front, were also destroyed by the boss (Siegel). The enemy was retreating in confusion and the situation had to be taken advantage of. Orders were given for two other tanks to follow on the left, and to cross the cornfield at full speed as far as a hedge and a stand of trees, 1,600 metres away. During the advance, the boss received anti-tank rounds from the right, through a stand of trees and informed the crew through the intercom. The driver reacted immediately, placing the tank in a good position to fire, after which a duel took place and five rounds were fired. Our tank too was hit by a second or third anti-tank gun and the crew baled out except for the radio operator who had been hit on the right side of his body, before the tank caught fire. The two other tanks which had stopped to fire were also hit, and remained standing 800 metres to the rear." In face, faced by the situation of C Squadron, B Squadron was engaged on the right flank of the former but received the onslaught of the Panzer IV's on its right flank. On top of that, *Ostuf.* Siegel was able to intervene in cooperation with an anti-tank gun from the 26th Grenadiers. Confronted by the disaster, Lieutenant-colonel Colwell reacted too late by not ordering the withdrawal of his two squadrons which were annihilated, together with D Company of the Queens Own Rifles. The Hussars lost 37 Sherman tanks and suffered 80 losses among them 59 killed or wounded including all the officers and nco's of B Squadron. The company of the Queens suffered 96 casualties. Thus it was that the energetic action of *Ostuf.* Siegel halted an important Allied offensive and caused severe losses to a battalion of tanks. The panzers were to become masters of the defensive.

Ostuf. Hans Siegel commanded the 8th. Company of the 12th SS Pz.Regt. which successfully counter-attacked at Mesnil-Patry.

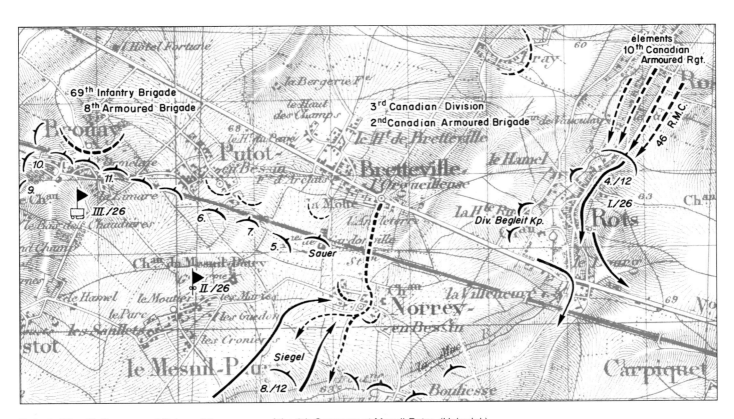

Defeat of the 4th Company at Rots and the success of the 8th Company at Mesnil-Patry. (Heimdal.)

Monday 12 June

A Panzer IV of the 2nd Batt. of the 12th SS. Pz.Regt.moving to take up a defensive position. Note the camouflage painted in a zig-zag pattern on the side protective plates. (PK Woscidlo/Author.)

The British attacks continued with the same intensity all along the front held by the Panzer Lehr Division mainly on the line Lingèvres - Tilly - Saint-Pierre. In spite of the British numerical superiority , the Panthers of the 1st. Battalion of the 6th Pz.Regt. had a successful engagement, in particular the 3rd. Company (Captain Schramm) stopped an enemy attack, destroying 20 Allied tanks, including seven in close combat.

Thus, a week after the Allied landings in Normandy, the German armoured divisions had been defeated in their primary task of throwing the invaders back into the sea within 48 hours. Several counter-attacks that were launched with too few resources and even a certain amount of improvisation, were stopped dead and brought only slender results. In addition, a grand offensive planned for the night of 10/11 June by all three panzer divisions then at the front, was cancelled because it would not have produced a decisive result. The panzers at the front were thus restricted to the defensive and to carrying out local counter-attacks in face of the seemingly irresistible Allied advance. The German commanders appeared just to hope that they could hang on.

There were only three armoured divisions to form a front in Normandy although there were others available, but the German high command remained convinced of a second landing in the Pas-de-Calais and was unwilling to release all the resources at its disposal. The 2nd. Panzer Division received orders to join the front in Normandy on 9 June and three days later it installed its divisional HQ at Lignou, south of Briouze in the Orne *Département*. The following day it joined the front on the left wing of the Panzer Lehr Division. On the other hand a battalion of heavy tanks, the *schwere SS-Panzer-Abteilung 101* was also en route for the front, but too late for the initial grand counter-attack.

Another Panzer IV from the same battalion on the move and the crew have placed a flag on the front panel for recognition by friendly aircraft. (PK Woscidlo.)

Uniforms worn by Army tank crews

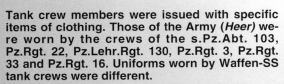

Tank crew members were issued with specific items of clothing. Those of the Army (*Heer*) were worn by the crews of the s.Pz.Abt. 103, Pz.Rgt. 22, Pz.Lehr.Rgt. 130, Pz.Rgt. 3, Pz.Rgt. 33 and Pz.Rgt. 16. Uniforms worn by Waffen-SS tank crews were different.

1. We see here the old pattern officers' field service **cap** and the tank crews' double-breasted black blouse introduced in 1934. This *Feldjacke* is the one of an officer cadet (*Oberfähnrich*) who were issued with officers' uniforms with the shoulder insignia of a warrant officer. The national emblem is an officers' one woven in aluminium wire.

2. Officers' pattern forage cap, tank crewmens' shirt and black uniform trousers. The black forage **cap** seen here was introduced on 27 March 1940. The bordering in aluminium wire and the national emblem (eagle with swastika) woven in the same material identify the wearer as an officer. The inverse braid "V" which surrounded the cockade should have been removed after 8 September 1942 but often continued to be worn. The dark grey two pocket **shirt** was of knitted material or jersey and was introduced on 23 June 1943. The shoulder boards (here, a lieutenant) were non-regulation and should not in theory have been worn with this shirt. The black **trousers** were tightened around the ankles by a draw-string : sufficiently long they were worn folded down over boots or left baggy over shoes.

(© Heimdal.)

3

4

3. The **cap** illustrated here was standard issue *(Einheits-Feldmütze)* adopted in 1943 to replace the forage caps. The officers' pattern was identified by the border braid in aluminium wire. The tank crews' protective **tunic** was introduced in 1942, tailored in a light sail-cloth in the so-called "pinkish green" colour. The cut was identical to the black one, but with two large pockets : one on the jacket and the other on the trousers. The rank insignia were on standard pattern shoulder boards or consisted of indications of special ranks introduced in 1942, in this case a junior warrant officer, sewn on the sleeve. Note also the insignia ("S" for a *Schirrmeister*) denoting a senior nco in

charge of a team acting in a support function. Such nco's could be found on the staff of a tank regiment in the headquarters company, the workshop company and in each of the two service companies.

4. The cloth forage **cap** is the pattern adopted on 27 March 1942. The national emblem is woven in grey wire in effect designed for nco's and other ranks, minus the "V" shaped braid. The protective tunic in cotton sail-cloth "pinkish-green" colour is the pattern adopted for the crews or armoured reconnaissance vehicles on 5 May 1941. The cut is identical to the black uniform pattern and the sleeve insignia is that of a corporal *(Gefreiter)*.

6

This one has been painted to match the camouflage of the tanks. Its use by tank crews was suppressed on 8 November 1943 but it continued to be worn by other personnel of the tank regiments. The field grey sail-cloth tunic was identical in cut to the 1933 pattern. The one illustrated was manufactured between 1943 and 1945 with six buttons. The shoulder boards are those of a sergeant (*Unteroffizier*) and the cuff insignia is that of an armoured unit radio mechanic (*Panzerfunkwart*).

(© Heimdal.)

5

5. The cap shown here is the *Feldmütze,* which replaced the 1940 pattern cap on 21 July 1942, issued to nco's and other ranks. The dark grey knitted and pocketless shirt was the pattern made for tank crews up until 23 June 1943 when it was replaced by the two pocket pattern (see page 65). The black **tie** was obligatory when walking out. Seen here with standard issue braces, the field grey sail-cloth **trousers**, introduced in 1942, were the summer campaign pattern.

6. The 1935 pattern steel helmet, manufactured during the last three years of the war with hammered-over rim.

Tank crew uniforms of the Waffen-SS

7

8

7. This **cap** is a standard pattern introduced in 1943 which replaced the Waffen-SS forage cap. The second type shown here had a single plastic button above which were sewn the insignia woven in aluminium wire - the Waffen-SS pattern eagle and death's-head. The Waffen-SS black uniform was adopted as from 1938 for the crews of armoured reconnaissance vehicles and it was issued to the first tank crews at the end of 1941. Its straighter cut was different from that of the army tank crews' tunics. The insignia of rank worn on the lapel is that of a *Sturmmann* (corporal) and the cuff insignia is that of the *Das Reich* Division (2nd SS Pz.Regt.).

8. This standard pattern officers' **cap** is distinguished from the other- ranks' model by its braiding and insignia in aluminium wire. All officers' caps had two buttons and the Waffen-SS pattern eagle was shown on the side that cannot be seen here. The dark grey knitted or jersey shirt with two pockets was introduced into the Waffen-SS on 15 August 1943. The black cloth trousers were of a different cut to those of the army, especially the pocket flaps.

(© Heimdal.)

9   10

9. The officers' forage **cap** was a pattern adopted by the Waffen-SS in 1940. The black cloth pattern was worn with double-breasted tank crew uniform, identified as that of an officer by its braiding and insignia woven in aluminium wire. The protective tunic in "pinkish-green" sailcloth was issued to the crews of armoured reconnaissance vehicles from 1 September 1941 : its cut was similar to the black pattern, and it was also worn by tank crews. The rank badges are those of an *Untersturmführer* (second lieutenant). The collar braiding in aluminium wire identifies the wearer as an officer.

10. The 1940 pattern forage **cap** is that worn by other-ranks. The two piece protective **outfit** is of the same cut as the black version, but made of camouflage cloth. The black slip-overs on the shoulder boards have the letters "LAH" embroidered on them showing that the wearer is a crewman from the 1st SS Panzer Regiment or a veteran of that unit (as were many in the 12th SS Pz.Rgt.).

(© Heimdal.)

11

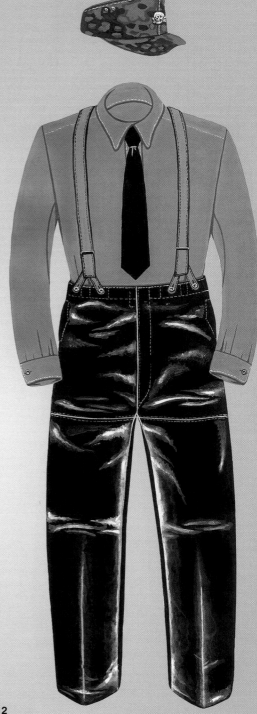

11. During its sojourn in the north of Italy from 1 August to 2 November 1943, the *Leibstandarte SS Adolf Hitler* Division recovered numerous items of Italian clothing. These leather uniforms were delivered to the Italian navy by the *Kriegsmarine* (German navy) and were taken for the tank crews of the 1st and 12th SS Panzer Regiments and the 101st. SS Panzer Battalion. They were very popular with the crews as they offered excellent protection against fire (common in tanks which were hit by a shell). Shoulder boards were often attached to these **jackets**, like these of an *Unterscharführer* (sergeant).

12

12. The reversible cloth camouflage **cap** was adopted on 1 June 1942. In theory no insignia were worn except a metal death's-head in the one illustrated. The brown shirt was a standard Waffen-SS pattern issued until 15 August 1943, when it was replaced by the dark grey two pocket model (illustration n° 8). Note the black tie and the leather trousers which were worn with the leather jacket already described.

(© Heimdal.)

14. This photograph was taken in Flanders during the winter of 1943/44 during the training of the 2nd Battalion of the 12th SS Pz. Regt. and shows a young *Unterscharführer* (sergeant) of that unit of Panzer IV's. His black cloth Waffen-SS tunic is buttoned up to the collar. The shoulder board of an *Unterscharführer* bears the woven and interlaced letters "LAH" and the cuff band "Adolf Hitler" indicates that he was a veteran of the 1st SS Pz. Regt. in the *Leibstandarte SS Adolf Hitler* Division, as was frequently the case with the initial cadres of the 12th SS *Hitlerjugend* Division. The sleeve eagle is woven in aluminium wire and the camouflage cloth cap issued after 1 June 1943 has metal badges.

(Bundesarchiv.)

13

13. The peaked service dress **cap** (*Schirmmütze*) with white binding was worn in the field without a chin-strap by certain officers. The reversible camouflage **overall** was introduced on 15 January 1943 to replace the pinkish-green sailcloth pattern (illus. 9) and is shown here with the spring side out. After the 15 February 1943, badges of rank were worn on the sleeve, in this example, an *Obersturmführer* (lieutenant). In January, this overall was replaced by the camouflaged sailcloth pattern (illus. 19). The belt shown is an army pattern.

(© Heimdal.)

14

22nd Panzer-Regiment

The 22nd Panzer Regiment was equipped with numerous obsolete tanks including captured French Somua S-35's (renamed Pf. Kpfw.35S [f]). 23 of them equipped the 2nd Battalion on the eve of the landings (instead of 54 a few weeks previously). These tanks painted with camouflage and carrying German markings were not particularly powerfull with their 47 mm guns.

Among the obsolete tanks available to the 22nd Panzer Regiment, this Panzer IV type "C" with short barrelled gun was seen at Saint-Martin-de-Fresnay just before the landings (see page 3) It was painted in a sand yellow finish and did not have side protection plates or any markings, with the exception of the names of the driver's and radio operator's girlfriends painted on the front. (see illustration on the facing page).

Above : After the defeat of their attack on 6 June, some of the tanks of the 22nd Pz. Regt. were dug in hull-down in defensive positions north of Caen. This one, "134", a Panzer IV type "H" from the 1st Company was knocked out and left where it was. It was entirely coated with well applied with *Zimmerit* cement except on the side protective plates (*Schürzen*), which were coated with a motley camouflage applied in large blotches by hand, including some white. The German crosses and identification numbers were stencilled.

Below : Tank crews often painted the names of their girlfriends on their vehicles. The following were to be seen in the 12th SS Pz.Regt. (Paula, Wilma, Berti, Steffi), in the 130th Pz. Lehr Regt. (Christel, Gerda, Hesla) and here from the 22nd Pz.Regt. with "Hedi" in white paint and "Elfriede" in white chalk on the other side.

(Paintings Heimdal/E. Groult.)

12th SS-Panzer-Regiment

The tank regiment of the 12th SS Panzer Division *Hitlerjugend* was one of the best equipped, in effect with nine companies, including an extra one of Panzer IV's in the 2nd Battalion. The one seen above was a Panther from the 3rd Company, the "304". It was the company commander's tank, *Obersturmführer* Rudolf von Ribbentrop, whose gun-layer was Heinz Freiberg. Varied camouflage was applied in that regiment, but in theory it had three colours : a base colour of sand with over-painting in brown and green. It would seem that, according to photographs and statements by veterans that this tank was only given a rapid paint job with reddish-brown curved patterns applied with a spray gun. The number "304" was hand-painted without a stencil and outlined in white. According to veterans, tanks of that company also carried red numbers outlined in white.

This Panzer IV of the 8th Company, the "837" was the tank of *Ustuf.* Jeran. On the 6 June it was lost and fell into the hands of the British. It can been seen on Page 35 "before" and "after". Its camouflage was quite motley, with large hand-painted numbers in black with a white border. Those of the 5th and 6th Companies also seem top have been similar as were the 9th Company tanks.

(Paintings Heimdal/E. Groult.)

The 130th Pz. Lehr-Regt. was widely dispersed along the front. The Ist. Battalion (Panthers) had already been loaded for service on the eastern front and only five Panthers went into battle on 10 June, the rest following several days later. "322" which is illustrated here was a 3rd Company Panther and which we have seen during training at Amboise in May 1944. These tanks were covered in *Zimmerit*, applied in squares and painted sand-yellow. The turrets of 3rd. Company vehicles were marked with very large identification numbers, hand-painted in red without stencil and outlined in white.

On the other hand the Panzer IV's of the 2nd Battalion were painted in a different manner with the armour plating covered with a three-colour pattern area by area. On this 6th Company vehicle the numbers are painted white with, on either side, the German cross (*Balkenkreuz)* and the personal coat of arms of the Prince von Schönburg-Waldenburg. There were numbers on the rear of the turret painted in black.

(Paintings Heimdal/E. Groult.)

I./Panzer-Lehr-Regiment 130

Panthers of the 130th Pz.-Lehr-Regt. on 10 June

1. These photographs were taken during the afternoon of 10 June near the farm known as Pallières at Mondaye (8 km. south of Bayeux). This time scale is confirmed by the following evidence : the last elements of the division had to withdraw shortly afterwards from Mondaye as a result of British pressure. We see here the Panther tanks of the Ist. Battalion of the 130th Pz. Lehr Regt. which appear to contradict the fact that the battalion had already been loaded on trains for the Russian front and only reached the Normandy front several days later. In fact, recent studies have shown that a section of five Panthers from the battalion were present right from the beginning of the deployment of the division in Normandy. Those are the ones we see in these photos which were destined for a propaganda report designed to demonstrate to the public how powerful the panzers were in the face of the Allied landings - even though that elite division only had those five Panthers available on the front. They are "A" models.

2. Instead of the black panzer uniform the Panther crews wore the green sailcloth version : the collar patches featured the traditional insignia *(Litzen)* rather than the death's-head of the panzer forces which seems to have been the norm in the 130th Pz.Lehr Regt. On the other hand, all are wearing the black forage-caps or standard caps.

3. Lieutenant Finsterwalder (identification uncertain) posing in front of the tank. He was killed on 11 June, a day after this photo was taken.

(ECPA.)

4. The five Panther type "A" tanks which arrived at Mondaye on 10 June are all present in this painting which was made on the basis of the photo report featured on these pages. : the muzzle brake of one of the tanks is in the foreground, two of the Panthers are in the middleground and two others behind them. They are covered in *Zimmerit* applied in large squared and painted a uniform sand colour without any additional camouflage.

5. The same location as it appears today.

(© Heimdal.)

I./Panzer-Lehr-Regiment 130

The Panther tanks of the Ist battalion of the 130th Pz.-Lehr-Regt. at Mondaye on 10 June

1. One of the five type "A" Panthers in position at Mondaye on the afternoon of 10 June. Note the retractable visor for the driver which was typical of that model. The *Zimmerit* (anti-magnetic cement) was applied all over the armour plating and grooved to form a pattern of squares to make it adhere better to the metal. The name of the driver's girlfriend "Gerda" is painted on the base of the seat on the hull. The tank is to the north of the farm.

2. The officer visible in the foregound was Lieutenant Steindamm. Note the special badges of rank worn habitually on the arm of the protective tunic.

3. In this photo, taken to the west of the farm, two other Panthers are in position. The first is a hybrid version : a type "A" turret mounted on a type "D" hull. It carried the name "Christel" and the other one (not visible in this photo), the name "Hesla". In the foreground the section commanders were assembled to study a map. The man on the right could be Lieutenant Gerstenmeier of the 3rd Company of the *Panzer-Aufklärungs-Lehr-Abteilung 130* (the divisional reconnaissance battalion).

(ECPA.)

4. The view corresponding to Photo no.1 as it is today

5. The view corresponding to Photo no. 3 as it is today.

(Heimdal.)

6. Uniform unique to 130th Pz.-Lehr-Regt. crews. The protective jacket is the same as that issued to members of the armoured reconnaissance units which was introduced on 5 May 1941. It does not seem that crews from the PLD generally wore the black Panzer uniform. In the same way the collar patches did not feature the death's-head insignia but instead carried the woven or embroidered plaits known as *Litzen,* which were peculiar to the PLD. (© Heimdal.)

A *Flakpanzer 38 (t)* armed with a 20 mm. cannon with which the anti-aircraft section of the 12 SS-Pz.Regt. was equipped. This vehicle type replaced in most of the tank regiments, the *Flakpanzer IV's* with 37 mm. cannon as laid down in the table of equipment known as *Freie Gliederung 44*. Nevertheless, the regiment was also equipped with the formidable quadruple barrelled *Flakvierling 38*. Here, the *Flakpanzer 38 (t)* has been spray-painted with large curved shapes in an olive-green colour.

(Painting Heimdal/E.G.)

Monsieur Angot, a farmer, recovered from his field near Norrey-en-Bessin, two bogey wheels from the track of a wrecked Panther of the 3rd Company of the 12th SS-Pz. Regt. The rubber tyres were still marked with the inscriptions "Continental", "Fulda" and 860/100 = D. These relics of the battlefield have been presented to the Museum of the Great Bunker at Ouistreham.

(© Heimdal.)

The failure of the panzers

(IWM.)

13 June to 20 July 1944

by Georges Bernage

101st SS Heavy Tank Battalion

1. In **May 1944** the 101st SS Heavy Tank Battalion was on exercise in the Beauvais area. The 3rd. Company formed up in a line of battle on an extended front, although the crews never had the occasion to use that formation during the Battle of Normandy

2. A crew from the 1st. Company adopted a crow as mascot. The three men are wearing the 1944 pattern mottled camouflage smock - the most widely used protective garment in the tank regiments of the Waffen-SS during the summer of that year. The man in the centre was the tank commander, *Junker* (officer candidate) Erwin Asbach, who, on 6 June commanded the Tiger « 124 ». This photograph was taken in May 1944.

7 June 1944. Wittmann's 2nd. Company of Tigers in the Morgny area of Normandy.

3. The alert having been issued, the battalion moved up to the front line. This photo was taken during the morning of 7 June on the N316 road between Bézu-la-Foret and Morgny in the north-east of Normandy.. « 221 » was the Tiger of the commander of the 2nd. Section, *Ustuf.* Georg Hantusch. The one in front was « 214 » (*Uscha.* Karl-Heinz Warmbrunn).

(BA.)

4. The 2nd Section tanks continued to follow the winding road : probably « 222 » above, with « 223 » visible in the middle ground (*Oscha.* Jurgen Brandt) and « 224 » just exiting the picture (*Uscha.* Ewald Molly).

5. Tiger « 131 » with *Ustuf.* Walter Hahn in the turret hatch, posing in front of the church at Morgny. It was followed by « 132 », (*Uscha.* Werner Wendt) and « 133 » (*Uscha.* Fritz Zahner).

(BA.)

9

Tuesday 13 June
Reinforcements arrived
Wittmann at Villers-Bocage

SS-Stubaf. Heinz von Westernhagen.

SS-Hstuf. Rolf Möbius.

SS-Ostuf. Michael Wittmann.

SS-Ostuf. Hanno Raasch.

(Photos coll. auteur et P. Agte.)

After the defeat of the frontal attack by the British 50th Infantry Division and the 7th Armoured Division in the Tilly-sur-Seulles area, Montgomery decided to outflank that obstacle to the west. In fact of the Panzer Lehr Division, the German front was gaping wide open. The breach was to be stopped by the 2nd. Panzer Division moving into the Caumont area as well as the 17th SS Panzergrenadier Division *Gotz von Berlichingen.* Those two divisions which were to reinforce the western wing of the German armour were on the way but had not yet arrived in the line. Thus, on 12 June at midday, the staff of the British Second Army decided to seize the opportunity. A report by the 22nd Armoured Brigade (7th Armoured Division) summed up the decision : "because of the difficult terrain and the resulting slow progress, it was decided that the 7th Armoured Division would attempt to turn the enemy position on the left of the American sector. The Americans were already to the north of Caumont and there was a chance of exploiting a success towards Villers-Bocage and if possible to occupy Hill 113." If successful, it was intended that the British armoured division would advance as far as Evrecy, followed by elements of the 5Oth Infantry Division and supported by a planned parachute drop by the Ist Airborne Division. Evrecy was only 3 km. to the south-west of Hill 112 which was destined to be bitterly fought over during the coming weeks. On **12 June at 1600 hrs.**, according to its orders, a battle group of the 22nd Armoured Brigade moved off towards Villers-Bocage, but the vanguard clashed with the German infantry supported by anti-tank guns near Livry. At 2200 hrs. that German strongpoint was eliminated but it was too late to continue the advance.

The Tigers to the rescue

In fact the I SS-Panzer-Corps had been informed of the threat but did not have the reserves to oppose it, except for the elements of its heavy tank battalion which were arriving during the evening of 12/13 June.

The 101st SS heavy Panzer Battalion had been alerted to move on 6 June and actually got underway in the early hours of 7 June. It had available 45 "E" model Tiger I's. The unit had its origins in the heavy tank company of the *Leibstandarte* Division which had been reformed in Italy during the summer of 1943 and from 1 November of that year had been engaged on the Russian front. At the same time a battalion of heavy tanks was being formed as from 19 July 1943, and in March 1944, the men of the 13th Section of the 1st SS Panzer Regiment were transferred to the new battalion, basking in the fresh glory of *Untersturmfuhrer* Michael Wittmann. After a period of training near Mons in Belgium, the battalion moved to the area of Gournay-en-Bray in the north-east of Normandy on 20 April 1944. Battalion HQ was at Crillon, the 1st Company at Saint-Germer-de-Fly, the second at Elbeuf-en-Bray and the third at Songeons.

The battalion commander was *Sturmbannfuhrer* Heinz von Westernhagen (Tiger 007), the Ist Company was commanded by *Hauptsturmfuhrer* Rolf Mobius (Tiger "105"), the second by *Obersturmfuhrer* Michael Wittmann, and the third by *Obersturmfuhrer* Hanno Raasch (Tiger 305). The CO of the 4th Company (reconnaissance, engineers and anti-aircraft) was *Obersturmfuhrer* Wilhelm Spitz and the workshop company came under *Pbersturmfuhrer* Gottfried Klein. Their boss, *Stubaf.* Von Westernhagen (known by his men as "Hein") was born on 29 August 1911 at Riga in Latvia and he joined the *SS Verfugungstruppe* on 1 October 1934 having been a Nazi party member since 1929 and of the *Allgemeine SS* (General SS) since 1932. He became an officer in the *Sicherheitsdienst* (security service) until he rejoined the army on 10 September 1938. After June 1942 he commanded the assault-gun company of the Ist SS-Pz.Div. (LSAH) and was at the time earmarked to command the 101st SS Heavy Tank Battalion. During the 1943 summer offensive *Zitadelle* in Russia he was severely wounded in the head on 6 July. Although formally nominated in command of the battalion from 5 August 1943, on account of his wound he was unable to take on his duties until he joined the unit at Mons on 23 February 1944. As far as the commander of the 2nd Company was concerned, Michael Wittmann, was born on 22 April 1914 at Vogelthal in the Palatinate and joined the *Leibstandarte Adolf Hitler* in 1937. After the campaign in France he integrated the new assault-guns into the unit, and after the Balkan campaign he gained his first successes in Russia, being commissioned as a second lieutenant on 21 December 1942. At the beginning of 1943 he was transferred to the heavy tank company of the 1st SS Pz. Regt. although only in command of a Panzer III (the "421"), but during operation *Zitadelle,* still in the same company, he finally got his own Tiger (the "1331"). In the autumn of 1943 he returned to the fighting in the East and on 14th January 1944 he was decorated with the Knights' Cross for having destroyed 66 Soviet tanks. Two weeks later he was awarded the "Oak Leaves" to his medal having upped his score to 88. He was thus promoted to *Obersturmfuhrer* (lieutenant) and took over command of the 2nd Company which essentially was composed of the men of the old 13th Heavy Company, all experienced veterans of the battles in the East.

Thus at around three o'clock in the morning of 7 June, the battalion's Tigers passed through Gournay-en-Bray en route for the Seine, and reached Morgny later that morning. It was there that a war correspondent took the series of photographs (which became well-known) at around 10 o'clock. But, when they arrived at Andelys, the battalion staff were forced to realise that the bridge over the Seine was unsuitable. This was an annoying situation which forced the battalion to head for Paris along the N14 road and caused a serious delay. The Tigers drove through Paris and staged a propaganda coup by roaring up the Champs Elysee to the Arc de Triomphe before continuing on to Versailles where they spent the night of 7/8 June : they were subjected to a hail of bombs and the workshop company registered the first losses. While the 3rd Company returned to Paris, the other two continued their march to Normandy at dawn on 8 June. Two days later the 2nd Company had only got as far as Argentan where it was attacked by fighter-bombers before carrying on to Falaise. That evening in spite of not having engaged in combat, the battalion had already suffered nine killed and eighteen wounded. The 2nd Company was followed by the 3rd and the whole battalion was dispersed.

By the evening of 12 June the battalion's Tigers had still not reached Villers-Bocage. *Hstuf.* Rolf Mobius had reached the south of Caen with his 1st Company and during the night drove a further dozen kilometres just to the north-east of Villers-Bocage, to the north of the N175 highway linking that place to Caen. He only had eight out of the fourteen Tigers available to his company, but was soon joined by Wittmann with a further six from the 2nd Company that had been able to reach the front. Artillery barrages forced him to move three times during the night until he finally took up a position to the south of the N175, to the east of Mobius. Exhausted by the five days on the road, the men were unable to sleep that night.

13 June. Wittmann confronted an entire armoured brigade

That Tuesday, 13 June, at five o'clock in the morning, the 7th Armoured Division restarted its advance with its reconnaissance elements in the lead (8th Bn. Kings Royal Irish Hussars with 40 Cromwell tanks, 6 Fireflys, 5 Centaur anti-aircraft tanks plus 8 scout cars). They were followed by a tank battalion (the 4th County of London Yeomanry , "the Sharpshooters", equipped with 55 Cromwells, 6 Shermans, 11 Honey light tanks, 5 Centaur AA, 8 Humber armoured cars and the 22 Armoured Brigade HQ. Then came an artillery battery (5th Royal Horse Artillery with 23 Sexton self-propelled howitzers), an infantry battalion (1/7th Queen's Royal Regiment with six 6pdr. anti-tank guns and six 3 inch mortars), a further tank battalion (5th Royal Tank Regiment with 42 Cromwells, 16 Shermans, 11 Honeys, 6 Centaurs and 8 Humber armoured cars), a battalion of motorised infantry (Ist. Bn. Rifle Brigade) and an anti-tank battery (the 260th). The battle group in the lead was followed by the rest of the division.. That same morning at 8 o'clock, Wittmann positioned his available Tigers to the south of the N175 : the tanks of *Ustuf.* Hantusch, (2nd Section commander), *Uscha.* Stief and Sowa and *Oscha.* Brandt and Lotzsch (the tracks of his tank were damaged). *Ostuf.* Wessel, the commander of the 1st Section was on the move and about to make contact with the others.

Wittmann saw that the head of the British column was in the process of leaving Villers-Bocage and starting to advance along the N175 towards Caen and approaching Hill 213, near his few Tigers which were in position around Haut Vents and Montbrocq, roughly 150 metres south of the road. "A" Squadron of the 4th CLY was already in a meadow below the hill with its Cromwell tanks. On the face of it there seemed to be little the few Tigers could do in the face of that British column of more than 200 tanks and numerous other armoured vehicles. But, while waiting for reinforcements the effect of surprise might make it possible to cause significant damage amongst the packed tanks, and at the very least, the wrecks of those destroyed would slow up the avdance.

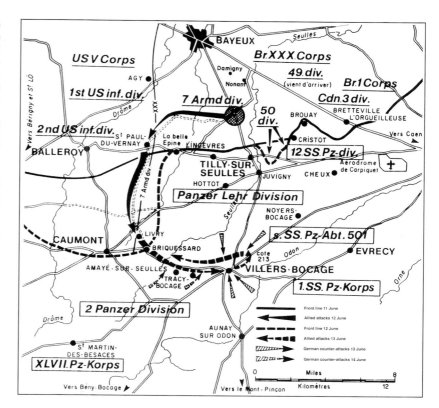

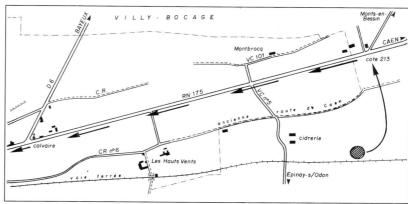

Maps above :

The attempt by the 7th Armoured Division to strike at the rear of the Panzer Lehr Division on 13 June

The route of *Ostuf.* Michael Wittmann's attack along the N175 towards the centre of Villers-Bocage

Left : Wittmann photographed on the afternoon of 13 June at the HQ of I SS Panzer Corps in the park of the chateau, at Baron-sur-Odon, a few hours after his victory at Villers-Bocage. He is wearing a black leather jacket and a cloth cap with a single button.

Right : This drawing from the German magazine "Signal" gives a good impression of Wittmann's attack on the British column along the N175. (Heimdal.)

Below, from top to bottom :

Positions of the two companies of the Tiger battalion to the east of Villers-Bocage. (Map Heimdal.)

British wrecks along the N175 ; half-tracks and a 57mm anti-tank gun. (BA.)

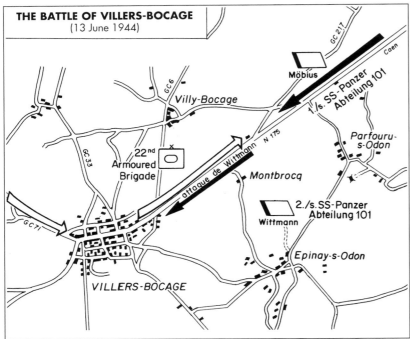

THE BATTLE OF VILLERS-BOCAGE
(13 June 1944)

If Wittman attacked towards Hill 213 he would thus isolate "A" Squadron of the 4th CLY from the rest of the British column. He therefore moved north towards the main road with his Tiger which had an engine problem : all the tanks had been subjected to a severe trial during the long march by road and several had broken down and been left behind. His Tiger had had engine problems the whole way, so he jumped out and took over the one behind, that of *Uscha*. Sowa, whose place he took. It was **0805 hrs.** (an hour later for the British) when Wittmann started his attack and this was how he described it later : "I could not collect my company together and it was necessary to act swiftly as I had to assume that the enemy had seen me and would destroy me on my start line. I set off in my tank, having given the other tanks in the company orders not to retreat but to stay where they were and hold their position. I thus surprised the English in the same way that they had surprised us. I first destroyed two on the right and then one to the left. Then I turned round to the left to get at the half-tracks in the centre of the regiment. I drove along the second half of the road and destroyed several armoured vehicles in front of me while on the move. There was unbelievable confusion among the enemy" (quoted in *Tiger* by P. Agte , Edns. Heimdal, p. 254). The following are the recollections of a tank commander of the 4th CLY, J-L Cloudsley-Thompson : "suddenly the "A" Squadron tanks caught fire and their crews abandoned them (...) Pat Dyas, the deputy commander, lined up his tank alongside mine. His forehead was bleeding. At that moment all the tanks in front of us were burning. Through the smoke I could make out the shape of a huge Tiger and I was not more than 25 yards away from it (22.875 metres). We loosed off several 75mm shells at it but they simply bounced off the massive armour plating of the Tiger. I fired with the 58mm mortar but on account of the smoke, they missed the Tiger which traversed its 88mm gun. Whoosh ! We were hit. I sensed a burning pain between my legs and was surprised to be wounded again. A jet of flame shot through the turret and my mouth was full of sand and burned paint. I yelled 'bail out' and jumped off the tank. As I was watching that my crew get out, suddenly a machine-gun opened up and I hit the dirt. The Tiger continued on and Dyas's Cromwell followed it down the street. (...) One heard a terrible racket from the centre of the village. I decided to get behind a wall behind the houses and try to find "B" Squadron. As we were moving off I saw Dyas on foot, a short distance away ; he was hoping to destroy the Tiger from be-

1. One of the Cromwells destroyed at the top of the Rue Clemenceau, facing east ("4" on the plan to the right). (BA.)

2. The observation Sherman of the 5th RHA with in the foreground, its dummy gun ripped off ("6" on the lower plan), destroyed by Wittmann level with the Hotel du Bras d'Or. (BA.)

3. Plan showing where the Cromwell tanks of Major Carr ("1" on the plan) and Lieutenant-Colonel Cranley ("2") were destroyed by Wittman's Tiger before carrying on down the street. (Heimdal.)

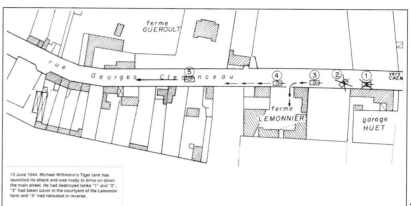

13 June 1944. Michael Wittmann's Tiger tank has launched its attack and was ready to drive on down the main street. He had destroyed tanks "1" and "2", "3" had taken cover in the courtyard of the Lemonier farm and "4" had retreated in reverse.

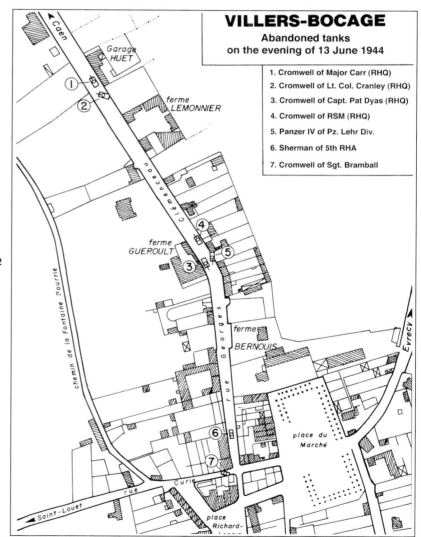

VILLERS-BOCAGE
Abandoned tanks
on the evening of 13 June 1944

1. Cromwell of Major Carr (RHQ)
2. Cromwell of Lt. Col. Cranley (RHQ)
3. Cromwell of Capt. Pat Dyas (RHQ)
4. Cromwell of RSM (RHQ)
5. Panzer IV of Pz. Lehr Div.
6. Sherman of 5th RHA
7. Cromwell of Sgt. Bramball

hind. He encountered it again after it has destroyed the rest of the regimental staff . The Tiger fired again and the second driver and the gun-layer were killed, but Dyas and his driver were able to escape unharmed". (quoted by P. Agte, op. cit. p259-60).

What had happened? Michael Wittmann, leaving the head of "A" squadron of the 4th CLY, had driven down the main road leading into Villers-Bocage in his solitary Tiger, firing as he went. His first shell hit the last "A" Squadron Cromwell and then he poured 88mm shells and machine-gun rounds into the half-tracks and other vehicles of the Rifle Brigade, section after section at point blank range without ever bothering to correct his fire. From Landes to the entrance to Villers-Bocage there was a long column of tanks, half-tracks and other armoured vehicles in flames, with bodies littering the ditches. According to some eye-witnesses (see *Tigres en Combat,* Heimdal, p. 38-39). He was supported by another Tiger camouflaged under the apple trees of a small orchard behind the wayside cross, which was able to intervene without changing its position. This reinforces the opinions of those who maintain that the column was attacked from both ends simultaneously. If that were the ca-

se, it could have been the Tiger of *Ostuf.* Wessell.

When Wittmann arrived in the actual village he was confronted by the four Cromwell tanks of the HQ of the 4th CLY : they were level with the Lemonnier

1. The Cromwell tank of Sergeant Bramball ("7" on the plan on the previous page) which caught fire in the Rue Curie and set a house alight.

2. Wittmann's damaged Tiger in the Rue Pasteur ("7" on the plan on page 90).

Oscha. Jurgen Brandt who destroyed three Shermans and several half-tracks.

the meanwhile, moved out of the courtyard of the Lemonnier farm. Dyas fired two 75 mm shells at the Tiger without being able to stop it, but a single round from the 88 mm gun put the Cromwell out of action, killing two of the crew. Captain Dyas jumped out of the turret to use the radio in the Cromwell of the regimental sergeant-major, previously put out of action by Wittmann. He made contact with Lt-Col. Cranley who told him that the situation was desperate : the remaining tanks of "A" Squadron were under attack from the rest of the 2nd Company Tigers which had come to rescue Wittmann.

Rottenfuhrer Lau recounted the engagement of the other Tigers : "the English tanks were advancing to the right in the direction of Caen and we could hear Wittmann firing along the road. I found myself without a tank commander in the turret, about 50 metres away from the road. I could see *Uscha.* Sowa standing where Wittmann had left him and what with the roaring of the tank engines and the sound of firing, it was difficult to make myself understood, but I shouted at him - 'Come here, Kurt, I haven't got a tank commander' . With him on board we drove up to the road where to our left was just a vast tangle of wreckage which was difficult to make out through the smoke. To the right we could see two Cromwells in the process of turning round and we knocked them out. All around us there were English troops frantically running around. We left the road in the direction of a sunken lane in order to obtain a better view to be able to cover the area and stopped the engine as it was overheating. Then we saw several of our troops in the process of rounding up the English. A Russian auxiliary from our field kitchen particularly distinguished himself in that task (...) In the meanwhile about a hundred prisoners had been collected in an open garage in front of our tank and while the men from our support units were searching them for weapons, we unshipped the machine gun from the turret and placed it on the hull. Between thirty and sixty minutes later some Tigers arrived from the direction of Caen and advanced towards Villers-Bocage. As they passed in front of us we could read off their recognition numbers : "111", "112", "122", "131" - it was our 1st Company." (P. Agte, op.cit. p. 257/258).

In effect, after Wittmann had advanced into Villers-Bocage, according to the orders they had been given, the other Tigers of the 2nd Company stayed where they were. *Oscha.* Jurgen Brandt (Tiger "223") destroyed three Shermans and several half-tracks as well as collecting 70 prisoners with his crew members. The other crews had managed to collect 160 more (see the account of Walter Lau above). The following is a further extract from the account of Wittmann himself : "I entered into the village and when I got to the centre, I received a severe hit from an anti-tank shell which immobilised my tank. I carried on firing at anything within range in the vicinity but I had lost radio contact with everyone as my tank was out of range. I decided to evacuate it and we took our weapons with us insofar as we could carry them, leaving the tank intact as there was a chance of recovering it. I managed to reach a divisional HQ about fifteen kilometres away. Several times I had to skirt around enemy armoured vehicles and I would have had the chance of destroying them at close range if I had had a suitable weapon, thus with a heavy heart I had to leave them. I got to the divisional HQ and reported both there and to corps HQ".

In fact, having reached the Place Jeanne d'Arc, turned round and destroyed Captain Dyas's tank,

farmyard at the entrance to the village, including the tank of Captain Pat Dyas (see the earlier account by J-L Cloudsley-Thompson). The first two Cromwells (those of Major Carr, deputy battalion commander and Lt-Col Cranley, the CO of the unit) were almost immediately knocked out by Wittmann while Captain Dyas took cover in the farmyard. Wittmann's Tiger continued along the main street of Villers-Bocage, the Rue Georges Clemenceau where he destroyed the two artillery observation Shermans of the 5th RHA (with dummy wooden guns) outside the Hotel Bras d'Or plus the armoured car of the intelligence officer and the medical half-track. Then, when he arrived in his Tiger at the Place Jeanne d'Arc, the lead tank of "B" Squadron of the 4th CLY, a Sherman Firefly commanded by Sergeant Stan Lockwood, was waiting for him. On seeing the Tiger, 200 metres away, with its turret traversed to fire into a side street, the latter fired four 17 pdr. shells at it. One of them hit the hull, producing a jet of flame. Wittmann replied by bringing down half a house on top of the Sherman, but assuming the presence of other tanks turned round, his Tiger hardly damaged. But, at the bend ion the Rue Georges Clemenceau he found himself face to face with Pat Dyas's Cromwell which had in

Wittmann abandoned his (in fact the "222" of *Uscha.* Kurt Sowa) in front of the Huet-Godefroy shop with the sprocket wheel which drove the track, damaged. During the battle he had accounted for 21 British tanks and 22 other armoured vehicles together with *Sturmmann* Boldt (loader), *Uscha.* Walter Muller (driver) and *Sturmmann* Gunther Jonas (radio operator).

Wittmann assembles reinforcements

On foot, passing northwards via Saint-Louet-sur-Seulles and Feuguerolles-sur-Seulles he reached the Chateau d'Orbois (a little more than six km) which housed the headquarters of the Panzer Lehr Division where he encountered Major Kauffman, the chief-of-staff. He made him aware of the seriousness of the situation of the German forces, threatened with being surrounded from Villers-Bocage. Wittmann also warned the HQ of I SS Panzer Corps, still at the chateau at Baron-sur-Odon. 12th SS-Pz.Div. was blocked with all its units around Caen. Major Kauffmann hastily assembled all the forces at his disposition and even sent his staff members to the northern edge of the village, supported by two 88 mm. guns and three howitzers (1). He also sent fifteen Panzer IV's to counter-attack, those of the 6th Company of the 2nd Battalion of the 130th Panzer Lehr Regiment (Captain Ritschell). They were led by the new battalion commander Captain Helmut Ritgen who had replaced the Prince von Schonburg, killed on 11 June. Ritgen recalled (2) : "I received orders from division to block the exits to the north of Villers-Bocage and be ready to counter-attack in the face f the British penetration eastwards from Villers-Bocage. The companies fighting alongside the 901st Panzergrenadier Regiment were unable to disengage. As I was driving south towards Villers-Bocage, General Bayerlein stopped me and gave me his orders. From there, accompanied by the general we moved towards the west, north of the stream. The walls of Villers-Bocage stretched to the south of us from where we were subjected to heavy anti-tank fire. Sergeant-Major Dobrowski received a direct hit and his tank caught fire but we were unable to make out the positions of the British anti-tank guns Without infantry and artillery support, any further progress would have been pointless and general Bayerlein ordered a withdrawal to Villy-Bocage."

The attack in the early afternoon

In the meanwhile the 1st Company of the heavy tank battalion (Mobius) had also become involved after the four Tigers of the 2nd Company had cleaned up the N175 leading into Villers. *Ostuf.* Wittmann in a staff car had joined up with the 1st Company near Hill 213. The commander of that company, *Hstuf.* Mobius received the following order : "Order of attack. Something is going to happen down there. Go and take a look with the company." He then met up with Wittmann and engaged two of his sections. The nine Tigers available to the company had passed four from the 2nd Company. Under of the command of *Ostuf.* Hannes Philipsen of the 1st Section, they were the Tigers "111" (Philipsen), "122" (*Uscha.* Arno Salomon), and "131" (*Ustuf.* Walter Hahn) seen by Walter Lau (see above). There was also the "113" (*Oscha.* Ernst), the "132" (*Uscha.* Wendt), the "133" (*Oscha.* Zahner), plus the Tigers of *Oscha.* Swoboda, *Oscha.* Bode and *Ustuf.* Lukasius. According to British accounts, Philipsen's Tigers intervened at about **1300 hrs.** (1400 German and continental time). From the ti-

me that Wittmann had withdrawn in the middle of the morning and the new attack on the centre of Villers-Bocage at the beginning of the afternoon, a relative period of calm reigned, during which time the British brought up reinforcements, installing machine-guns, PIAT's, mortars and 57 mm anti-tank guns.

The Tigers of Mobius's company were joined by the 14 Panzer IV's of the 2nd Battalion of the 130th Pz. Lehr Regt. and according to several eye-witness accounts, a dozen of them took part in the counter attack together with the Tigers. The following is the recollection of one of them, Corporal Leo Enderle of the 6th Company (3) : "before the counter attack started we followed the road, along which lay the wrecks of tanks and transport vehicles. When I stuck my head out of the tank I could also see dead bodies. A despatch rider who came out of a side road, braked violently and fell onto the road in a state of horror. The attack on Villers-Bocage had to be delayed for at least a half hour while the tanks were positioned to the right and left of this main axis. A few tanks were placed to left and right of the village to capture any troops found there who might try to escape. We drove on into the village and two Tigers moving over a cross-roads were destroyed by a self-propelled gun positioned down the street on the left. Our first two Panzers had been sent rapidly to the cross-roads. They went over it and having disappeared from our view because of the bend in the street, they were hit by anti-tank fire. We heard over the radio that the first one had been destroyed while the second had reversed in spite of having been warned several times not to go over that cross-roads, and also took a hit. The shell entered from the left and exited on the right. We thought that no member of the crew would get out alive, but after a moment the loader's hatch opened and one of our comrades came out head first and sprung down onto the street before disappearing into a side street, where, according to other witnesses, he bled to death. I was in the third tank, thus just before the cross-roads and we were advancing so as to be able to cover each other. The tank on the right advanced, covered by the one on the left, and so on, taking turns. Our tank was on the right, directly before the cross-roads and could not be hit

(1) See P Agte. op.cit., p. 255.
(2) J.-P. Perrigault. *La Panzer-Lehr-Division*, Heimdal, p. 181.
(3) Quoted by P Agte. op.cit., p.256.

Ostuf. Hannes Philipsen who led the attack by the 1st Company. He destroyed three enemy tanks before his own met the same fate.

Ustuf. Walter Hahn who commanded Tiger "131".

One of the 1st Company Tigers destroyed at the bottom of the Rue Pasteur, just after the Place de l'Hotel de Ville ("10" on the plan on page 90). It was probably Philipsen's "111" which was hit while leading the attack. In the background can be seen the Panzer IV ("9" on plan, page 90) and the second Tiger ("8" on plan page 90). (BA.)

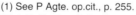

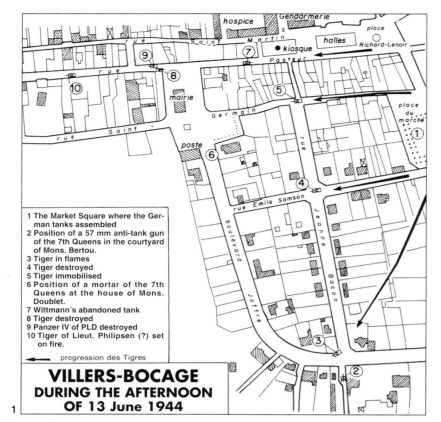

1 The Market Square where the German tanks assembled
2 Position of a 57 mm anti-tank gun of the 7th Queens in the courtyard of Mons. Bertou.
3 Tiger in flames
4 Tiger destroyed
5 Tiger immobilised
6 Position of a mortar of the 7th Queens at the house of Mons. Doublet.
7 Wittmann's abandoned tank
8 Tiger destroyed
9 Panzer IV of PLD destroyed
10 Tiger of Lieut. Philipsen (?) set on fire.

← progression des Tigres

**VILLERS-BOCAGE
DURING THE AFTERNOON
OF 13 June 1944**

by the enemy. The firing from the front sounded clearly but that coming from the left was deafening." Another account quoted by P Agte, (4) complements the above. Just behind Corporal Enderle's tank (the third) was that of Sergeant Rother of the 5th Company of the 130th Pz. Lehr Regt. His gun-layer, Hans Burkhardt recalled that they drove past the column of destroyed vehicles and then just before entering Villers-Bocage : "on the left at the edge of a wood I saw another two Tigers in position, one of which was apparently destroyed. The crew was still there, several of whom were wounded and one unfortunately dead. After a short moment for observation, we rolled slowly into Villers-Bocage. After a few hundred metres we arrived at a cross-roads (author's note - level with the town hall). When our first tank went over the cross-roads it received a hit from an anti-tank gun placed on the left, in such a way as it could only be seen when one was actually in the middle of the crossing. It was knocked out and the second one suffered the same fate. When the third one and us in the fourth arrived there we heard the order of our commander over the radio : 'Close hatches. Tanks advance!' and we were ordered to drive to the right. A group of two or three Tigers then passed us, went over the cross-roads and knocked out the anti-tank gun. I presume that the first Tiger was also destroyed but I am not sure. It was said later that a Tiger had simply driven over the enemy anti-tank gun. Everything happened so quickly and the scene was played out in a few minutes".

As far as the Tigers of the 1st Company were concerned, the first four entered into Villers-Bocage with that of *Ostuf.* Philipsen in the lead, destroying in the process eight British tanks which were trying to make their escape. According to eyewitness accounts by civilians and British sources (5), the counter-attack by the Panzer IV's and the Tigers formed up on the Market Place and then spread out in several directions towards the west. As they moved into the town which was stoutly defended, Philipsen's Tiger was destroyed by a direct hit (6). "Hans Philipsen managed to get out of his burning tank uninjured, climbed into another one and continued the fight". Thus the Tigers found themselves engaged at close quarters in an area which the British had prepared for the defensive. Tiger "112" of *Oscha.* Heinrich Ernst was destroyed and Ernst himself was killed, close to a Panzer IV of the 2nd Battalion of the 130th Pz. Lehr. Regt. which itself was knocked out in the Rue Pasteur, just after the Place de l'Hotel de Ville. The destroyed Tiger slightly further on which had brewed up, was probably that of *Ostuf.* Philipsen.

According to British accounts, a Cromwell tank saw appearing a few metres from it, on the corner of the

(4) Op.cit., p. 257.
(5) *Tigres au Combat,* Heimdal, p. 42/43.
(6) Account by W Hahn in P. Agte, *op.cit.,* p. 258.

---

1. The plan show how the attack by the Ist. Company of the 101st Heavy Tank Battalion fanned out. (Heimdal.)

2. Looking from the Place de l'Hotel de Ville we see a destroyed Tiger ("8" on the plan above). It was probably the "112" of *Oscha.* Heinrich Ernst with its turret turned to the 9 o'clock position. Beside it sits the wreck of a Panzer IV of the 2nd Battalion of the 130th Pz.Lehr-Regt. ("9" on the plan above), probably that of Sergeant-Major Dobrowski who was killed in that action. (BA.)

3. Rear view of the first Tiger which could be the "111" of Philipsen seen on the previous page. Note the traces of the fire provoked by Bill Cotton on the *Zimmerit* coating of the turret. (BA.)

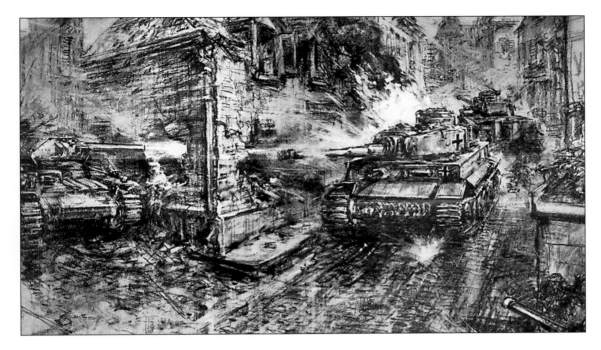

A drawing from the *Illustrated London News* dated 1 July 1944, showing the way the tanks had to fight each other in Villers-Bocage. Sergeant Bobby Bramball fired effectively through a window. Both the German and the British press at the time gave abundant coverage to the battles for Villers-Bocage.

(Coll. William Theffo.)

Rue Pasteur and the Place de l'Hotel de Ville, a Panzer IV followed by two Tigers. It fired at the Panzer IV at almost point blank range, stopping it and setting it on fire. The Cromwell moved into a small side street before the Tigers could line up on it.

The two Tigers drew back a bit and fired armour piercing shells through the houses trying to hit the British tank and then ceased fire. The first Tiger continued on and was hit on the left track (Philipsen's tank). Unable to steer he careered into the Lepiètre clothing shop, bringing down the building with the impact (today no. 18 Rue Pasteur). Lieutenant Cotton who had observed the scene from a neighbouring building, thought that the tank had been evacuated and approached it with a blanket soaked in petrol intending to set it on fire, but, to his great surprise the tank "moved" and Hannes Philipsen baled out.

The first tank destroyed there, the Panzer IV from the 2nd battalion of the 130th Pz. Lehr Regt. had come to rest in front of the Jouin hat shop (roughly in front of no. 39 in the present day Rue Pasteur). The second Tiger, that of *Oscha.* Ernst, destroyed beside the Panzer IV a little after the destruction of the first two tanks, succeeded in blocking the Rue Pasteur, hindering a further advance by the other tanks. The victors were the Queens with their anti-tank guns and PIATs, the crew of the Cromwells with their 75 mm guns and the Firefly of Sergeant Bob Moore of "B" Squadron who hit the panzers on their right sides.

As described by Patrick Agte (7), an anti-tank gun fired from a side street until a tank pushed down the house on the corner, crushing the gun. Three other Tigers spreading out behind the initial advance were unable to get through the narrow streets in the town centre (rue Georges Clemenceau then Rue Pasteur) but entered into the attack through the parallel roads to the south where the surroundings were more open, consisting of individual house set in small gardens.

Thus, except to the south, the advance was not easy. In fact the three Tigers were destroyed when crossing the Rue Jeanne Bacon, at right angles to the central street, by an by an anti-tank gun installed by the British in Mons. Bertou's workshop bet-

ween 10 and 11 o'clock that morning. The first Tiger of *Uscha.* Amo Salomon ("122") was hit at almost point blank range on the corner of Boulevard Joffre and Rue Jeanne Bacon; although wounded, Salomon managed to escape from the tank. The Tiger had been hit when it showed itself between two houses, and disabled, it crossed the street and mounted the pavement on the corner of the street and the boulevard on the boundary of Mons. Bertou's garden where it caught fire. A second Tiger was stopped 200 metres further to the north where the Rue Emile Samson crossed the Rue Jeanne Bacon, by an anti-tank gun which was located in a garden just on the right. It was hit by an impact which immobilised it. According to Mons. André Marie, the ammunition inside the Tiger was exploding throughout the afternoon. A photograph shows the wreck of the vehicle with the gun barrel recoiled inside the turret and the left track damaged at the level of the front drive sprocket wheel,

(7) P. Agte, p. 258.

The Tiger destroyed on the crossroads of Rue Jeanne Bacon and Rue Emile Samson ("4" on the plan on the facing page). It was hit by a shell from a 57 mm anti-tank gun ("2" on the plan) which could enfilade the streets. The gun barrel has recoiled into the turret and the left track has been hit level with the sprocket wheel. (BA.)

probably by the shot which managed to immobilise it 300 metres to the north of the gun in Mons. Bertou's workshop, a third Tiger was destroyed at the crossroads with the Rue Saint-Germain but was able to be recovered.

Thus the tanks which once again had been sent in to the attack without infantry support had to withdraw on account of the fire of the British "tank destroyers". The testimony of Sergeant Bobby Bramball (8) of the "Sharpshooters" (4th CLY) describes exactly how the Panzer IV and the Tiger were knocked out at the bottom of the Rue Pasteur : "My section, the 3rd of 'B' Squadron got orders to intercept a breakthrough the southern part of the town to come to the aid of 'A' Squadron. So, we set of with my tank in the lead and with Lieutenant Bill Cotton in command. Bill was a small stocky guy, afraid of nothing, a good boss. When we got into the town the whole place was full of the sound of firing mainly concentrated around the square leading off the main street (author's note - Place de l'Hotel de Ville). Soon three German tanks (author's note - a Panzer IV and two Tigers) came down the main street. I was certain that the lead tank was a Panzer IV (author's note - Sergeant-Major Dobrowski's) although several thought it was a Tiger, but I fired at it and I am certain that it was not. In fact I missed it as the range was too short for laying the gun accurately. Luckily a 6 pdr. anti-tank gun had been placed in position and it was able to destroy it. At any rate the one behind was definitely a Tiger. I managed to reverse a bit and was able to see through the window of the house on the corner. I don't know how many times we fired, but from one moment to the next, we were able to put it out of action, I assume at around midday. All over the town we could hear the noise of machine-guns and anti-tank rounds. During the afternoon news arrived that the Queens had been attacked by tanks and infantry from the south. The third German tank - also a Tiger - reached the corner of the square and in the meanwhile I had been able to lay the gun. Without the gun-sights as the range was too short, but by looking along the barrel to a mark on the wall of the house opposite. When the Tiger covered that mark, we fired and it was all over. It began to rain in buckets. One of the tanks started to burn and either the crew baled out or had been killed, but the Germans were able to return and tow away their tanks." Bill Cotton went

(8) In P Agte. *op.cit..*, p. 260/261.

(9) Figures presented by Henri Marie in *Tigres au combat*, p. 59.

to try and set the Tiger on fire which was that of *Ostuf.* Philipsen.

The British withdrawal

Faced by the German counter-attacks the position of the British in Villers-Bocage had become increasingly untenable, all the more so because the remainder of the 7th Armoured Division in reserve to the east near Amayé-sur-Seulles was being subjected to attacks coming from the north (elements of the Panzer Lehr Division) as well as from the south where elements of the 2nd Panzer Division had arrived after a forced march. The grenadiers of that division were nearby but the tanks were still well to the rear. The remaining units of the 7th Armoured Division which were still intact were threatened with being surrounded, and the divisional commander, General Erskine and the commander of the 22nd Armoured brigade, General Hinde, ordered a withdrawal westwards to more favourable positions around Livry, following the Villers-Bocage - Caumont road in the opposite direction to which they had driven down early that morning.

The balance

The intervention by the Tigers of the 101st. Heavy Tank Battalion supported by elements of the Panzer Lehr Division, as well as the threat posed by the arrival of the initial elements of the 2nd Panzer Division cancelled out all the hopes that had been placed in the offensive of the 7th Armoured Division. Between Hill 213 and the lower part (west) of Villers-Bocage, the 22nd Armoured brigade had lost (9) :

27 tanks - 20 Cromwells, 4 Firefly and 3 Honey

28 other armoured vehicles - 14 half-tracks (mostly from the Rifle Brigade), 14 carriers as well as several soft-skinned vehicles. To these figures must be added - a Sherman from the Royal Horse Artillery (RHA), **nine armoured vehicles** of the 11th Hussars and several light tanks of the 8th Hussars. On top of this there were the losses of numerous anti-tank guns.

Obersturmbannfuhrer Michael Wittmann was credited with 21 British tanks plus numerous other armoured vehicles as were listed in the citation for the award of the "swords" to add to his Knights' Cross with Oak Leaves, signed that same day by *Obergruppenfuhrer* Sepp Dietrich. Thus his total score had risen to 138 tanks and 132 anti-tank guns destroyed! He could also have been credited

One of the two assault-guns of the 17th SS Panzer Battalion destroyed on 13 June by the paras. Of the US 101st Airborne Division and Combat Command "A" of the US 2nd. Armoured Division.

with : several tanks from A Squadron of the 4th CLY (Cromwell, Firefly, Honey), the observation Sherman of the 5th RHA, several light vehicles and the ambulance half-track. *Obersturmfuhrer* Hannes Philipsen had destroyed three tanks and *Oberscharfuhrer* Jurgen Brandt had disposed of three Sherman (Firefly) and several half-tracks.

Compared with this impressive score the German losses were 6 Tigers and the 2 Panzer IV's from the 2nd Batt. of the 130th Pz. Lehr Regt. including "634" at the edge of the town. The 1st Company of the 101st Heavy Tank Battalion suffered several killed : *Oscha.* Heinrich Ernst and Hans Swoboda, *Uscha.* Robert Zellmer, *Rottenfuhrer* Hermani, *Sturmmann* Hruschka and four other men. Several tank commanders were wounded : *Ustuf.* Lukasius, *Uscha.* Salamon and Langer, plus seven men. From the 2nd Company, three men and *Rottenfuhrer* Eugen Schmidt had been wounded.

Fresh reinforcements : the assault-guns from the G.v.B.

That 13 June which saw the intervention by the Tigers of the 101st. SS Heavy Tank Battalion, even though the tanks of the 2nd Panzer Division were still far away, other armoured reinforcements arrived on a sector of the front from which they had so far been absent, facing the American divisions around Carentan.

The 17th SS-Panzergrenadier-Division *Gotz von Berlichingen,* differed from a normal panzer division in that instead of a tank regiment, it only had a battalion of self-propelled assault-guns. The one assigned to the G.v.B. division was the 17th SS Panzer Battalion and its men wore the black uniforms of the armoured troops. That unit had been formed in October 1943 and for training purposes was stationed in the area of Tours, Angers and Parteney in December. It was commanded by *Sturmbannfuhrer* Ludwig Kepplinger who was born on 31 December 1911 at Linz in Austria. He started his career in an Austrian mountain regiment, but had to resign on account of his political activities. He rejoined the Austrian Legion in Bavaria and then the SS *Verfugungstruppe* in 1935. In 1938 he was an *Oberscharfuhrer* and a section commander in the 6th Company of the *SS Standarte Deutschland* in Munich. After the annexation of Austria he was transferred to the *Der Fuhrer* regiment. On 10 May 1940, *Hauptscharfuhrer* Kepplinger was in command of a special raiding party of eighteen men who captured a fort in Holland and accomplished various other exploits, in the course of which he was seriously wounded. For those actions he was awarded the Knights' Cross, the first Waffen-SS nco. to be so decorated. As a second lieutenant in the 10th Company of the *Westland* Regiment (SS-Division *Wiking*) he was awarded the German Cross in gold for service in Russia on 28 February 1942. Once again severely wounded, he took command of the 2nd Battalion of the SS Panzer Ersatz Regiment in Riga, and following the accidental death of *Sturmbannfuhrer* Kniep, he replaced him in command of the 17th SS Panzer Battalion.

His deputy was *Ostuf.* Hasselmann. The anti-aircraft section of three self-propelled quadruple barrelled 20mm flak guns was commanded by *Hscha.* Domacher. The staff had three command tanks. The three companies were equipped with 42 *Sturmgeschutze* (assault-guns) model 40 type G, giving 14 each. Hans Stober, author of the divisional history (*Die Sturmflut und das Ende,* Munin Verlag. 1976) speaks of 17 StuG IV per company which apparently contradicts the official war establishment. The commander of the 1st Company was *Ostuf.* Dedelow, the 2nd was *Ostuf.* Hormann and the third was under *Ostuf.* Brittinger.

On 13 June a battle group of the *Gotz von Berlichingen* counter-attacked from the south towards Carentan to relieve the 6th Airborne (*Fallschirm-Jager)* Regiment commanded by von der Heydte. The G.v.B. artillery commenced the opening barrage at **0530 hrs,** and fifteen minutes later the assault-guns and the grenadiers set off to recapture Carentan behind a creeping barrage. At **0900 hrs** the eastern edge of Carentan was reached in the area around the station, but there were plenty of American units in the rear of the attackers and the parachutists who had been cut off. At **0950 hrs.** the attack was stopped dead and the Americans counter-attacked in turn with tanks from CCA (combat command "A") of the 2nd Armoured Division. Threatened by the tanks the withdrawal to the start line commenced at **1045 hrs.** by way of the RN171. The 1st Section of the battalion lost two assault-guns, one of which was the "133" commanded by *Ustuf.* Simon who was killed along with most of his crew. In the evening after the defeat of their attack, the G.v.B. Division took up new defensive positions along a line running from the south of Carentan to the swampy meadows of Gorges. The offensive had only lasted a few hours and a bitter defensive campaign ensued with the assault-guns having to support infantry strongpoints.

Opposite. *Sturmbannfuhrer* Ludwig Kepplinger, the commander of the 17th SS Panzer Battalion which counter-attacked against Carentan on 13 June.

101st SS Heavy Tank Battalion

1. This Tiger of the battalion was admirably camouflaged in a sunken lane.

2. Tiger « 211 », the Ist. Section commander's tank, *Ustuf.* Georg Hantusch, seated on the right in overcoat, of the 2nd Company commanded by Wittmann.

3. Another shot of « 211 » which was towing « 231 » as a result of a breakdown. The latter tank has traversed its turret to the rear (at 6 o'clock) to avoid its gun barrel hitting the turret of the towing tank. One can clearly make out the insignia of the I SS Panzer Corps on the left at the front of the hulls of the two tanks. Standing on the left of « 211 » was its driver, *Sturmmann* Erlander. These two photos were part of the same photo report.

4. *Uscha*. Balthasar Woll who had been Wittmann's gun-layer in Russia for which he had been awarded the Knights' Cross for 80 victories. In Normandy he had his own Tiger, "212" in Wittmann's company. The photo was taken in May 1944.

5. An M10 tank destroyer (unit unknown) knocked out in the Villers-Bocage area, being examined by a junior officer from an Army (*Heer*) tank unit, probably the 3rd Pz. Regt. in the 2nd Pz.-Div. which arrived there shortly after 13 June.

6. This tank officer admired the effect achieved by German anti-tank shells on the turret of the M10. The man is wearing a tank crew blouse, sailcloth trousers and the old style soft field cap which had been standard pattern before 1938 but continued in use. On his arm can be seen the badge awarded for the destruction of a tank in close combat with a hand-held weapon : attached under the eagle on his chest is the German Cross in Gold, known as the "fried egg" by the troops.

7. A soldier demonstrates how the shells penetrated.

(BA.)

Lingèvres 14 June.

The 151st Brigade was launched into an attack on Lingèvres and Verrières at 0900 hrs on 14 June. The 9th Durham Light Infantry entered Lingèvres after several hours fighting in woods to the north of the village. The British advance was halted for the price of the destruction of the 6th Company of the 902nd Panzergrenadiers and at 1130 hrs. a detachment of Panthers from the 1st Battalion of the 6th Panzer Regiment counter-attacked. Six of them were eliminated by the 4/7th Dragoon Guards. The Panzer Lehr Division finally abandoned the place around 1700 hrs.

1. Near Lingèvres on 14 June, soldiers of the 6th DLI give first-aid to wounded members of the PLD - here a tank crewman wounded in the head.

2. A Sherman of the 4/7th Dragoon Guards knocked out beside the Lingèvres church which had received at least five direct hits on its frontal armour. The Panther "225", situated almost facing it had nothing to do with its destruction as it was Corporal Johnson's tank knocked out at midday by another Panther

3. Panther « 225 » suffered a wrecked track from a direct hit by Sergeant Harris's Sherman Firefly (tank commander in the 4th Section commanded by Lieutenant Morrison of « A » Squadron of the 4/7th DG. The Panther finished up against the Lingèvres war memorial.

(IWM.)

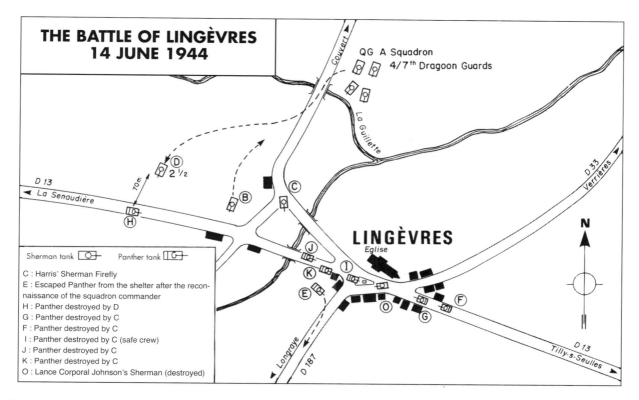

THE BATTLE OF LINGÈVRES
14 JUNE 1944

QG A Squadron
4/7th Dragoon Guards

Couvert

La Guillette

D 13
← La Senaudière

D 33
Verrières

D 2½

70 m

B

C

H

LINGÈVRES
Eglise

J

I

K

E

O

G

F

N

D 13
Tilly-s-Seulles

Longraye

D 187

Sherman tank ☐ Panther tank ☐

C : Harris' Sherman Firefly
E : Escaped Panther from the shelter after the reconnaissance of the squadron commander
H : Panther destroyed by D
G : Panther destroyed by C
F : Panther destroyed by C
I : Panther destroyed by C (safe crew)
J : Panther destroyed by C
K : Panther destroyed by C
O : Lance Corporal Johnson's Sherman (destroyed)

Above : Plan showing the positions of the six Panthers destroyed in Lingèvres on 14 June. (Plan Bernard Paich/Heimdal.)

Below : Panthers "J" and "K" on the plan which were pushed into the ditches on either side of the bridge 200 metres west of the church at Lingèvres where they remained for two years. Sergeant Harris's Sherman Firefly was 90 metres in front of the Panther on the left, behind the trees.

Panthers of the 1st Battalion of the 130th Panzer Lehr Regiment destroyed on 15 June.

1. British infantry marching up to the front, pass a Type "A" Panther destroyed on 15 June in the Tilly-sur-Seulles sector. All the rear part has been incinerated causing the disappearance of the *Zimmerit* coating.

2 and 3. Another type "A" Panther of the battalion, destroyed during the night of 15/16 June, without a doubt near Hottot when the battalion attempted to recapture the village where the commanding officer, Major Markowski's tank, was also knocked out during the counterattack. A powerful shell, possibly fired at point blank range impacted at the angle of the turret. Note how the antimagnetic *Zimmerit* paste was applied in squares, incised with a tool.

(IWM.)

1

2

3

98

The 1st Battalion of the 12th SS-Pz. Regt. at Fonteney-le-Pesnil (report by SS war correspondent Pachnike).

4. A type "G" Panther in the centre of the village of Fonteney-le-Pesnil, three km east of Tilly-sur-Seulles on the road linking Caumont-l'Eventé and Caen. In the foreground, a grenadier of the *Hitlerjugend* Division is looking toward the British front in the direction of the road leading to Cristot. That sector had been handed over to the *Hitlerjugend* by Panzer Lehr with effect from 9 June. In the background, the village church which has lost the bell loft of its tower.

5. A type "D" Panther, an older model, arriving along the road leading in from the north. This one was "219", a tank from the 2nd Company commanded by *Ostuf.* Gaede. That company, while engaged in a counter-attack to the north-west of Fonteney-le-Pesnil towards Hill 102, destroyed seven tanks of "B" Squadron of the 4/7 Dragoon Guards. These photographs could well have been taken at the end of that successful counter-attack during which Gaede's company lost five wounded, an nco and four other-ranks. The photos were released by the German censor on 3 July, making the actual date of 11 June plausible. (Departemental Archives of Calvados)

5

6. "219" taking up position, probably to relieve the type "G" Panther.

(Photos coll. auteur/ Heimdal.)

6

10

The counter-attacks between 14 and 24 June

Wednesday 14 June

The 101st SS Heavy Tank Battalion

During the previous night the 7th Armoured Division withdrew to the hamlet of Livry at Briquessard and to the hamlet of Torteval at les Orailles. On the Wednesday, Villers-Bocage was completely cleared of any remaining British troops who were still there. Further to the west the battalion's Tigers fought it out with the 7th Armoured Division, which subsequently retired to the Amayé-sur-Seulles area.

The 130th Panzer-Lehr-Regiment at Lingèvres

The attacks by the 50th Infantry Division redoubled in intensity in the area of Tilley-sur-Seulles, Lingèvres, La Senaudière and La Belle Epine. At the crossroads in La Senaudière in spite of the support rendered to the 902nd Grenadiers by the Panthers of the 1st Battalion of the 130th Panzer Lehr Regiment, the 1st Dorsets from the 231st Brigade seized control of that strategic point and beside them the 151st Brigade moved up to attack Lingèvres. Starting at 0900 hrs the 6th Durham Light Infantry Fought for six long hours against the 902nd Grenadiers to take the small wood to the north of the village. A heavy artillery barrage preceded the final assault by the 9th Durhams on the village itself during which the 6th Company of the grenadiers was more or less annihilated in trying to contain the advance of the British into the centre of the village. Then the PLD Panthers intervened and at 1030 hrs, one and a half kilometres to the north, a Panther and an assault gun pounced on a Sherman and brewed it up. After that, three further Sherman's of the 4/7 Dragoon Guards were destroyed by the Panthers.

During the assault on Lingèvres, five sections each of three Shermans of "A" Squadron the 4/7 D.G. infiltrated into the centre of the village and each of the sections had one Sherman Firefly variant fitted with a 17 pdr. gun which was equivalent to the Panthers' 75 MM. Sergeant N Harris commanded such a tank and he was to excel against the Panthers from the PLD. Elements of the Ist Battalion of the tank regiment of the PLD , probably the 2nd Company commanded by Lieutenant Steindamm ("225" was one of the Panthers destroyed in Lingèvres) were engaged against the British. At **1130 hrs.** (British time), Lieutenant Morrison's Firefly (1) appeared alongside the church and scored a bullseye on the first Panther. At **midday,** Sergeant Harris observed that Corporal Johnson's tank was hit by a Panther and went up in flames ; it had arrived from the east and blazed away with all its weapons. Harris opened fire and stopped that second Panther. At around **1300 hrs** a third Panther was reported, camouflaged in a barn whence it withdrew in the face of the Du-

rham's attack at **1400 hrs** Shortly afterwards a Panther moved slowly out of a small wooded valley just outside the village - the first 75mm armour piercing shell from a Sherman was fired at it but it only caught fire with the second round. Captain Stirling who commanded the tanks of the Dragoon Guards saw some other Panthers to the west of Lingèvres at ranges of between 600 and 1,200 metres, below the road from Lingèvres to La Belle Epine. Three more, following the one that had been destroyed, arrived on the left along the road that ran in from the west to the village centre, after crossing the small stream known as La Guillette. They steered straight towards the Firefly of Sergeant Harris ! The first of the three was hit by a shell from Lieutenant Morris's Sherman which only succeeded in setting a camouflage net and some baggage stowed outside, on fire. The resulting smoke camouflaged the tank sufficiently for it to proceed towards the centre of village where it arrived within range of the 17 pdr. of Sergeant Harris who also put a round into the rear compartment. Then the second Panther ("225) appearing in turn, presented its stern on the right of the Firefly. "225", still moving; traversed its turret towards Sergeant Harris's tank, but his gun-layer, Mc-Killop, was quicker off the mark and scored a hit on the sprocket wheel of the left-hand track at a range of 500 metres. The Panther, hit while travelling at high speed finished up entangled with the village war memorial. Harris then traversed to the right, his turret at 3 o'clock and knocked out the third Panther near a small bridge, bringing it to a halt but without setting it alight. Thus Harris in a single day, managed to destroy five out of the six Panthers accounted for in Lingèvres and by the end of the day, the villages was firmly in the hands of the 50th Division.

Towards the evening the Panzer IV's of the 2nd Battalion of the 130th Pz. Lehr Regt. formed up to counter-attack towards Lingèvres but a heavy artillery barrage so damaged the periscopes and radio antenna of Captain Ritgen that the attack was called off.

Thursday 15 June

The Tigers suffer heavy losses

During the previous night, 22nd Armoured Brigade retired nine km to the north-east of Caumont l'Eventé. Four Tigers from the 1st Company of the 101st SS Heavy Tank Battalion were sent to pursue the British who were withdrawing northwards, destroying five tanks and several anti-tank guns in the process. A witness of that engagement, *Uscha.* Wendt, commander of Tiger "132", remembered (2) : "At dusk a dispatch rider guided me to the other 1st Company tanks near Hill 213. Under the command of Philipsen we attacked in a northerly direction with four Tigers, crossing a landscape cut up by numerous hedgerows.

---

(1) A detailed account of these engagements was published in issue 85/86 of *39/45 Magazine* pp. 33-38.

(2) P. Agte. *op.cit.* p. 272.

Brought to a halt by one of these I received a hit, probably a hollow charge, which penetrated the armour and projected a flaming mass into the interior, immediately filling the turret with flames. Evacuation ! But, I was snared by my headphones and throat microphone. Lowering my head I ripped out the leads. That short moment was sufficient to burn my hair. We all managed to get out of the tank and my gun-layer also had severe burns, but we were able to administer first-aid at an aid station".

A little further to the east, the 3rd Company had finally arrived but had been subjected to a terrible ordeal. It had reached Falaise on 13 June and the following day moved up to the front line by sections. The Tigers were camouflaged in the gardens of Evrécy to the left of the road and the supply vehicles were to the right. This is how *Sturmmann* Ernst Kufner (3) remembered the events : "At around midnight, *Ustuf.* Amselgruber, the commander of the 3rd Section, Tiger '331', put me on sentry duty. *Ustuf.* Gunther, in command of the 1st Section, Tiger '311' and a holder of the Knights' Cross was in position about 20 metres to the left. As dawn broke on 14 June , a few enemy aircraft were in the sky, observing the Evrécy sector. The crews of the four Tigers and their comrades from the supply trucks were mostly sleeping in the open air under their vehicles. It was about 1 o'clock in the morning when my sentry duty started and all was quiet. All that could be heard was the distant rumbling of artillery and the growling of aircraft engines - then suddenly the trees, the vegetation between the tanks, the houses and the church of Evrécy began to burn from phosphor bombs dropped by the aircraft. I woke up the tank crews who were sleeping underneath and we leapt inside the tanks. We heard the company commander order us to start the engines and move the tanks out. Our driver tried to fire up the engine, but in vain as the starter motor was broken and we had to leave it where it was. Looking through the visors we could see that everything around us was burning. Our driver saw that Usha. Gunther's tank was on fire. Those were twin-engined bombers which had dropped their loads on us and on Evrécy. Twenty or thirty minutes passed until everything was over and it took us all our strength to open the hatches which were covered with a layer of earth 20 cm. Thick. The houses in the village were still burning. We could not hear out comrades and did not see them again. Having repaired the starter motor we drove as far as the war memorial. After a few hundred metres the engine started to overheat as the ventilation grilles had been blocked with earth. Near where we found ourselves there were vast bomb craters, big enough to swallow a Tiger. At dawn on the 15 June we set to search for our comrades. As far as I can recall, the assistant armourer appeared, his coat completely in shreds. He had sought refuge in a bomb crater and had been lucky, but we found no trace of our friends from the supply column. The three other Tigers had been destroyed ; that of *Uscha.* Gunther had received a direct hit and was completely gutted. All we found of the crew were a few shreds of singed uniform, buttons and scraps of bone - nothing else. The company commanders tank, (*Ostuf.* Hanno Raasch, '105') had received a direct hit on the gun barrel which wrenched off the turret which was lying beside the tank. The three men inside had been thrown out with it and were badly burned - the radio operator and driver were dead.

(3) Agte. *op.cit.*, p. 278.

The third Tiger had driven out into the open but after about 300 metres it fell into a deep sunken lane, six or seven metres lower, killing all the crew. Our mates from the supply train who were sleeping in the open were all killed except for the assistant armourer. As for me I had been lucky to replace the radio operator who had been killed in *Ustuf.* Amselgruber's tank. I had been lucky to leave my position the previous dawn as the radio operator in the company commander's tank as his operator was also killed."

Thus, without having fired a single shot, the 3rd. Company suffered severe losses. During that single night of terror in Evrécy, eighteen were killed and eleven wounded, the equivalent of six Tiger crews. The total losses of the company between 13 and 15 June were one officer, four nco's and 18 other-ranks killed, plus one officer, five nco's and eight other-ranks wounded, all in all a grand total of 37. The company commander, *Ostuf.* Hanno Raasch was among the wounded, and more seriously, *Ustuf.* Alfred Gunther had been killed. That veteran nco. from the assault-gun battery of the 1st SS Pz. Division who had gained fame during the battle of Kharkov at the beginning of 1943 which he was awarded the Knights' Cross on 3 March of that year. He was the symbol of the company which thus lost its two principal officers. That same day, having lost his own tank, *Uscha.* Wendt, of the 1st Company was given the task of taking the remains of his comrades killed at Villers-Bocage, to Evrécy, where they were buried in the battalion's grave plot The 1st and 2nd Companies suffered twelve killed between 13 and 15 June, making a total for the whole unit of 35 killed and 33 wounded during that period.

The Panthers of the P.L.D. at Hottot

While the British were being constantly reinforced the units if the Pz. Lehr Div. were suffering a constant drain of both men and material. The British advanced on a broad front to the south of the road from Balleroy to Tilly and took the village of Hottot; the 69th Infantry Brigade attempted to progress to the east of that place towards the hamlet of Lion Vert, threatening to sever the lines of communication of the 1st Battalion of the 902nd Panzer Grenadiers. General Bayerlien issued orders to recapture Hotto on the evening of 15 June, allocating the task to 1st and 2nd Companies of the 1st. Battalion of the 6th Panzer Regiment under the orders of Major Markowski, the battalion commander. The two Panther companies had infantry assigned to accompany them,

This photo shows the wreck of Tiger "311" in which *Ustuf.* Alfred Gunther was killed at Evrécy during the night of 14/15 June.

The *SS-Ustuf.* Alfred Günther.

The *SS-Sturmmann* Ernst Kufner.

The *SS-Uscha.* Werner Wendt .

the 2nd and 3rd Companies from the 902nd Grenadiers. Markowski drove at the head in his command tank, a *Befehlspanzer V*, followed by the 22 panthers in a wedge shape as if on an exercise, with the grenadiers sitting on their engine casings. Shortly after setting off the tanks crossed a shallow ravine and appeared in front of the first houses of Hottot which were subjected to a barrage from the divisional artillery, the shells whistling over the heads of attackers before exploding in the village. But the British infantry were prepared to withstand an assault having tucked themselves away in cellars, at the foot of hedgerows and in the ruins of the houses. They greeted the attackers with a hail of fire directed at the tanks and the grenadiers who had dismounted and were following them. "Fire free !" shouted Major Markowski into his microphone and the Panthers' guns opened up on the British anti-tank pieces and machine gun nests whose hiding places could be spotted. Suddenly a Cromwell tank appeared from behind a hedge, opened fire on the command tank and missed. Markowski replied and managed to immobilise the enemy tank which fired a second shell which landed right in front of the command tank, throwing up a cloud of splinters and stones. Markowski then delivered the coup de grace, hitting the Cromwell in the hull just below the turret, causing it to explode ten metres in front of the command tank. In the meanwhile the other Panthers had become involved in the battle, neutralising the defenders with the help of the grenadiers and penetrating into the village. In manoevring, the Panthers collided with the houses which collapsed on top of them in a tangle of masonry and roof beams. The street fighting lasted throughout the afternoon as the grenadiers neutralised the defensive posts one after the other while the tanks drove deeper into the village. Major Markowski scored a second victory but his own tank was hit, forcing him to transfer to another Panther. The British were firing at the tanks from the cellars with their PIAT's and the Major ordered the abandonment of his tank as the radio operator had been killed and both he and his gun-layer had been wounded. Several more British tanks were destroyed and the last resistance was eliminated as the grenadiers established control of the village and prepared to defend it from the north, having received artillery reinforcements. Two hours later, however, Lt-Gen. Bayerlein felt obliged to withdrew the Panthers still in Hottot as Tilly had been attacked in force, having been subjected to a preliminary bombardment from land and sea based artillery which had flattened the place. Colonel Gerhardt, the commander of the 130th Pz. Lehr Regt. had to commit all his reserves ; the 1st Battalion Panthers and the 2nd Battalion Panzer IV's, but they proved insufficient and the *Jagdpanzer IV's* (self-propelled anti-tank guns) from the 3rd Company of the 130th *Panzerjager-Lehr-Abteilung* (anti-tank battalion) had to be called upon. With one of those redoubtable well-proven machines, Sergeant-Major Stolz and his gun-layer, Sergeant Eduard Job, knocked out three British tanks and two anti-tank guns. His section commander, Lieutenant Schonrath accounted for another three while Sergeant-Major Duckert added two Cromwells to his score. In spite of repeated assaults by the two British divisions, the 49th and 50th, Tilly remained in the hands of the Pz. Lehr Division. On the evening of 15 June, the following night the first VI's appeared in the sky and those new weapons give a glimmer of hope to the Germans fighting at the front.

Ostuf. Hannes Philipsen who was killed on 16 June at Cahagnes, having survived the destruction of his tank a few days earlier.

Friday 16 June

The Tiger battalion suffered new losses

Two sections of the Ist. Company of the 101st SS Heavy Tank Battalion were engaged that day near Cahagnes, to the west of Villers-Bocage, against elements of the 7th Armoured Division. One of the section commanders, *Ostuf.* Hannes Philipsen was killed, as *Ustuf.* Hahn, who took part in the fighting, remembered (4) : "Two days later on 16 June, we set off for an attack near Cahagnes where Hannes met his death. Our tactical group of four tanks under his command attacked with the support of grenadiers and initially the advance went well. We repelled the enemy from a village and as we drove out, we were subjected to such a density of artillery and anti-tank fire such as I have never again experienced in my life. Hannes's vehicle received two anti-tank rounds and caught fire. My tank was about 20 metres away and I saw how he and one of his crew members, apparently uninjured, baled out of the tank and tried to get away. Then a shell impacted nearby and I saw Hannes fall and lie still. I jumped out of my tank to be near him, but when I arrived I saw that it was too late. Several shell bursts had given him an end without suffering. We laid his body on my tank and carried it back to the company after the battle". Philipsen's Tiger was hit twice by anti-tank shells on the way out of Cahagnes, as he emerged from a sunken lane. His driver, *Uscha.* Sturhahn, and his radio operator were unable to escape from the burning Tiger. Philipsen together with his loader and his gun-layer attempted to get under cover in the sunken lane under intense shelling. About 50 metres behind his tank a shell exploded and he received the splinters in the stomach area. Once again the battalion suffered the loss of a competent officer.

Saturday 17 June

At dusk the evening before, the Supreme Commander in the West, Field Marshal von Runstedt was warned of a visit by Hitler. On the Saturday at 0900 hrs he was received at "W II", the headquarters specially installed at Margival. Hitler was accompanied by Field Marshal Jodl and von Runstedt by Field Marshal Rommel. The latter stated that "sooner or later the front will rupture" and went on to add that the Allies intended to break out "to the south in the direction of Paris, with a subsidiary operation via Avranches to seal off Brittany. Hitler replied with an endless speech about the new special weapons, one of which, the VI had been fired for the first time at England during the night of 15/16 June. They were also shown photographs of the Me262 jet aircraft that was still not available.

It was necessary to counter-attack, as that would counter the Allied offensives, and the two most effective armoured divisions had to draw up a balance. Up to the 16 June, the "HJ" Division had accumulated 1,419 casualties while as far as combat ready tanks were concerned it could still field 52 Panzer IV's and 38 Panthers, giving a total of 90 left out of the initial 164. As far as the repair of vehicles concerned, especially the tanks, the adjutant of the 12th SS Pz. Regt., *Hauptsturmfuhrer* Georg Iseke, explained in an account recorded by Hubert Meyer (5) : "particular recognition is due to the regi-

(4) P. Agte. *op.cit.*, p. 273.

(5) H. Meyer, *12 SS Panzer-Division "HJ"*, Heimdal, 1991, p. 256.

mental workshop company and the battalion repair sections. Because of Allied air superiority they had to install themselves in woods for camouflage. All movement and in particular the repair of damaged tanks could only take place at night. It was in this respect that the excellent cooperation between the troops and the repair crews became apparent. Recovery of tanks often had to take place under enemy fire. Right from the beginning of the campaign, the recovery tractors were reinforced by captured Cromwell tanks which served as towing vehicles after their turrets had been removed. 20 ton cranes were used for lifting off turrets in order to repair damaged guns".

For its part, Panzer-Lehr-Division could tot up its successes from the 6 June to date : 137 Allied tanks had been destroyed, 12 officers, 300 nco's and other -ranks had been captured, but the fighting was costing them 60 casualties a day.

That same day the experiences of the crews of the 8th Company of the 130th Pz. Lehr Regt. were an illustration of the daily realities in the frontline. At dawn the British launched an attack on the sector defended by the 2nd Battalion. Four Panzer IV's of the 8th Company had been dug in at the front for the last two days, those of Sergeant Schulz, Westphal (a veteran tank buster), Sergeant Pausche and on the right flank, Captain Felmer. The heavy preliminary barrage took Second Lieutenant Stohr in "801" by surprise, who was in reserve two kilometres to the rear with the tanks of the 6th. and 7th Companies. One of the crew members, *Panzeroberschutze* (crewman 1st class) Heinz Loewe, was having his "farmer's" breakfast and the fried potatoes leapt out of the pan as he he threw himself under the tank to take shelter. The bombardment lasted two hours and at midday a despatch rider arrived. One of the men from "801" collected the mess tins of the five crew members and went off to collect food from the other side of the road, but as he made his way back the artillery opened up again. Once again the food was lost but he did manage to save the cigarette ration. The gunners fired in relays until night fell.

Sunday 18 June

Tilly under a hurricane of fire

After a heavy barrage the evening before, at dawn a veritable hurricane of fire descented on the positions of the PLD and especially on Tilly where 19 civilians perished. To the east, Cristot was evacuated and then occupied by the 146th Brigade. The 56th Independent Brigade and elements of the 50th Northumbrian Division attacked Tilly in the centre where the grenadiers of the 2nd Battalion of the 901st Panzergrenadier Regt. were supported by the 9 assault-guns of the 316th *Funklenk-Kompanie* (remote controlled explosive charges) commanded by Lieutenant Mainhardt. Finally, at **1945 hrs**, supported by numerous tanks, the infantrymen of the 56th Brigade forced their way into Tilly, confronted by the grenadiers entrenched in the ruins of the place. The Panthers of the I/6th Panzer Regiment launched a counter-attack, under the command of Captain Jahnke who had replaced Major Markowski, wounded at Hottot. But they were unable to restore the situation and General Bayerlein ordered the front to be shortened to a new line running from Mantilly to Sagy. The town of Tilly, more or less obliterated by the bombardments, was definitively abandoned. Further west, an attack launched by three battalions from the

231st Infantry Brigade (50th Division) against the Chateau de Cordillon, north-east of Hottot, was defeated thanks to a counter-attack by the Panthers of the 1st Battalion.

The arrival of the 3rd Panzer-Regiment

Even though the first elements of the 2nd Panzer Division started arriving at the front between Caumont l'Eventé and Villers-Bocage from the 13th June, the initial units of its tank regiment (3rd Pz. Regt. did not appear until five days later, on 18 June.

The 3rd Pz.-Regt. was one of the first regiments in the German armoured forces : it was officially formed as a Panzer unit in 1935 although it had previously existed disguised as the 12th Cavalry Regiment. Assigned to the 2nd Panzer-Division, it took part in all the campaigns : Poland, France, the Balkans, Russia (centre), and recruited in Austria from its depot in Vienna. The division left the Eastern front in December 1943 for the region around Amiens in France. On 6 June at 0200 hrs. when it was put in a state of alert, it was still in Picardy, although it was destined for the Pas-de-Calais where the German high command still believed in another landing. On 9 June the division finally received orders to relocate to Normandy in the area of Sées and Argentan, south of Falaise. As all the bridges over the lower Seine had been destroyed it was necessary to detour via Paris and take to the roads. The regiment had 98 Panzer IV's, 79 Panthers and 10 assault guns from the 301st Panzer Flak Battalion and moved via Poix, Beauvais, Paria, Versailles, Dreux and l'Aigle to reach Argentan. On 13 June while the first elements of the division had arrived at the front to the east of Villers-Bocage, the tank regiment had only detrained to the east of Paris to continue the journey by road. The first tanks only arrived on 18 June having been delayed by fighter-bomber attacks.

Projected counter-attack

Following Hitler's lecture on 17 June, plans were prepared for the launching of a counter-attack to hit the junction of Second British and First US Armies in order to cut the bridgehead in two and set about the destruction of the two armies.

Hstuf. Georg Iseke was the adjutant to the commander of the 12th SS Pz. Regt., serving at the Chateau de Rauray where regimental tactical HQ was installed from 9 to 26 June. The rear HQ was at Grainville-sur-Odon, the regimental hospital was at the southern limit of Evrécy (7 km. from Rauray) and the workshop and supply companies were in a wooded area near Grimbosq (about 14 km distant).

Below. A rail transport loaded with Panther tanks en route for the Normandy front. The soldiers are wearing Army uniform so it could well be the 1st Battalion of the 3rd Pz. Regt.

(Musée Mémorial de Bayeux.)

1. The 8th Company (equiped with Panzer IV type H) of the Panzer Regiment 3 during a training in the area of Amiens (winter 1943-1944). (BA.)

2. The *Spiess* (company's warrant officer) of a company (probably the 8th) of the II./Pz. Rgt. 3 during the same exercise in Picardie. (BA.)

On **20 June** issued its comments on two studies of the war in the west, submitted the previous evening by Field Marshal Rommel : "I) The Fuhrer's intention is that a concentrated attack by 1, 2, 9, 10 SS, 2 Pz. and Pz. Lehr will be launched, leading to the destruction of the American forces in the Balleroy area (Vth US Corps). That is why the relief of 2 Pz. and PZ. Lehr by infantry divisions is necessary. Communicate the movement and timings."

"2) Before that the enemy installed to the east of the Orne must be eliminated by the strongest means possible before the land forces participating in this operation will be available for the main offensive." (War Diary , Fifth Panzer Army, 63 181/44. Teleprinter message OB West to Panzer Group West).

The following day, **21 June**, Field Marshal Rommel laid down the dispositions for the attack which would be under the overall command of Panzer Group West. On the **right**, I SS Panzer Corps with 12th SS Pz. and Pz. Lehr : **centre**, XXXXVII Pz. Corps with 2nd Pz. plus 276 and 277 Inf. Divs. : **left** (west), II SS Pz. Corps with 2, 9 and 10 SS Pz. Divs. The II Corps would also take part on the western flank towards the Cerisey Forest. The attack, however, would not be able to be launched before ten to fourteen days (shortly before the beginning of July) because of the absence of certain units (II SS Pz. Corps with 9th and 10th SS Pz. had still not arrived) and the lack of ammunition. His report stated that : "the attack to the east of the Orne depends, according to the Fuhrer's oral exposition, on the preliminary condition of the elimination of the naval artillery. Without that step, I have persuaded myself yesterday evening, that any attack is condemned to be defeated." Rommel considered that it was indispensable to engage 21st Pz. and the 16th Luftwaffe Field Division to the east of the Orne while at the same time it was necessary to maintain the attacks to the east and the west of the river.

On **24 June** the situation in the Cotentin was grave, Cherbourg was about to fall and there was nothing that could be done to avoid it. Von Rundstedt refused to release the forces for a counterattack to relieve the great port because they were needed for the great offensive planned for the beginning of July. He recommended that : "it should be examined if, after the success of the attack on Balleroy and the area to the north-west of that place, it would be possible to follow up the offensive in the direction of Carentan. Until the start of the grand attack, the sector around and to the

east of Caen remains the most important for OB West".

As far as General Montgomery was concerned, he had issued his directive no. M502 for the continuation of the fighting in the bridgehead on 18 June. His Second British Army was given the task of advancing on : "Aunay-sur-Odon and Evrécy, as far as the bridges over the Orne between Thury-Harcourt and Amayé-sur-Orne inclusive. These operations are to start on 18 June and reach their climax on 22 June when VIII Corps will have achieved its mission of establishing a bridgehead to the east of the Orne."

Thus, as of the 22 June, a competition between the British and the Germans began for the start of their attacks. Starting on the 19 June, a terrible summer storm had put a stop to the arrival of Allied reinforcements and retarded the British offensive. The elements were on the side of the Germans, destroying the Mulberry harbour at Omaha Beach, although the storm had blown over by 21 June. On the other hand, the Germans could not contemplate getting underway before ten or eleven days. 12th SS Pz., Pz. Lehr and 2nd Pz Divs. Were on the defensive, could not be relieved by infantry divisions and were thus unavailable. The 2nd SS Panzer Division *Das Reich* was still on the way and only a few of its elements had been able to assemble at Torigny, 12 km to the south of St-Lo. The 1st SS Panzer Division was on the road from Belgium and would not arrive at the front, bit by bit, for a further week. The II SS Panzer Corps with its two divisions, the 9th SS *Hohenstaufen* and the 10th SS *Frundsberg,* had been relieved as part of the North Ukraine Army Group, and been loaded onto trains on 12 June but on 20 June the armoured corps was still a long way from being operational. On top of all this, certain divisions had not been able to finish refitting (1 SS and 2 SS) and were thus understrength.

The British attack which had been due to start on 23 June was delayed by the storm but not enough to enable the panzers to engage before Montgomery's offensive. On that same day, *Obergruppenfuhrer* and Waffen SS General, Paul Hauser, arrived at Seventh Army HQ and reported that his II SS Panzer Corps would be assembled around Alencon for the 25 June. To prepare the assembly of the attacking forces, Seventh Army (according to the War Diary of Fifth Panzer Army, appendix 12) would move the 16th Luftwaffe Field Division to relieve 21st Panzer and Panzer Lehr and 2nd Panzer would be replaced by the 276th and 277th Infantry Divisions. That would free three armoured divisions which would be joined by the two from II SS Panzer Corps and the Ist SS Pz. Div which was about to arrive.

The storm, however, had abated and reinforcements and supplies were flowing in to the beaches again. On 20 and 21 June the Allied forces had been weakened to such an extent that a German attack would have stood a good chance of success, but they were minus four armoured divisions and the other armoured units engaged at the front had not yet been relieved. Montgomery had won the speed race. Tomorrow he would attack, throwing the panzers back onto the defensive and pushing them back. The first great turning point in the Battle of Normandy had occurred that evening and the second would take place within a month.

3. The crew of a Panzer IV from the 2nd Battalion of the 3rd Pz. Regt. busy refuelling. To do the job the men had to remove one of the side « skirts ». The large-toothed rail can be seen on which these 5 mm. thick side protection plates were hung. The marking « 4L » indicated the fourth plate on the left side. (BA.)

4. A good frontal view of a Panzer IV, the most manufactured tank in the German army, its turret at « two o'clock ». Note the trident symbol on the right mudguard, emblem of the 2nd Pz. Div. (BA.)

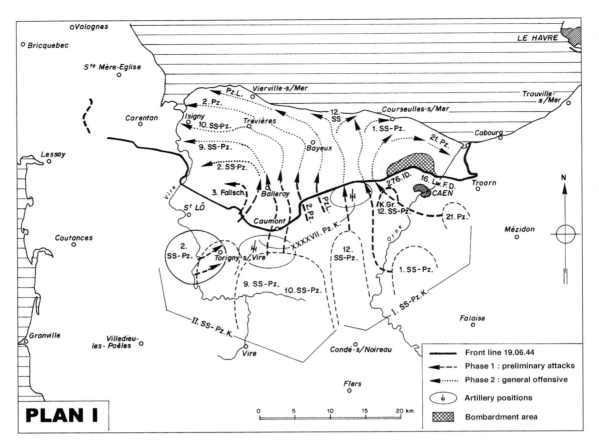

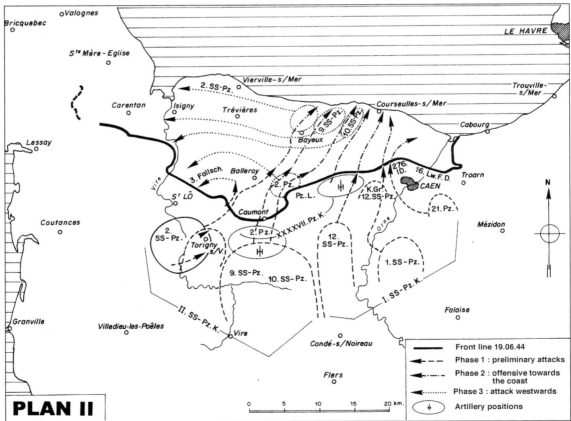

Plan I - This proposed a preliminary engagement by II SS and XXXXVII Panzer Corps to bring them up level with I SS Pz. Corps. All the divisions would then advance northwards towards the sea before turning to the east and west. A powerful artillery concentration would pin down the British forces around Caen.

Plan II - It was envisaged to pivot the armoured corps in the rear areas of the British and Canadians, to turn them towards the US sector where the Allied forces would be squeezed up into the Cotentin peninsular. (Cartes J.-L. Leleu - B. Paich/Heimdal.)

11

The Battle for the Odon 25 to 30 June

Operations Martlet and Epsom

At dawn on 25 June, Montgomery launched an extensive operation to the west of Caen. His VIII Corps was to attack positions held by 12th SS Pz. Div. down a narrow corridor running from Mesnil-Patry in the west to Saint-Manvieu in the east. That main attack was to be preceded by a secondary offensive in the Rauray area (Saint-Pierre - Fonteney-le-Pesnel) to eliminate the threat to the right flank of the main attack.

On 25 June that attack on the Rauray area was launched by the 49th (West Riding) Inf. Div. and the 8th Armoured brigade. Their task was to capture the high ground around Rauray and to follow through to Noyers-Bocage and Auray-sur-Odon, using their 9 infantry battalions and 4 armoured ones. To oppose them the Germans had two infantry battalions (the 3rd of the 26th Grenadiers of 12th SS Pz., and the 1st of the 901st Grenadiers from Panzer Lehr) supported by the Panzer IV's of the 8th Company of 12th SS Pz. Regt. The ratio of forces was 4/5 to 1, and in addition, the operation was supported by the firepower of 900 artillery pieces and the guns of three cruisers offshore. This was the operation code-named Martlet, preceding the main offensive known as Epsom.

The following day the attack on the Saint-Manvieu area was launched by the 15th (Scottish) Infantry Division supported by the 31st Tank Brigade and the 11th Armoured Division with further support from the 4th Armoured Brigade group and the 43rd (Wessex) Infantry Division. These units had the task of advancing along an axis passing through Saint-Manvieu, Esquay and Amayé-sur-Orne. The British had 22 infantry battalions and 11 armoured ones which could only be opposed by three infantry battalions of the "HJ" division (the 1st and 2nd of the 26th Grenadiers and the engineer battalion, and 4 tank companies (5th, 6th, 7th and 9th) which tilted the balance firmly in favour of the Allies - almost ten to one !

12th SS Panzer still had 58 Panzer IV's and 44 Panthers ready for action, and since 6 June it had lost 36 and 19 respectively, half of which had been totally destroyed but the others had been recovered and would be repaired in a short or long term. The Panzer IV's of the 2nd Battalion were well hidden in defensive positions behind the grenadiers in the following order of companies from west to east - 8th, 6th, 5th, 7th, and 9th The 1st Battalion Panthers were held as a fighting reserve around Noyers-Bocage.

On 25 June at **0500 hrs**, and just as the sun was rising a thick mist arose, reducing the visibility to not more than four or five metres, the British attack was launched after a furious preliminary barrage. The Hallamshire Battalion found itself the target of the Ist. Bn. of the 902nd Grenadiers and the 3rd Bn ; of the 26th SS Grenadiers supported by a few Panzer IV's of the 8th Company (Ostuf. Siegel) as they advanced towards Fontenay-le-Pesnel. One of the Panzers was destroyed by a new form of anti-tank ammunition with a discardable "sabot". Elsewhere, on the left (east) the 11th Bn ; The Royal

Scots Fusiliers had also moved into the attack but had dug in at the north-west corner of Fontenay after having lost their way in the mist. Further west the break-through by the 146th Brigade was more solid on the right wing of Panzer Lehr, and the tanks of the 6th, 8th and 9th Companies were sent in to retrieve the situation. But, during the day the positions of the 901st Grenadiers had been penetrated to a depth of three km : giving the British the chance to advance through the breach as far as Noyers-Bocage, thus arriving in the rear of the 3rd Bn. of the 26th Grenadiers. Therefore the Battle Group (Kampfgruppe) Wunsche was thrown into the struggle. Commanded by Ostuf. Max Wunsche, it consisted of the 1st Bn. of the 12th SS Pz.Regt. plus elements of the 3rd Bn. of the 26th Grenadiers and the divisional reconnaissance company. Starting off from Tessel-Brettevillette, their attack was directed on Fontenay with the 2nd Panther Company (Ostuf. Gaede) in the lead. At the latter's request, Ustuf. Schroder commanded the lead section, but the British resistance stiffened to the west of Tessel and the lead Panther was knocked out, Schroder being killed as he was evacuating his tank. At **22.30 hrs** it had proved possible to advance as far as 500 m from the road which ran through Fontenay and regain contact with the left flank with the 3rd Bn. of the 26th Grenadiers. On the other hand it had proved impossible to contact the right flank of Panzer Lehr. The 6th and 8th Companies of 12th SS Pz. Regt. had destroyed at least five British tanks and the 1st Bn ; had restored the situation. The regiment's casualties amounted to 23 : an nco and six men killed, an nco and twelve men wounded plus an officer and one man reported missing. For the following day, 26 June, I SS Panzer Corps ordered a counter-attack, for which the Tiger battalion would be sent in

Obersturmfuhrer Helmut Gaede commanded the 2nd Company of the 12th SS Pz. Regt. He took part in the attack by *Kampfgruppe* Wunsch late on 25 June. This photo was taken during the autumn of 1943 at the Mailly camp.

Ostubaf. Max Wunsche (right), congratulates an *Oberscharfuhrer* who had shot down five Allied aircraft with his light anti-aircraft gun. In the background, *Hstuf.* Schlauss, can be seen who was the signals officer in the tank regiment of the « HJ » Division. Photo taken by the SS war correspondent Stollberg.

as reinforcements. The 1st Bn; of 12th SS Pz. Regt. would be back in action but also with four companies from the 2nd Battalion. The division had kept back the 9th Company to keep up observation from the western edge of the airfield at Carpiquet. Max Wunsche spent the whole night preparing his battle group for the attack the following morning, but the British had an ugly surprise in store for him.

Monday 26 June

At dawn the *Kampfgruppe* Wunsche set off from Rauray to attack in the direction of the Bois de Tessel, but their advance coincided with the British attack. The signals officer of the 1st Battalion, *Ustuf.* Rolf Jauch, was wounded during the engagement : "Our attack faltered and we were shot at from three directions at once. We had a problem with the gun of our Panther and together with my gun-layer, I climbed down to detach a spare part from another Panther which had been destroyed on the eastern side of the small valley. On the way we were shot at from the right and my gun-layer, Gumpert, was killed outright. I was hit on my right elbow and lightly in the stomach area, but managed to get back to my tank with the part. Jorgensen, the battalion commander, advised me to withdraw eastwards and from there to the south because it would not be possible to transport me in an ambulance. Through the hedgerows I managed to reach the road along which we had advanced towards Tessel-Brettevillette that morning, and from there, during the afternoon, I was picked up by an ambulance and taken to the first-aid post, and from there to the divisional casualty clearing station." (1)

While the *Kampfgruppe* Wunsche was busy to the west between Tessel, and Fontenay, the main attack started further to the east, preceded by a formidable artillery barrage. At **0730 hrs** the 15th

(1) Account by R. Jauch quoted by H; Meyer in -*12th SS Pz. Div "Hitlerjugend"*. Heimdal, p. 271.

1. "948" a Panzer IV of the 9th Company of the 12th SS Pz. Regt. The numbers on the turret were painted in black with a white border which was unusual, as in theory the regiment did not have a fourth section. The divisional insignia can be seen on the front of the hull of the tank which was well protected under the apple trees. (BA.)

2. Another Panzer IV from the same section, knocked out at Esquay-Notre-Dame towards the end of June. The two white marks on the gun barrel denoted victories. (DR.)

3. A Sherman wrecked in Fontenay-le-Pesnil, perhaps after a duel with the Panther on the left, which belonged to *Kampfgruppe* Wunsche. The photo was taken on 27 June. (IWM.)

(Scottish) Division waited behind the curtain of steel which would creep forward 90 metres every three minutes. They were to attack with two brigades up : the 46th on the right supported by the tanks of the 7th RTR and the 44th on the left with the 9th RTR. Kurt Meyer who was at the HQ of the 12th SS Pz.Regt. at the Chateau de Rauray, remembered that the barrage stopped for ten minutes on the line of objectives, in his book *Grenadiere* : "It started to rain and thank God, that got rid of the '*jabos*' (fighter-bombers) - but what was going on? - the earth appeared to be about to open up and engulf us. Within the space of a few seconds, all hell was let loose. Rauray was nothing but a mass of ripped up trees and wrecked buildings."

With that hail of metal the grenadiers were wiped out in their foxholes and the inexorable advance of the Scots began : towards 1100 hrs. the Glasgow Highlanders reported that they had taken the northern part of Cheux and by **1130 hrs** had passed through the village, although the resistance was proving fierce and fanatical. At the time, when all available tanks were need to stem the offensive, *Kampfgruppe* Wunsche was still engaged with the fighting to the north of Tessel. However, the 7th Company of 12th SS Pz.Regt. was in position to the west of the northern part of Cheux where it was able to watch the road from Fontenay to Caen, and nearby was the 5th Company. The following is an account by the commander of the 3rd Section of the latter company, *Ustuf.* Willi Kandler : "When we set off, we saw to our left on the high ground leading from Mesnil towards Cheux, numerous armoured vehicles of different sizes. In turning to reach our old position in the middle of some hedgerows, we became involved in a savage duel with the enemy anti-tank guns, provoking successes and losses. When crossing a few metres in front of my tank, *Uscha.* Buchholz, who had his head sticking out of his turret had it blown clean off by a direct hit. As a group of British tanks had already penetrated into Cheux, withdrew fighting over two or three fields surrounded with hedges and took up new positions on either side of the road from Noyers to Cheux (RD 83). I myself with four of five tanks of my section, positioned myself slightly to the south of them. Suddenly, on the way to that new position among the hedges, *Oscha.* Junge fell upon some Shermans which were advancing south-west along a parallel lane and destroyed five of them at point blank range. (2)

To the left, in front of *Kampfgruppe* Wunsche, the tanks of the 4/7 Dragoon Guards had only got as far as the Bordel stream to the west of Tessel, where they were stopped by the fire of the Panthers. The British threw in a fresh tank battalion, the Sherwood Rangers Yeomanry, who confronted the Panzer IV's of the 6th Company of the 12th SS. *Uscha.* Berner was in charge of the company workshop and was waiting for the tanks to return : "During the absence of the fighting unit, one tank and the workshop train under my command, waited under cover. The tanks had not been away for long when the enemy tried to break into our position with infantry supported by armour. Our tank entered the fray but had to retreat under enemy pressure. The *I-Gruppe* (workshop train), which among other tasks had to ensure the protection of our tank, was pinned down by machine-gun and rifle fire : two men were wounded. When the pressure became even stronger, we had to abandon the company

HQ. When I tried to leave in my old VW *Kubelwagen,* my cap was torn from my head by a rifle bullet but I continued to wear it as a sort of lucky charm until I was severely wounded in Hungary. We were already at the rear limit of our waiting area when, literally at the last minute, our tanks reappeared, put in a counter-attack and freed our area." (3)

At **midday,** the positions situated in the areas in front of Fontenay-le-Pesnil as far as Saint-Manvieu had been submerged, and British tanks and infantry were already in Cheux. Elements of the 2nd Battalion of the 12th SS had managed to stop the tanks near to Haut-du-Bosq but they were under threat from enemy armour to their west. In the west, *Kampfgruppe* Wunsche had managed to strangle the break-through towards the south. The real danger of a break-through lay to the south-east of Cheux towards the Odon crossings, near Verson or to the south of Tourville but the "HJ" division did not have sufficient reserves to deal with this problem, even though the Tigers of the 101st SS Heavy Tank Battalion had been promised by Corps HQ as well as a company of tanks and another of assault guns from 21st Pz. Div. At **1300 hrs** the 11th Armoured Division attack on Gavrus got underway with a tank battalion, the II/Fife and Forfar Yeomanry and on Tourmaville with the 23rd Hussars. A third armoured battalion followed behind, the III/Royal Tank Regiment (RTR). To the west of Cheux the FFY became embroiled with the II/12th SS Pz.Regt., and the tanks and infantry of the "HJ" Division, split up into small battle groups attacking constantly , barred the route from Cheux towards the bridges over the Odon to the 227th Infantry Brigade. The position at Haut du Bosq held out and the 227th Brigade attack was finally halted by the assault-guns furnished by 2Ist Pz.Div.

Regarding the attack by the 2nd Gordon Highlanders to the south of Cheux, it was repelled by two Tigers. The 3rd Company of the 101st Heavy Tank Battalion, commanded by *Ustuf.* Amselgruber, had been transferred to Grainville-sur-Odon, 2.5 km south of Cheux by orders from I SS Panzer Corps. Two Tigers, one of which was Amselgruber's, pitched into the onrushing British column without infantry protection. He accounted for three tanks of the 9th Royal Tanks who were supported by a company from the Gordons, and the British stopped the attack after suffering heavy casualties. A little further to the east, a lone Tiger brought the attack by the 227th Brigade to a halt near Mobus, where *Hstuf.* Mobius's 1st Company became involved.

In the centre, the Salbey stream was a final obstacle before the Odon, and *Ostuf.* Hans Siegel, commanding the 8th Company of 12th SS Panzer Regiment gained recognition by defending that line. Between 1600 and 1700 hrs he moved off to the north-east of the Chateau du Rauray to refuel, accompanied by three other Panzer IV's from his company. His crew hardly took the time to drink a mouthful from the can because the battle had been raging since dawn. There, they encountered their regimental commander, Max Wunsche who told them : "our front has collapsed on the right wing. You must go there right away and try to slow up the enemy attack south of Cheux". There were no infantry available to accompany the tanks. Hans Siegel recalled : "the engines roared into life, hatches were closed down, guns and turrets were cleared for action. Our commanders last words were drowned by the rattle of our tracks". Without losing any time, Hans Siegel left with his four

Ustuf. Willi Kandler who commanded the 3rd Section of the 5th Company of 12th SS Pz. Regt. (Coll. auteur.)

Ustuf. Rolf Jauch, signals officer of the Ist Bn. of 1 SS Pz.Regt.

Uscha. Heinz Berner, commander of the company workshop of 6/12th SS Pz.Regt.

(2) Account cited by H. Meyer, *op.cit.,* p. 276.

(3) Account cited by H. Meyer, *op.cit.,* p. 277.

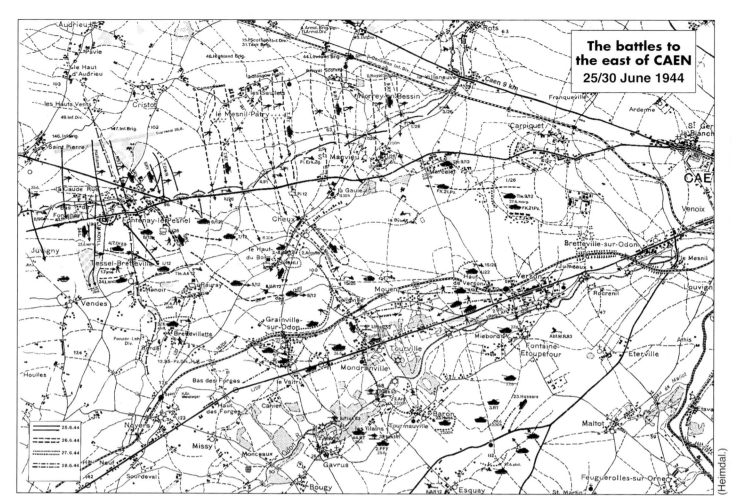

The battles to
the east of CAEN
25/30 June 1944

Ostuf. Hans Siegel who
was ordered to hold the
line of the Salbey with
four Panzer IV's from
his 8/12th SS Pz. Regt.

Command of the re-
mainder of the company
was entrusted to Her-
bert Hofler, commander
of the 1st Section.

tanks, leaving the rest of the company positioned around Rauray, in the charge of Herbert Hofler, commander of the 1st Section. Siegel drove cross country and reached high ground on which was a prominent tree. This dominated in front of him facing northwards, the small road between Cheux and Grainville-sur-Odon. To his left was the small Salbey stream which was normally nothing more than a trickle but it had been swollen by the abundant rain and its banks had become marshy. He identified his targets, opened fire and three British tracked carriers were knocked out on the road level with the Salbey stream, one of them going up in flames. Carefully he rejoined the road which in those days did not have a tarmacadam surface. It was little more than a narrow track bordered by tall trees running north from the stream, which has since been widened by cutting in to the verges. At **1800 hrs** the four Panzer IV's advanced in a file along the track. Siegel positioned three of them in a field on the left, in a line facing north, 300 metres to the north of the stream, well concealed behind the hedgerow with only their guns poking through the foliage. His own tank stayed on the track also facing north. At **1805 hrs** he went off on foot on a reconnaissance in the field on the right, where he saw four 10.5 cm. howitzers from one of the regimental artillery batteries. Their crews had been driven to ground by the British attack, were short of ammunition and had taken shelter in a small dugout where Hans Siegel found them. It was necessary to wait for nightfall until the tractors could be brought up to retrieve the guns, so he went back to his own tank in the lane where he met up with the patrol he had sent out into the field on the left. They told him that they had stumbled on elements

of the 26th Panzergrenadier Regiment (in fact from the 2nd Battalion) on some high ground, who had been overrun by the British attack. They said that they were unable to establish a link with the four tanks as there were not enough of them. Siegel noted : "thus we found ourselves right on the front line without contact to either flank, and the enemy had withdrawn, probably to the southern edges of Cheux. The breach had been stopped up and the mission accomplished". At **1900 hrs** he decided to go himself to make contact with the grenadiers who were a few hundred metres to his left. He followed a hedgerow until he arrived at a dug-out made of wood and covered with earth, similar to the one where he had found the gunners. It turned out to be the battalion headquarters of *Stubaf.* Bernhard Siebken who commanded the II/26th SS Panzergrenadiers and Siegel went back to his tanks. Darkness fell and it was raining in torrents soaking through everything. The men were drenched and the ground soaked up the rain. Siegel could not establish radio contact with anyone to get permission to retire. The night was as black as ink. Suddenly a VW *Kubelwagen* turned up by the Salbey bringing a container of food for the 20 odd crewmen of the tanks, and one man from each crew was detailed to collect food for himself and his four comrades. Siegel seized the opportunity to write out a message to regimental HQ, saying that he has maintaining his position having completed his mission. A quarter of an hour later (it was by then around **2300 hrs**) another *Kubelwagen* arrived and headed for Siegel's tank. In it was *Stubaf.* Schops who commanded the 2nd Battery of the artillery regiment of the "HJ" Division. They had a discussion and decided to evacuate the howitzers at around

110

one o'clock in the morning and as there were no tractors available to tow them out, they would use one of the tanks. The *Kubelwagen* was unable to turn round as Siegel's tank was blocking the way and the lane was far too narrow, but with strong arms and in four moves it was heaved round to face in the right direction, south, towards Grainville-sur-Odon. Suddenly they heard a shout of "hands up" Silhouettes surged out of the bushes towards the group which split up and ran for cover behind the tank, which in an instant was alone in the middle of the lane. In a reflex action, Siegel made a jump for the throat of an enemy who was shouldering his automatic rifle to fire. With his left hand he grabbed the man by the neck and brought him to the ground, knocking away the rifle with his right. The triangular bayonet actually went through the right leg of Siegel's leather trousers. The British soldier fired and emptied his magazine through the trousers, grazing the German's legs. The two men were rolling about on the ground and the soldier, half strangled, cried out : "help me, help me". At that moment one of his comrades appeared but missed his target. Siegel's adversary cried out : "Ohh. I'm wounded", and collapsed. Siegel stood up and realising he still had his pistol, drew it and emptied the magazine into the silhouette of the other British soldier who disappeared into the hedge as silently as he had come. Siegel remembers : "the silence was ghostly. Only the rain fell on us from the tops of the trees and the blood pulsed in out temples". He returned to his tank but ten metres away he saw *Stubaf*. Schops gravely wounded, with blood streaming out of his neck, so he dragged him into shelter under the tank. Having given his orders, he went towards the tank on his left, reloading his pistol : "suddenly I saw two flat steel helmets on top of the tank outlined against the night sky. I was by then beside the tank and I saw the two silhouettes straining to pull open the turret hatch which was being pulled shut at the same time by those inside. It made a rhythmic clatter : open, shut, open, shut. One of the men then asked, in English, for a grenade. I thought, 'just you wait boys', and quite calmly, as if on a firing range, I raised my pistol. Two shots at point blank range and the turret was liberated». There were several more similar incidents during that turbulent night until at around **midnight,** Hans Siegel gave orders for one of the Panzer IV's to tow the howitzers back to Grainville. He recommended the crew to drive slowly and not to make too much noise, not wanting the enemy to became aware of their activities. He left ahead of them in *Stubaf*. Schop's *Kubelwagen,* taking the latter with him who he believed to be wounded but was probably dying. (Siegel later found out that Schop's jugular artery had been cut and that he had lost a lot of blood). Siegel knew that the tactical HQ of the regiment was going to be moved from the Chateau de Rauray where it had been since 9 June, to Grainville-sur-Odon, the location of the rear HQ, two km. south-west of Rauray. So he set off southwards and found the headquarters installed in a farmhouse close to the mediaeval church. He parked his vehicle in front of the building, handed over Schops to the medics. And went in to report. Max Wunsche was there in a darkened room, studying the maps spread over the table by the light of a flickering candle. The windows had been blocked off by cupboards because of the danger of blast. This is what happened according to Hans Siegel's own account : "staff and other officers overcome by tiredness, supported themselves on the backs of chairs or were stretched out on couches. Someone gave me a cup of coffee which did me so-

me good. The door creaked and almost silently by contrast with the noise of battle, an *Oberscharfuhrer,* commander of an anti-aircraft section that was in position beside the railway line (light railway that ran from Caen, through Grainville to Vire, which no longer exists today), stumbled in, saluted hastily and announced breathlessly that he had heard the noise of engines and tracks of approaching armoured vehicles. Max Wunsche glanced at me enquiringly and he said to the nco : 'calm down - they are our 8th Company tanks that are towing in the guns', and then to me : 'Siegel, get back right away, give out your orders and keep your eyes open. Good luck'. I filed out leaving half my cup of coffee." (4)

Tuesday 27 June

The Allies had been ashore for three weeks.

To continue with Hans Siegel's story, at around **0400 hrs** he made contact again with his neighbours on the left. There was nobody to his right after the withdrawal of the gunners. After about 300 metres he almost fell over the sentries who were asleep beside the bushes, covered by tent cloth. In the HQ bunker of the 26th Grenadiers it was the same scene : everyone slept, exhausted. On his way back he attempted to take the men up, mentioning the possibility of an attack. At around **0430 hrs** he was in sight of the field in which were his tanks, when suddenly, enemy shells started up their "harvesting" again : "They were firing in salvoes, over our trees and the shells were landing behind us. Happily, far enough away from us. The sodden ground simply absorbed the shells which did not explode and made a loud 'plop', sending up columns of mud and stoned which formed a macabre background. But from where I was I saw that the tanks wanted to escape from the deluge of shells, and suddenly they started to move off, one after the other. I ran towards them but they backed away from the hedgerow. The stupid idiots would soon be in full view of the enemy. But somebody noticed me and saw my frantic signs that they should stop. I had gone off and in the command tank the crew thought that I was not coming back and decided to escape the shelling. I sent them back to their positions as the enemy attack was getting underway. The British infantry (HLI) advanced from the high ground to the south of Cheux accompanied by some tanks slightly behind them (2nd FFY). We let them approach our positions and I gave orders to only fire with the coaxial machine-guns so as not to reveal the presence of the tanks. The frightened British infantry advanced cautiously and we let them get right up close to us. Then I gave the order to open fire and we let rip with our four machine-guns. We were acting from experience and as envisaged, they panicked and ran back, only to be hit again by our streams of bullets. We opened up with our main armament when the tanks arrived with the second wave of infantry, and again were successful without suffering any loss on our side. The crews of the knocked out tanks baled out from the burning and exploding wrecks, while the survivors turned about and retreated back to the high ground with the infantry."

The night patrol that had infiltrated Hans Siegel's position had imaginatively reported back that they had found "Tigers" (the silhouette of the Panzer IV was similar, especially at night) and had overesti-

(4) The complete account was published in issue no. 64 of 39/45 Magazine.

mated the power of the small force of tanks. When dawn broke, Siegel asked for reinforcements and ammunition. The attack got underway again but that time further to the right towards Colleville (2nd Argylls). At dawn the 15/25th Grenadiers had been crushed by the 2nd Gordons supported by the 23rd Hussars. That was where the danger was coming from and Siegel was forced to move his tanks out from their hiding places and position them in the field to the right, where they could observe any attempt to outflank them from the east. The time by then was around **0930 hrs.** Hans Siegel recalled the events : "through binoculars one could see an amazing group of infantry who were slipping off their heavy rucksacks and sitting down, at a range of 1,200 metres. The tank on the left fired a round which was a direct hit. Flames and explosions. Human bodies were thrown into the air with their arms and legs windmilling before falling back to earth like stones. We thought they must have been engineers equipped with explosives on their way to blow up our tanks. A litte later the expected attack got underway again, this time more to the right. This third assault suffered the same fate as the other two. We let them get close and once again we wiped them out. By then there were a dozen tanks burning in front of us, but then I saw a tank, probably a Sherman, level with me to my right although it was difficult to make out the turret through the branches with the periscope. I thought that it had not spotted us, represented no danger and that the shells lost their power through the branches anyway. It was by then about **1030 hrs** and the fourth wave started its attack, and that time they seemed to have more tanks. The situation was the same but during a frontal duel with the tanks a shell suddenly impacted from the right. I wanted to exit via the turret hatch on top, but found myself caught up by my microphone cable. I then decided to get out after the loader on the right, but found myself face to face with the radio operator who could not use his own hatch because the gun was on top of it and blocking his way out. I jumped backwards and pushed the radio operator out of the hatch and for a few seconds I was in the middle of the flames. I lost consciousness but in jumping I found myself in the fresh air. I still had the microphone cable which I could not get rid of because of my cap and I found myself hanging from the tank in the process of strangling myself while machine-gun rounds impacted against the hull. I managed to free myself with a desperate effort that broke the cable which was as thick as a thumb. I found the rest of the crew in the sunken lane where the events of the night had happened, with the exception of the driver, *Sturmmann* Schleweis, who had remained in the burning tank, probably wounded or killed by the impact. His hatch was free and he could have got out. The gun layer was lying on the ground and on fire. The other crew members, themselves partially burned, covered him with their bodies to extinguish the flames. Unlike the others he did not have leather clothing and was wearing a camouflage overall because it was he who had been sent to replace the gun-layer who had been sent back to the rear. Those leather outfits which had been taken from the Italian navy had been handed out to us by Max Wunsche who knew full well the protection that they offered. They saved quite a few lives, but the gun-layer died later from his wounds in hospital. Like the others I did not suffer immediately from the burns to my face and hands, but the enemy attack was still in progress and there was no question of staying where we were. The three other tanks had seen nothing of the drama which had taken place, and were in action against the enemy. Powerless, I

was in the middle of them and saw with joy and relief that their commanders, all of them nco's were fighting bravely and that their firing was accurate. Almost every round was a direct hit. They were well protected behind their screen of natural vegetation and only their muzzle flashes revealed their presence. Then the turret hatch opened and a head appeared, blackened by powder, marked by fatigue and unrecognisable, shocked by the sight of his superior officer whose head resembled more and more a boiled potato. I handed over command to the senior *Uscha.* I collected up the wounded in the *Kubelwagen* and drove to the HQ at Grainville. The regimental commander, Max Wunsche, patted me on the shoulder and the medical orderlies gave us all morphine shots."

A company of Panthers from the 2nd Panzer Division arrived to relieve the few tanks from the 8th Company at around **midday** and the actual relief took place at 1400. Siegel explained to the army captain commanding the company where to position his tanks, but the latter, condescendingly declined to follow the wise advice, preferring to advance in full view of Cheux, losing seven of his Panthers in a very short span of time. For his decisive actions at Mesnil-Patry on 11 June and on the Salbey on 27 June, Hans Siegel was awarded the Knights' Cross on 23 August 1944. He said : "at Mesnil-Patry I was successful because I was more watchful than my enemies, but here, I was wrong to ignore the tank I had seen to my right. I simply forgot about it and it was me who had not paid attention. In war, it is the fastest one who wins."

As Siegel recalled, some reinforcements arrived, among which were the Panthers from the 3rd Panzer Regiment, to strengthen the weak positions of the "HJ" Division which had suffered heavy casualties that day. The casualty report of 12th SS Panzer Regiment for 26 June, listed 4 nco's and men killed, and 5 officers, 9 nco's and 28 men wounded, with none missing. The positions had to rely on the tanks still in working order : 30 Panzer IV's and 17 Panthers as well as the tanks and assault guns of the two companies from 21st Panzer Division.

As far as the engagement of the Panthers from 2nd Pz. Div. was concerned, as outlined by Hans Siegel, a captain from the I/3rd Pz.Regt. came up from the St-Lo area during the night and was able to make contact at around 0900 hrs. His 17 Panthers had remained more to the west, near the positions of the 5th Company of the 12th SS Pz.Regt. before relieving Siegel's tanks and by attacking, reestablishing the situation south of Cheux. Siegel had noticed to his right the preparatory moves by the 2nd Argylls in the direction of Tourville and had considered that prudence dictated positioning his tanks on the right to take that second attack in the flank. That, however, was contrary to the orders given to the captain from I/3rd Pz. Regt. who was to attack along the road running from Haut-du-Bosq to Cheux. His attack which was due to start at **0930 hrs**, sowed confusion in the area, destroying several guns before being brought to a halt by the loss of six Panthers from his company. A report by the 49th Division indicated that a radio operator from the 4th Company of the 3rd. Pz.Regt. who had been captured had spoken of the loss of 4 Panthers out of the 17. As there was only one company from the regiment, in this case the 4th was it involved in two different actions with the loss of 6 tanks near Cheux and four others elsewhere ? It is impossible to determine the facts in the light of current knowledge.

The British VIIIth Corps had not achieved its objectives at dawn and restarted its offensive. The 10th

Two wrecked Panthers south of Cheux on 27 June. They could well be two of the tanks from I/3rd Pz.Regt. sent to relieve Siegel's Panzer IV's. Six Panthers from that company were destroyed during the attack on Cheux. (IWM.)

Highland Light Infantry (HLI) attacked to the west supported by the 31st Tank Brigade, with the aim of crossing the Odon near Gavrus. The 2nd Argyll and Sutherland Highlanders attacked to the east with other tanks from the 31st Tank Brigade to cross the Odon south of Tourville. The 11th Armoured Division provided its 27th Armoured Brigade in support of this fresh attack. To the west of VIIIth Corps, the 49th Infantry Division continued its offensive towards Rauray and then on to Brettevillette, Hill 124 and Noyers.

The 10th HLI in attacking towards Gavrus via Grainville suffered from the German machine-guns and mortars which caused casualties among that Scottish battalion. It came to a halt and announced that its passage was blocked by four "Tigers" south west of Cheux, which were in fact, Ostuf. Siegel's Panzer IV's. They remained all day on their start line, suffering 112 casualties, which was a measure of the importance of Siegel's tanks.

Even thought the 10th HLI was blocked by a few tanks it was a different story further to the east, where the 2nd Argylls were able to make progress into a vulnerable sector of the German defences and Colleville was captured with the support of tanks from 23rd Hussars (11th Armoured Division). At around **1700 hrs** the two lead sections of the 2nd Argylls reached the bridge over the Odon near Tourmaville which they found intact, and an anti-tank gun was unable to hinder their crossing. By **2000 hrs** two companies of Argylls were on the south bank of the Odon and two hours later the whole battalion and the tanks of the 23rd Hussars were safely over. Even better, a company from the 8th Rifle Brigade with some of the tanks of the 23rd Hussars had already advanced towards Hill 112 and by nightfall they had stopped between Baron-sur-Odon and the Hill.

Further to the west, as a result of the resistance put up by Siegel's Panzer IV's along the Salbey, the British decided to try to outflank the position where they were confronted by the tanks of the 5th Company of the 12th SS Pz.Regt. At 1100 hrs while out

on foot to show the position of a target (an enemy macjine-gun) to Ustuf. Willi Kandler (commander of the 3rd Section) who was looking out of his turret, the company commander, Ostuf. Bando, was killed by a volley from the gun which hit him in the back of his head. Kandler told the other two section commanders, Porsch and Kunze, of the death of their company commander. Shortly afterwards, Kandler's own tank was knocked out, and of the five that had been in the line in the morning, only three were left at the end of the day. Having changed tanks, Kandler's new gun-layer was Willi Schnittfinke from Cologne (see pages 25 and 26). During the afternoon three Shermans appeared to the right of the three tanks of Kandler's section, and at a range of 600 metres they did not appear to have spotted the panzers. Kandler gave their targets to his two tank commanders : "Biback, you take the one on the right ; Jurgens, yours is the left hand one and I'll have the one in the middle. If possible without making a noise, drive in second gear up onto the ridge near the hedgerow. You will fire together, each destroying your indicated tank and then return into your hiding places. Biback got stuck in a sunken lane, when the bottom of his hull jammed on a tree stump. The three Shermans were on fire and Kandler also had to destroy Biback's tank. Panzers got back safely into their hiding places. (5)

With regard to the Tigers of the 101st SS Heavy Tank Battalion, eighteen tanks in full running order took part in the heavy fighting, but were destroyed one after another in trying to stem the headlong British advance. This was what Hstuf. Mobius, commander of the Ist Company had to say : "I had been engaged between the two lines with my tanks for three days. Under enemy fire I lost them one after another until there were only three of us left, one minus its gun. I myself hindered a British penetration by knocking out six tanks from a sunken lane. Together with Ustuf. Amselgruber's tank I attacked an armoured column and

(5) W Kandler's account quoted by H Meyer. op.cit. p. 286.

Uscha. Bobby Warmbrunn slipped through the British lines with his Tiger on 27 June.

destroyed three tanks, but I had problems with loading and was myself knocked out by ten tanks. Both Amselgruber and I had to bale out." "*Uscha. Bobby*" Warmbrunn of the 2nd Company also had memories of that day : "On 27th June I passed through the enemy lines to discover what was going on, a mission for which, with the agreement of my crew, I had volunteered. When we reached a rise in the ground I found myself confronted by a Squadron of 30 Shermans which loosed off a hail of shells and all my systems were knocked out. My driver reacted as he had been taught and placed the Tiger in the enemy's dead angle and thanks to his skill, the manoevre was a success. Together with the crew I passed right through the middle of the enemy, and in spite of the loss of the Tiger, the operation had been worthwhile." That account is revealing about how the Tigers were used during the battle of Normandy. With a thickness of armour of 100 mm. on the front of the hull and on the plate surrounding the gun, and 80 mm on the upper side plates of the hull and the turret, these 56.9 ton monsters armed with the redoubtable KWK 36 L/56 88 mm gun could stand up to an enemy hugely superior in numbers. Their exceptional specification ensured that the crews had great confidence in their tanks as demonstrated by Bobby Warmbrunn's account.

The British decided to bring forward reinforcements to protect the flanks of their bridgehead over the Odon. Thus the Gordons marched on Tourville-sur-Odon but they fell in with a panzer positioned on the RN 175 roughly 500 metres east of the village which was able to enfilade them and knock out the British tanks one after another. Could this have been the Type "D" Panther seen in the photo below just at the exit of Tourville ?

To the west, the 49th Division had succeeded in taking Rauray after a hard struggle, thanks to the engagement of the 70th brigade supported by tanks. There, the III/26 had been helped by a section of Panthers from I/12th SS Pz. Regt. while another section had backed up the 13/26th The 13th 15th and 16th Companies of the 26th SS Panzergrenadiers had been stiffened by the Panzer IV's of 6/12th SS Pz.Regt. and a section of the 9th Company of the same 2nd Battalion. Some of the Pan-

thers of the 1st Battalion had left for Grainville. That day the losses of the tank regiment rose to 49 : 2 Officers, 2 nco's and 10 other ranks killed; 2 officers, 6 nco's and 17 other ranks wounded.

As far as reinforcements arriving at the front were concerned, other than the I/3rd Pz.Regt. of which we have already described the unfortunate engagement of a company south of Cheux (the battalion reported the destruction of 14 Allied tanks for the day), the 4/22nd Pz.Regt. was engaged north-west of Verson. In other respects the 2nd SS Panzer-Division "*Das Reich*" finally arrived at the front with some of its units and a battle group, *Kampfgruppe* Weidinger (also known as *Kampfgruppe "DF"* as *Ostubaf.* Weidinger was the commander of the *Der Fuhrer* Regiment) which assembled to the east of Noyers preparatory to counter-attacking the following day at Grainville-sur-Odon. Essentially the battle group consisted of two battalions of grenadiers, the 1st of

Der Fuhrer Regiment which had left behind it an evil reputation around Oradour-sur-Glane and the 1st Battalion of the *Deutschland* Regiment. The divisional tank regiment, 2nd SS Pz.Regt. had still not arrived and would not become engaged until the beginning of July in the St.-Lo area.

The 2nd SS Panzer Regiment was formed in 1942 as the tank regiment of the 2nd SS Panzer Division "*Das Reich*". In June 1944 its official war establishment was 174 tanks : 54 Panzer IV's, 78 Panther (Panzer V's) and 42 assault-guns to compensate for the incomplete quantity of Panzer IV's. It was commanded by *Obersturmbannfuhrer* Christian Tychsen who was born on 3 February 1910 at Flensburg, near the Danish border. He joined the SS *Verfugungstruppe* (SS-VT) in 1938 he was in a signals battalion with the rank of *Obersturmfuhrer*. He took part in the campaign in the West where he was awarded the Ist and 2nd class Iron Crosses, after which he was transferred to the reconnaissance group of the SS Division "*Reich*", taking part in the attack on Russia in 1941. The following year he took command of the 2nd Battalion of 2nd SS Pz.Regt. and leading it at the recapture of Kharkov he was decorated with Knights' Cross on 28 March 1943, gaining the Oak Leaves on 10 December

This Type « D » Panther, a rarity which one could still find among the Panther battalions during the Battle of Normandy was wrecked beside the RN175 at Tourville-sur-Odon . It could either be from the I/3rd Pz.Regt. which had been engaged in that area on 27th June or a tank from the I/12th SS Pz.Regt. Given the fact however, that it was an out of date model, Eric Lefèvre attributes it to I/3rd Pz.Regt. But the second hypothesis is equally credible : see the Type « D» Panther from 2/12th SS Pz.Regt. On Page 99. A Type « D » Panther had neither a turret top periscope nor a machine gun in the front of the hull. In any case, the Gordons were stopped by a tank in position on the RN 175 east of Tourville-sur-Odon on 27th June, and could it have been this one ? (IWM.)

and taking command of the whole regiment. He was a tough fighter, cool and efficient and was killed on 28 July 1944. He was replaced by the commander of the 1st Battalion, Rudolf Enseling. But although it had been earmarked to take part in the counter-attack on 19 June, the regiment was only able to engage one company (the 6th) after the 5 July. As far as the rest of the regiment was concerned, the 1st Battalion could only enter the line on 10 July !

Wednesday 28 June

The Allied attack was to continue in several directions. The plan was that the infantry would fight their way westwards to improve the positions in the Odon valley and the armour would continue the engagement to the south east to take control of Hill 112.

At **0330 hrs**, starting from Colleville, the 9th Cameronians attacked westwards and finally captured Grainville-sur-Odon. But a little further north, the position along the Salbey continued to hold out throughout the day. Another attack also started from Colleville, but to the south, before turning to the west to enlarge the corridor in which the British were fighting. The 7th Battalion Seaforth Highlanders, supported by Churchill tanks advanced westwards down the RN175, but they suffered severe losses when counter-attacked by part of the Weidinger *Kampfgruppe*.

Moreover at dawn, the 159th brigade (a part of 11th Armoured-Div.) had relieved the 2nd Argylls from their positions in the bridgehead south of the Odon near Tourmauville, so that they could move to the west down the Odon valley over difficult ground, to gain control of the area. A reconnaissance patrol reached the two intact bridges near Gavrus which were not guarded by the Germans and the 2nd Argylls who advanced along the river were on the south bank before nightfall, giving the British control of three bridges.

As far as Hill 112 was concerned, the 23rd Hussars advanced towards the summit but came under fire from the tanks of 12th SS Pz.Regt. in position in the area to the south of Fontaine-Etoupefour and in the small woods north-east of Baron-sur-Odon. At around **midday** the Hussars had occupied the northern part of the wide summit but were running short of ammunition. They were confronted among others, by the 5/12th SS Pz.Regt. which had departed from Haut-du-Bosq early that morning, reaching Esquay at around 0900 hrs. and then the small square wood (*kastenwaldchen*) at the base of the Hill. The company was under the command of *Ustuf*. Porsch. The following is the account of one of his section commanders, *Ustuf*. Willi Kandler : "All we had left were four tanks which were commanded by *Ustuf*. Porsche, *Ustuf*. Kunze, *Hscha*. Muller and myself. (With the exception of Muller all the tank commanders were officers, because, to ensure quality of command the available tanks were given to the highest ranks when there were more crews than tanks available - author's note). The remaining tanks were unavailable either as a result of losses in combat or breakdowns. Porsch, the company commander wanted to make a second attempt to capture the "*Kastenwaldchen*" and the summit of the hill. We set off from our start line in the valley and drove straight ahead for the wood at **midday.** Very quickly my gun-layer informed me that we had a problem with the gun's electrical firing circuit and we had to stay behind the other three tanks as they manoeuvred, to effect repairs, which was a rot-

ten situation for me. Muller also remained behind Porsch and Kunze. I heard Kunze's voice over the radio, evidently addressing those remaining behind : "Don't hang about. Panzers advance'! Kunze's tank was knocked out 200 metres before the wood, which stopped the attack and the three remaining panzers rolled back to their start line. Kunze's driver, *Sturmmann* Groter and the radio operator had been able to bale out. Groter was very shaken and said : 'the shell went right between my legs." It is astonishing how I have been able to remember such details even while I was worried about the fate of my friend Kunze. I intended to reach his tank by whatever means possible. Also at around midday, four tanks from the 6th Company, under the command of *Standartenoberjunker* Kurt Muhlhaus set off for a reconnaissance from the south-east towards Hill 112.

At **1530 hrs** the tanks of the 23rd Hussars were relieved by the 3rd Royal Tanks and another tank battalion from the 29th Armoured Brigade, the former arriving via the northern slope of the Hill at **1700 hrs** The 5/12th SS Pz.Regt. took part in another duel between the Panzers and the Allied tanks and 36 of the latter were counted abandoned on the summit of the hill. The engine of Kunze's tank was still running and a recce. established that there was someone dead inside. In fact, when night fell, a team set out to recover the body : "It was Kunze's tank. The loader, Howe, was sitting there, his big blue eyes wide open and his face covered in blood. Kunze himself was dead, crumpled up in the commander's seat and the shell appeared to have hit him directly in his back. To his left, the gun layer was also dead. The engine had been running since midday."

At dawn the 29th Armoured brigade had fielded 165 tanks to which the tanks of the 23rd Hussars should be added, to confront 30 Panthers and Panzer IV's on the top of Hill 112. 2/12th SS Pz.Regiment claimed to have destroyed 21 tanks. The regiment had lost that day an officer and six men killed, two nco's and 15 men wounded.

On the other hand, to the west of Verson, 4/22nd Pz.Regt. mounted a counter-attack westwards towards Colleville, into the flank of the British salient. Their Panzer IV's drove in single file as they got near the level-crossing to the north of Mouen, where the lead tank destroyed three British ones. With the support of grenadiers, they took the northern part of Mouen from "C" Company of the Monmouthshires. The British suffered heavy casualties and were surrounded. Tiger tanks were also involved near Verson.

Thus on that particular day, the British had continued to try to reinforce their foothold on Hill 112 as well as to extend the bridgehead over the Odon, helped by the capture of two more bridges. The stiffness of the German resistance, however, surprised the British commanders. The tanks of the 12th SS Pz.Regt. refused to concede Hill 112 which was to be fought-over furiously during the coming days. On top of all this, counter-attacks were launched at the flanks of the British salient : by battle group Weidinger from the west and especially the Panzer IV's of the 4th Company which enabled the recapture of Mouen. The Tigers which were engaged in the area, were all too often isolated and were knocked out one after the other. The following day was to see the engagement of II SS Panzer Corps.

That army corps consisting of two armoured divisions, brought two tank regiments into the line. The 9th SS Pz.-Div. "*Hohenstaufen*" had a tank regiment equipped with three different types of armou-

Ostubaf. Christian Tychsen, commander of the 2nd SS Pz.Regt. who was killed on 28 July 1944.

Stubaf. Rudolf Enseling who commanded the 2nd Battalion. He took over command of the regiment when *Ostubaf*. Tychsen was killed.

Ustuf. Karl-Heinz Porsch, commander of 5/12th SS Pz.Regt. who was killed on 9 August 1944 to the north of Falaise.

Ustuf. Kunze who commanded one of the 5th Company tanks on 28 June during the fighting for control of Hill 112.

Ostubaf. Otto Meyer who commanded 9th SS Panzer Regt. and was killed on 28 August 1944.

Ostubaf. Otto Paetsch commanded 10th SS Panzer Regt, and was killed on 16 March 1945.

red vehicle : Panthers, Panzer IV's and assault-guns. The 9th SS Panzer Regiment was formed at the Mailly camp in 1943 and had been engaged in front of Tarnopol in Galicia between 11 April and 9 June 1944 where it lost a number of Panzer IV's and assault-guns, although the Ist Battalion with the Panthers had remained behind at Mailly. The regimental commander, *Ostubaf.* Otto Meyer, had been decorated with the Knights' Cross in front of his troops on 4 June. The complete regiment with its Panther battalion was earmarked for participation in the Battle of Normandy. On 28 June, the theoretical strength consisted of a regimental hq with 8 Panthers, the 1st Battalion with 76 Panthers (battalion hq with 8 and four companies (numbered 1 through 4) with 17). But at this time, the total of Panthers is only 28 !

The 2nd Battalion was a mixed one (*gemischt*) consisting of headquarters with 8 Panzer IV's, 5th and 6th Companies each with 22 Panzer IV's while the 7th and 8th Companies were each equipped with 22 mark III assault-guns. The total complement for the regiment was thus 44 assault-guns, 50 Panzer IV's and 28 Panthers giving a total of 122 armoured vehicles. **(see note above).** Otto Meyer was born on 23 December 1912 at Moldenit in Schleswig and killed on 28 August 1944 at Duclair, during the Seine crossing. The 1st Battalion was commanded by *Stubaf.* H Bollert, the 1st Company by *Ostuf.* Friederich, the 2nd by *Hstuf.* H-Ch Sailer, the 3rd by *Ustuf.* Herden and the 4th By *Hstuf.* Flor. The 2nd Battalion commander was *Hstuf.* Rennert, the 5th Company, *Hstuf.* Hunke, the 6th, *Ostuf.* Th Grimm, the 7th by *Ostuf.* K Frohlich and the 8th, by *Ostuf.* Rennert.

The other armoured division in the corps was the 10th SS Panzer *"Frundsberg" which* also had its tank regiment partly equipped with assault-guns. The 10th SS Panzer-Regiment had been formed in early 1943 in Lorraine and had then been sent to the Eastern front in the spring of 1944 where it participated in the campaigns of the II SS Panzer-Corps in Galicia before being transferred to Normandy. On 1 June it was a particularly weak unit comprised of only the four companies of the 2nd

Battalion – headquarters with 3 Mark III command tanks, two companies with Panzer IV's (39) and two assault-gun companies (38), giving a total of 80 armoured vehicles. The Panther battalion remained behind at Mailly. The regimental commander was *Ostubaf.* Otto Paetsch, born on 3 August 1909 at Rheinhausen in the Rhineland. He was awarded the Knights' Cross on 23 August 1944 for his actions in the Battle of Normandy at the head of his regiment, and was killed on 16 March 1945 at Altdamm on the Oder. His 2nd battalion was commanded by *Stubaf.* Leo Reinhold.

On the other hand, the Corps was still awaiting the arrival of its Heavy Tank Battalion, the 102nd SS which only appeared at the front twelve days later.

Thursday 29 June

Even though the II SS Armoured Corps should have been used for the grand counter-attack towards Bayeux and the coast (see pages 105/6), it only arrived at the front to help block the British attack and still without its battalion of Tigers. Furthermore, the other units which should have taken part were conspicuous by their absence : 2nd SS Panzer-Division was only present with one battle group and the remainder joined the front in dribs and drabs. 1st SS Panzer was also only present with one battle group which did become involved in the Verson area, but the rest (including the tanks) only appeared several days later. Thus the battle became a speed competition and any decisive counter-attack by armour was rendered impossible by the indecision of the German high command, and above all by the difficulties incurred in bringing fresh units into the front line. The Allied air forces had destroyed the railway network leading to the front, the Seine bridges downstream from Paris and the key road junctions. Fighter-bombers attacked mercilessly every vehicle moving by day, restricting the movement of armoured columns on the road to a few night hours. They could only cover a maximum of 100 kilometres in three hours, interrupted by frequent breakdowns, overheating engines and worn out track links. To cap it all, at that season the

Assault-guns of the *Hohenstaufen* Division on exercise during the autumn of 1943. The vehicles have already been camouflaged, the German crosses painted on but no numbers are visible. The 7th and 8th Companies of 9th SS Pz.Regt. were equipped with such machines. (ECPA.)

nights were comparatively short. The Normandy front was a long way for 2nd SS Panzer which had to come from the south-west, or 1st SS which had to move from Belgium. As far as II SS Panzer Corps was concerned, a number of its units were only transferred from Galicia after 12th June and had to be detrained in Lorraine. Thus on the 29th June, 23 days after the initial landings, the Germans' armoured counter-attack had finally grounded and they were forced onto the defensive, confronted by an enemy able to reinforce the bridgehead and who had a very powerful strike force available. If the tanks were having difficulties in reaching the front line, ammunition and fuel also had difficulty in getting through. Often Panthers exploded and caught fire easily because their fuel tanks contained more petrol vapour than petrol.

In spite of these problems the Panzer Corps received its first orders : "A) Defend the actual positions ; B) Preparation of a concentrated counter-attack for the purposes of destroying the American forces present in the Balleroy area, as well as the enemy situated east of the Orne ; C) Preparation of a counter attack directed against the flank of the deep enemy penetrations – 1) from the Caen area and from the west in a south-easterly direction." (6) With regard to point A) it was ordered in the evening at 1700 hrs : "1) Panzer Group West intends intends to attack at dawn on 29 June with II SS Panzer Corps (9th and 10th SS Pz.Div.) from a start line Gavrus/Noyers to capture the area around Baron, Mouen and Cheux, and to crush the enemy which has penetrated beyond the Caen/Villers-Bocage road." For that attack II SS Panzer-Corps was subordinated to I SS Panzer Corps. That ambitious attack, too pretentious in the prevailing circumstances, sounded good. However, the German chain of command had been modified the day before, at 1000 hrs General Dollmann committed suicide although it was officially stated that he had died of a heart attack. He was replaced in command of Seventh Army by *Obergruppenfuhrer* Hausser who gave up command of II SS Pz.Corps, handing over to *Gruppenfuhrer* Bittrich who had previously commanded 9th SS Panzer *Hohenstaufen*. He in turn was replaced by *Standartenfuhrer* Thomas Muller who had been in command of the 20th SS Panzer-Grenadier-Regiment. In spite of all this, II SS Pz.Corps was unable to start at the time foreseen.

That day the VIII Corps intended to enlarge the bridgehead over the Odon , clean out the areas already conquered and when the 15th Scottish Division had carried out its task, the 11th Armoured Division would advance towards the Orne in conformity with the plan. On the German side, the attack by II SS Pz. Corps, which was to bear the brunt of the effort, had been due to start at 0600 hrs. but on account of delays in forming up, it was not able to get underway until 1400 hrs ! The other German units involved had to wait for the Corps to start and thus it was the British who attacked first.

The morning was clear and the cloudless sky belonged to the RAF. The 129th brigade kicked off by recapturing Mouen before 1100 Hrs On the other hand at the Gavrus bridge, the 2nd Argylls were crushed in their bridgehead under the fire of the German mortars. As from **0440 Hrs**, the 44th Royal Tanks attempted to take Esquay in the flank. At **1015 hrs** the 8th Rifle Brigade supported by the 3rd Royal Tanks attacked the small wood 300 metres to the east of Hill 112, known to the Ger-

(6) KTB Pz.AOK 5 ehem. Pz.Gr. Westn Ia I-Teil, 2. Ausf., 10.6-8.8 1944. Anlagen Ob.Kdo.H.Gr.B, Ia Nr. 4072/44 g. Kdos.

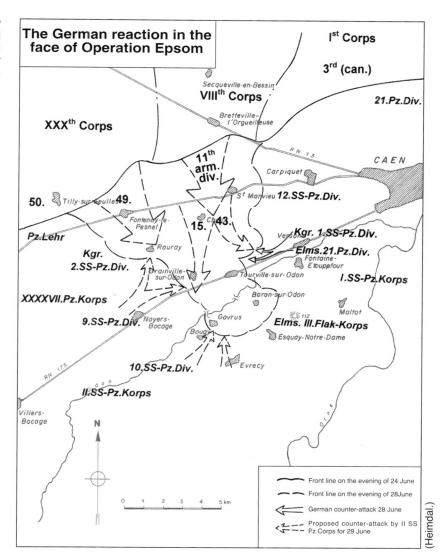

The German reaction in the face of Operation Epsom

	Front line on the evening of 24 June
	Front line on the evening of 28June
	German counter-attack 28 June
	Proposed counter-attack by II SS Pz.Corps for 29 June

(Heimdal.)

mans as the *Kastenwaldchen*. A few tanks from the 12th SS Pz. Regt. intervened at at around **1100 hrs,** they had to withdraw in the face of the superiority of the British force which thus held the wood. At the same time the tanks of the 3rd RTR attacked to the south and the south-west from the area to the north-west of Hill 112, but they encountered six Tigers (which may well have been Panzer IV's as the two types were often confused in reports) which crushed the British tanks.

The II SS Panzer Corps got underway at last at **1430 Hrs** 9th SS Panzer attacked on the Noyers/Cheux road, on the right of *Kampfgruppe* Weidinger, supported by its 9th SS Panzer Regiment. Initially it made good progress and retook Rauray on the left wing and Grainville on the right with the assault-guns of the 7th Company entirely on the right wing. However, the Panthers of the 1st Battalion which were assembled in the Bois des Forges together with the 3rd Company of the 20th Grenadiers, preparatory to an attack on Cheux, suffered a bombardment by 100 Lancaster bombers on their start line, and although the losses were slight their attack was cancelled. Although the main attack started off well enough, a tremendous barrage of shells from tanks and anti-tank guns and massive intervention by naval artillery was able to halt the advance towards Bayeux and the coast from Rauray and Grainville. For its part, the 10th SS Panzer-Div. attack got underway in a state of confusion and not all

Ostuf. Franz Riedel, commander of 7/10th SS Pz. Regt.

Stubaf. Leo Reinhold, commander of the 2nd Bn. 10th SS Pz. Regt.

its units has been told about the changes to the timetable, and the story of the 7th Company of the tank regiment is a good illustration of the problems. The company commander, *Ostuf.* Franz Riedel remembered that first engagement (7) : "On 29 June 1944, I received this order – "Attack at 0700 hrs on Hill 113 and follow on towards Gavrus". Our forming up area was at Evrecy. My company was to form the spearhead for the offensive with the 5th and 6th companies guarding the left and right flanks. What I was not told was that the attack had been postponed until 1000 hrs. because a grenadier regiment had not yet arrived in the assembly area. All the others had apparently been told in time, but not me. As a result, the attack went in at the prescribed time and our panzers rolled towards Hill 113, our assigned objective. A British armoured unit had obviously received orders to attack at the same as me, because after only a few hundred metres, a large number of Shermans crossed our line of advance below the hill. In a twinkling of an eye, the shells spat out from our guns and eleven of the Shermans brewed up on the hill. I was leading the company in my tank and because the range was calculated precisely, my gun-layer, Ewald Menzel, destroyed five of the enemy tanks. As for us, we only lost one tank, unfortunately that of the commander of the 1st Section, U*stuf.* Hilpert, who was seriously wounded and his driver killed. Because the British failed to recover quickly enough from the shock of our surprise, we naturally charged in among them and they fled with our tanks in hot pursuit. Our score would undoubtedly have been much higher, but in their retreat, the British rapidly swamped the area with a thick blanket of smoke and to pursue them would have been fatal. Then, to our astonishment we saw a motorcycle combination careering towards our tank at a crazy speed. In it was our battalion commander, *Stubaf.* Leo Reinhold, waving his arms excitedly and shouting out – "what exactly are all these explosions ?" At the same time, somewhat disconcerted he looked at the burning Shermans and went on in a calmer tone – "what the blazes have you done with those there?" After I had explained the situation naturally his face lit up. » By ensuring an essential part of the day's victories, that success gained at the expense of the 44th Royal Tank Regiment (10th Armoured Brigade) enabled the capture of Hill 113.

That preliminary engagement by a panzer company, preceded the attack by the division which got underway at **1430 hrs** Gavrus was taken by the grenadiers of the 21st SS Panzer Grenadier Regiment but was lost again after a counter-attack by the Scots. That stopped the offensive and because of the intense artillery bombardment, the corps commander, *Gruppenfuhrer* Bittrich signalled that the line reached at 1900 hrs after the capture of Gavrus, Grainville and Rauray, was to be abandoned because of the intensity of the artillery bombardment. The *Hohenstaufen* thus had to concede the territory it had occupied.

Friday 30 June

The Allies had succeeded in bringing 20 infantry and 5 armoured divisions into the Normandy bridgehead as well as several brigades and independent units. That gave a total of 850,279 men,

148,803 vehicles and 570,505 tons of supplies which had thus far been landed. A German breakthrough was no longer possible in view of the conditions. However, the II SS Panzer Corps attack was to continue and had to take place before dawn to avoid suffering from the artillery and the Allied aviation. Its objectives were Hill 112 and the villages of Esquay, Gavrus and Grainville. The Hohenstaufen set off at 0020 hrs. but as the British had reinforced their defences, the attack soon ran out of steam, while in its sector the *Frundsberg* engaged its tanks. At dawn the 2nd Battalion of 10th SS Pz.Regt. crossed the Guigne between Avenay and Vieux and established itself on the high ground, its start line for taking part in the assault on Hill 112. The German artillery opened up on the summit, crushing the positions of the 8th Bn. The Rifle Brigade. Elements of the *Hitlerjugend* and *Frundsberg* divisions went over to the attack, supported by their respective tank regiments and were complete masters of the hill by the middle of the morning. But that did not stop them from being the objects of persistent fighting.

Thus the attacks by VIII Corps and II SS Panzer Corps ran headlong into each other. The British were forced to suspend their assault and go over to the defensive in an attempt to hold on to their gains, especially the crossings over the Odon and the approaches to Hill 112. On the german side there was no longer any talk about grand counterattacks. On the contrary, after the failure of the attack on the previous day under the fire of the Allied artillery, the Germans had to realise that it would not be possible to split the British and American armies apart, and all they could do was to block the VIII Corps offensive. The commander of Panzer Group West, General Geyr von Schweppenburg realised that Montgomery intended to use up the German armoured divisions through attrition in defensive battles and being consumed by a crushing material superiority. He therefore submitted his ideas to General Hausser, commander of Seventh Army (8) : the evacuation of the northern part of Caen, establishment of a new line of defence running from south Caen and the Orne passing via Avenay to Villers-Bocage and the Caumont area, leaving II SS Panzer Corps on that line and retiring 12th SS Panzer and Panzer Lehr to refit in reserve, beyond the range of the naval artillery. OKW refused to even consider what it regarded as an admission of defeat and turned down flat the suggestions. Counter-attacking remained the order of the day. That evening, *Hohenstaufen* reported the tally of its available tanks : 22 assault-guns (64.7 % of the war establishment), 9 Panzer IV (26.5 %) and 27 Panthers (39.7 %) which amounted to only 58 tanks.

Hill 112 - Saint-Lô

On Saturday **1 July**, a final attempt was to be made to reabsorb the British salient on the Odon. That same day the *Hohenstaufen* reported the victories of its 9th SS Pz.Regt. : 13 Allied tanks destroyed by its Panzer IV's and Panthers, and 49 by the assault-guns. The latter, forming the 7th and 8th Companies were the units of the regiment which achieved the highest scores. But under the fire of the 20 times superior enemy artillery, the attacks once again were halted and the units of II SS Panzer Corps were regrouped and placed on the defensive. That 1 July, the number of tanks available

7) Account by Franz Riedel in *Die Hellebarde*, no. 5, p. 53, quoted by J-L Leleu in *10. SS- Panzerdivision "Frundsberg"*. p. 65

(8) Noted by H Furbringer in *9 SS Pz. Div "Hohenstaufen"*, Heimdal. p. 285.

in 9th SS Pz.Regt. were : 19 assault-guns, 10 Panzer IV's and 19 Panthers. Up to I July inclusive that regiment had suffered the loss of 151 personnel (62 killed, 74 wounded and 15 missing in action), plus 6 Panthers, 16 Panzer IV's and 10 assault-guns destroyed. The losses of that regiment in terms of men and material for three days of fighting were quite considerable and due to the power of the Allied material. Between 29 June and 6 July, however, the regiment's tally of victories was considerable and rose to 68 British tanks written off : the assault-guns destroyed 16 Churchill Mark III's, 16 Churchill Mark II's, and 16 Shermans ; the Panzer IV's accounted for 5 Churchill Mark II's and 8 Shermans, and the Panthers had destroyed 4 Churchill and 2 Mark IV's. On the other hand the workshops had repaired many tanks and the numbers available had risen. 19 assault-guns, 12 Panzer IV'' and 37 Panthers were operational.

After the British offensive and the German counter-attack were brought to a halt, a period of relative calm intervened. Along the Odon, the high ground spread around Hill 112, barred the way to the Orne valley upstream from Caen, remained in dispute. However, one of the panzer divisions, Panzer Lehr, was due to leave the sector. On 29 June at 2200 hrs it was placed under the orders of XXXXVII Panzer Corps, commanded by General of armoured troops Hans von Funk, and the following evening, the relief of its units by the

276th Infantry Division began. It reached its new sector, the area north-west of St-Lô during the night of 7 July. During the period from I June to 30 June the division had lost 24 Panzer IV's, 23 Panthers, 2 assault-guns and a tank destroyer. After its arrival in the new sector, the division was to mount a counter-attack to the north along the Vire river as far as the Vire-Taute canal, to block the American advance, cut them in two and eliminate any adversaries south of the canal. This attack, to be launched on 8 July, the day after the arrival of PLD in the area was to be backed up by 17th SS Panzer Grenadier Division on its left flank. Moreover the *Das Reich* Division was also engaged in the area although still waiting for its tanks, except for the 6th Company which was already at the front.

As a result of the failure of the II SS Panzer Corps counter-attack, General Geyr von Schweppenburg had to pay the price. Hitler had decided on his sacking during the night of 1/2 July, and his replacement was an eminent armoured warfare specialist, General of Panzer Troops Heinrich Eberbach who had previously commanded the 4th Panzer Div. and XXXXVIII Corps. Moreover, on 3 July Field Marshal von Rundstedt was also sacked and replaced as OB West by Field Marshal von Kluge.

Thus on 7 July the PLD prepared to face the American threat between Carentan and St-Lô, while further to the east, the battle for Caen got underway.

General der Panzertruppen Baron Geyr von Schweppenburg (left) who commanded *Panzergruppe West* who was sacked on 2 July. His replacement was *General der Panzertruppe* Heinz Eberback (right).

1. A type « A » Panther, the « 204 » , hit beside the D173 road between villages of Rauray and Fonteney-le-Pesnil. Eric Lefèvre has attributed it to I/3rd Pz. Regt. which was fighting in the area at the time. This is quite possible as the identification numbers were carefully applied with a stencil which was not the case with the tanks of the I/12th SS Pz.Regt (see the « 219 » at Fonteney-le-Pesnel.

2. 3 and **4.** British troops ands vehicles passing the wreck of « 214 ».

In photo no. 3 one can see on the rear left, the hole punched by the shell which penetrated the 40 mm thick plate and caused the petrol tank to explode. The protective plate over the track has been torn off.

5. A Tiger « E » belonging to the 101st SS Pz. Battalion captured in running order near the Chateau de Rauray (?) and taken over by crewmen from the Nottingham Sherwood Rangers Yeomanry. The front of the tank bears the scars of numerous impacts which failed to penetrate the 100 mm And 110 mm thick armour plate.

I./1st SS Pz.Regt.

On leaving Belgium, the *Leibstandarte Adolf* Hitler arrived at the front in Normandy between 17 and 23 June 1944. A war correspondent took this series of pictures of the Ist Battalion of the tank regiment in transit through Paris. The photos are of Type « G» Panthers. Note the application of the *Zimmerit* paste and the original camouflage which consisted of large blotches in several colours, applied like the plates of a tortoiseshell and are plainly visible in the photo below. Note the German cross (*Balkenkreuz*) roughly painted on the side of the hull in front (photo 1). In the same photo, the two crewmen are wearing different uniforms. The one on the left is wearing one made of Italian camouflage cloth while the one on the right is dressed in 1943 pattern overall over his trousers and the collar of a black shirt is showing at the collar.

The Type « G » Panthers continued their move to the front in Normandy by driving along the Champs Elysées. The Panther already seen in photos 1. and 2. can be recognised in photo no. 3. with the two crewmen , one in the 1943 pattern overall and the commander in the Italian camouflage material. Note the design of the camouflage paint on the back of the tank. Other Panthers can be seen with identical camouflage in the same series of photos, but there are no numbers visible on the turrets so it is impossible to say to which company they belonged.

(Photos Bundesarchiv.)

12

4 to 10 July
Caen - the final assault

Oscha. Richard Rudolf, a section commander in the 9th Company of the 12th SS Pz.Regt. was on the defensive with his Panzer IV on the edge of the airfield at Carpiquet when he destroyed six Shermans. He was awarded the Knights' Cross on 18 November 1944.

For more than a month, the 21st Pz.Div. and more importantly, the 12th SS Pz.Div. had managed to block off any Allied advance to the north and north-west of Caen. Operation Epsom had failed to capture Hill 112 and achieve a break-through to the Odon, south of Caen, but it had created a salient which would render the final assault on the capital of Lower Normandy that more easy.

Carpiquet 4 July

Montgomery needed to extend the salient which would allow him to attack Caen from several directions at once, and that was the object of Operation Windsor, launched on 4 July, to take Carpiquet to the west of the city. To confront the Canadian offensive there were 50 odd grenadiers of the 3 "HJ" Division from the 26th Regiment and a few Panzer IV's of the 9th Company, under the command of *Hstuf.* Buettner, positioned in the south-east of the airfield. The Canadians went into the attack twice and reached the hangars at the southern end of the airfield, and during those battles, *Oscha.* Rudolph knocked out six Shermans. One of the latter was at the north of the airfield and Rudolf attacked it from the hangars at the south. The Canadians were thrown back to their start line and for his successes, Rudolf was awarded the Knights' Cross . *Ustuf.* Modes of the 9th Company was wounded during those actions. Also in the area to the south were elements of the 2nd SS Pz.Div. *Das Reich,* still in process of arriving at the front, including a few tanks. *Uscha.* Herbet Kraft of the 2nd SS Pz. Regt. related his experiences (cited in *12th SS Panzer Division "Hitlerjugend".* Heimdal, page 324) : "we had had to remain whole days inside the tanks without getting out, and during a pause in the fighting, I stretched myself out under the tanks to relax my numbed limbs. After about ten minutes the enemy opened up an infernal artillery barrage. My mates, who knew I was underneath, could not move for fear of crushing me and it was impossible for me to scramble up onto the tank. Suddenly I saw four young grenadiers who were carrying a badly wounded comrade through the middle of the explosions and I yelled at them to take shelter under the tank, which is what they did. One of them explained that they had to bring the wounded man as quickly as possible to the dressing station as he had been hit in the lower part of the body and was losing all his blood. To make carrying him easier they asked for a blanket which I had with me. They placed the casualty in the middle of it and ran off through the barrage. I saw them disappear through the smoke and did not hold out much hope for them. Three days later I bumped into a young *Sturmmann* and when we spoke I recognised him as one of the young grenadiers who had wanted to carry the casualty to the dressing station. Smiling happily, he told me : "we got him there".

The Canadian attack failed to make progress against the determined defenders and at **2100 hrs** the 8th Canadian Infantry Brigade suspended its operations . The 1st Bn. of the 26th Grenadiers was relieved by the grenadiers of the "LSSAH" and at **midnight** the III/1st SS Pz.Regt. went over to the attack.

The journey to the front of the Ist. SS Pz.Regt.

That regiment was in the process of refitting and training in Belgium when the Allied landings took place. As from 17 June, it was an incomplete unit that was loaded onto trains destined for the Normandy front. The journey, however, was a difficult one and it was necessary to detrain and continue by road. Divisional headquarters was at Bagottière in the commune of Moutiers-en-Cinglais, 20 km south-west of Caen and only the 1st SS Panzer-Grenadier-Regiment was able to reassemble to the south of Caen on 28 June (the unit that was to become involved at Carpiquet). As far as the 1st SS Panzer Regiment was concerned, after crossing Paris (see photo report), it arrived at intervals and was frittered away by being fed into the front line in dribs and drabs during the following days. Thus, on 10 July the 7th Company (*Ostuf.* Wolfel) was in action at Bully and during the evening of 12 July, the 5th Company (*Ostuf.* Kremser) reached Vieux to be put at the disposal of I SS Panzer Corps. The regiment never had more than half its complement of tanks in its area of command.

It was commanded by *Ostubaf.* Jochen Peiper, born the son of an officer in Berlin on 30 January 1915. Attracted by the profession of arms he joined the SS *Verfugungstruppe,* becoming a corporal and then a sergeant, before being sent in April 1935 to the SS officers' academy at Brunswick. He was promoted *Untersturmfuhrer* (second lieutenant) and joined the *Leibstandarte* as a section commander. In April 1938, Peiper was promoted to *Obersturm-fuhrer* (Lieutenant) and was attached to the *Reichs-fuhrer-SS* (Himmler) as liaison officer with the SS-VT, where he remained until May 1940, in the meanwhile marrying one of Himmler's young secretaries. He then went back to the LSSAH and experienced his baptism of fire while commanding the 11th Company as Mont de Watten, near Dunkirk on 25 May. At the end of the campaign in France he was awarded the Iron Cross 1st and 2nd class and promoted *Hauptsturmfuhrer* (Captain). On 1 November 1940 he again reported for service with Himmler as principal liaison officer and at the end of May 1941, accompanied the latter on a visit to the concentration camp at Mauthausen. In August he returned once again to the LSSAH, shortly after the start of Operation Barbarossa, where he made his name as commander of the IIIrs. Battalion (armoured) of the 2nd SS Panzergrenadier Regiment, particularly during the battles for the recapture of Kharkov in February 1943 which gained him the Knights' Cross on 9 March the same year. During the winter of 1943-44 he again rose to prominence by decimating four Soviet divisions for which he received the Oak Leaves (the 377th German soldier to be thus decorated, on 27 January 1944. He was then at the head of the 1st SS Pz.Regt. with the rank of *Sturmbannfuhrer* (major) and during the move to the front line, he was an *Obersturmbann-*

1. 1st SS Pz.Regt. was refitting in Belgium when the Allied landings took place. The photo shows a SdKfz 7/1 tractor mounting a quadruple barrel anti-aircraft gun. On the back of the trailer can be seen the regimental tactical sign on the left and on the right, the divisional emblem. (BA.)

2. A Panther from the regiment traversing a small Flemish town, passing a signboard bearing the word « Peiper ». (BA.)

3. Another regimental Panther passing the lens of a war correspondent. As in the photo of the previous tank, spare track links have been fitted to strengthen the turret. This forced the crews to place the identification numbers (in this case, the « 327») on the side of the gun mantlet instead of their habitual position on the turret. (BA.)

4. *Ostubaf.* Jochen (Joachim) Peiper, the commander of 1st SS Pz.Regt. This photo was taken in Normandy during a ceremony for the award of decorations.

fuhrer (lieutenant-colonel). The 1st Battalion of his regiment (Panthers) was commanded by *Stubaf.* Kuhlmann and the 2nd (Panzer IV's) by *Stubaf.* Kling. The unit was still incomplete on 10 June and only had 45 Panzer IV's and 54 Panthers available.

8 July : Operation Charnwood

Finally, Carpiquet had fallen into the hands of the Canadians and the jaws of the vice tightened around Caen. For Operation Charnwood which was to herald the final capture of the city, Montgomery had massive resources at his disposal : three infantry divisions (3rd Canadian, 3rd British and the 59th British) backed up by considerable artillery support, amounting to 115,000 men to confront 10,000 Germans. The Allies thus had a superiority of eleven to one, and in addition, the operation was to be preceded by a carpet of bombs on the northern outskirts of the city.

In the area of attack assigned to the 3rd (Canadian) Division in the north-west, the village of Buron was the prime objective.

In the evening of **7 July,** everything was ready. The three divisions which were to mount the attack had the support of 350 tanks divided up between two armoured brigades, and the supply of ammunition was considerable, so that at the end of the first day, each gun would have fired 13 tons of shells. At 2100 hrs. Typhoons carried out rockets attack on targets around Buron and at 2210 hrs, 500 heavy bombers dropped their loads over a wide area to the north of Caen. The sky was on fire, the spectacle terrifying and the result devastating. The German defences, however, were to a large extent in front of the target area and the carpet of bombs succeeded in devastating the city of Caen, causing in the process, severe losses among the civilian population. Unfortunately for the Allies the bomb craters were to impose serious delays on the advancing troops, and the effect of the bombardment was totally negatives except for the psychological boost to the morale of the Allied troops.

On 7 July, Panzer Group West reported to Army Group B the number of tanks fit for action in the 12th SS Panzer Regiment : 37 Panzer IV's and 24 Panzer V's (Panthers). Several more tanks were able to be got back in running order, even though on the eve of the Allied offensive, the companies of 12th SS Pz.Regt. were fated to fulfil a defensive role. The 5th Company with five Panzer IV's, under the command of *Ustuf.* Kandler, was in position at the north and west exits of Buron, and with four Panzer IV's, led by the company commander, Porsch, at Gruchy. The 3rd Company, at full strength, formed an offensive reserve near the wa-

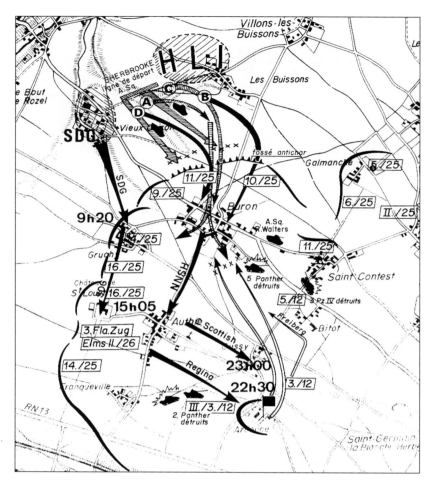

On 8 July to the northeast (**note – northwest ?**) of Caen the Highland Light Infantry went over to the attack supported by the tanks of the Sherbrooke Fusiliers. When the Panthers of the 3/12th SS Pz.Regt. tried to oppose that offensive, seven of them were destroyed.

ter tower to the west of Caen, ready to intervene northwards. The 9th Company with five Panzer IV's was on observation duty at the extreme eastern limit of Carpiquet airfield. The 1st, 2nd and 4th Companies were in observation around Bretteville-sur-Odon and Eterville, while the 7th Company had been withdrawn to rest.

On the **8 July**, at 0420 hrs the 7th Canadian Reconnaissance Regiment left Rots in 50 Humber armoured cars , heading for Carpiquet to simulate an outflanking movement to the south of the German lines. At **0730hrs** the artillery opened up on Gruchy, Cussy, Authie and Buron, strafing the German front for 61 minutes. Then the Highland Light Infantry of Canada went into the attack, supported by the tanks of the Sherbrooke Fusiliers.

The German front line was held by elements of the 25th SS Panzer Grenadier Regiment ("HJ" Division) supported by the Panthers of the 3rd Company of the tank regiment.

Von Ribbentrop's company returns to the front

After having suffered heavy casualties in the attack on Norrey on 8 June (see pages 48 to 54 in Part I), the 3rd Company of 12th SS Pz.Regt. was withdrawn from the front line and its ten remaining Panthers were distributed among the other companies of the I Battalion to make good their losses. The survivors of the company were sent back to their base station at Harcourt in the Eure department where they had been before 6 June. A small memorial to their dead had been erected in the park of the chateau in the form of a simple wooden cross on which the names have been burned in. Signifi-

cant in view of the horrible death most of them endured, burned alive in their tanks. Several of their comrades, Korte, Hoffmann and Paul Rawe were mainly involved in the erection of the memorial. On 18 June, the tank commanders and their drivers were sent to the camp at Mailly, as the company was to be reequipped with 17 brand new Panthers. Hardly surprising when one considers that the company commander was the son of the *Reichs* Foreign Minister. Those tanks were unloaded in Paris on 25 June and continued by road to Harcourt. On 5 July the company received orders to rejoin the front line. The combat element passed through Caen and on the evening of 6 July, reached the northwest of the city near the Abbaye d'Ardenne, to form an operational reserve. The following evening the crews watched the bombardment of Caen and *Ostuf.* Rudolf von Ribbentrop returned to take command. On the morning of 8 July and the three sections of Panthers were ready : the 1st Section was commanded by *Ustuf.* Bogensperger, the 2nd by *Ustuf.* Alban and the 3rd by *Ustuf.* Mathis.

That morning Mathis's section had taken up a covering position to the east of Authie and Franqueville. There were four Panthers facing west, towards two places which were about to be captured by the Canadians. The crew of the section commander's tank, the "335" had hardly slept at all. That Panther had joined the front at full speed and a pebble had got between one of the bogey wheels and the rubber tyre, which had to be replaced in the middle of the night. The wheel in question was on the inside of the running gear and nine other wheels had to be removed to get at the damaged tyre. The workshop had produced a spare, but on the Panther there were inside and outside wheels, and it was of course the wrong one. Gunther Gotha, the gun-layer of "335" who was not a born mechanic will never forget that night of 7/8 July when they had to remove the tyre from the spare running wheel and force it onto the original one, a lot of effort and fatigue before being able to take up their position at in the front line. The life of a crewman was a hard one with many exhausting hours spent in routine maintenance before the tank could experience brief moments of battle.

The second tank was commanded by *Uscha.* Hermani, and with him as crew were Nanning Lorenzen (gun-layer), Heinz Korte (loader), Horst Bandow (radio operator), and Heinz-Hermann Lammers (driver). The latter came from Celle in Lower Saxony, as did Heinz Korte who sat beside him in the tank and blond gerd Krieger. The four tanks waited a long time facing west and observing, until the Canadians attacked from Authie and the Panthers opened fire on the Shermans of the First Hussars. But suddenly they were subjected to a barrage from the enemy artillery. In changing position to avoid the hail of shells, one of the four Panthers received a direct hit and there was no news of the fate of the crew. The section commander, Mathis, tried to report in by radio, but was unable to get through. In the meanwhile the 1st and 2nd Sections were engaged at Buron and by then it was the middle of the afternoon and they were facing up to the Canadian offensive., but after a long wait the order came through to withdraw to the Abbaye d'Ardenne. This was how Gunther Gotha remembered the events : "Shark, come in, Shark, come in." The voice of *Ustuf.* Mathis echoed in my headphones. – "Bandow, try again." We did succeed in getting in contact to a certain extent. – "Attention, 3rd Section. Withdraw on the road that runs behind us. Reassemble down there." – "Gotha, see to it that the enemy infantry don't join us. Keep them at a distance with

The 3rd Section of 12th SS Panzer-Regiment consisted of four tanks.

● The first tank was hit and burned out on 8 July between Authie and the Abbaye d'Ardenne. Its commander was *Ustuf.* Mathis, *Sturmmann* Gunther **Gotha** was the gun-layer (**1**), the loader was Gerhard Kaub and the driver was *Strm.* **Alisch** (**2**).

● The driver of the second tank was Herbert **Niebisch** (**3**).

● The commander of the third tank (hit twice on the evening of 8 July, having destroyed five Canadian tanks) was *Uscha.* Josef **Hermani** (**4**), his loader was Heinz **Korte** (**6**), the gun layer was Nanning **Lorenzen** (**5**), the radio operator was *Strm.* Horst **Bandow** (**7**) and the driver was *Rttf.* Heinz-Hermann **Lammers** (**8**).

● The identies of the crew of the fourth tank, destroyed by artillery near Authie on 8 July, are unknown.

your machine-gun." "Our tank rolled slowly as far as the road".

At that stage the section commander's tank was in the lead and Hermani's tank was a hundred metres behind. The third tank, driven by Herbet Niebisch decided to reverse into a sunken lane. Gunther Gotha's account continues : "Through my visor I saw alongside the road, a ditch full of wounded grenadiers from the 25th Regiment, and I got out of the tank to try to help them. I noticed their faces with the waxy pallor of death, their eyes showed me what terrible suffering they had endured during the previous few days. Many had dirty blood-soaked bandages but not a complaint came from their lips. I helped an *Unterscharfuhrer* (sergeant) whose left shoulder and arm were shattered, to lie down beside the turret, and he whispered 'thanks'. He shut his eyes and I could see how he clenched his teeth together to subdue the pain. Then suddenly, the order 'Panzer, march !' clambered back into the turret, but the fatigue of the last few days made itself felt, and putting on my headphones and throat microphone, I tried to sleep." Behind in Hermani's tank, the driver, Heinz-Hermann Lammers who was looking through the thick glass of his visor, noticed that after having driven several hundred metres, suddenly an anti-tank shell came in from behind and to the left, and slammed into *Ustuf.* Mathis's tank. Gunther Gotha again : "Two loud shocks ! Direct hit ! Instantly I thought, 'we must bale out'. I leapt upwards intending to exit through the top. But then suddenly a burning fireball entered the turret. I lowered my arms and tried to protect my face (thanks to that he saved his eyes). Then I heard the cry of an animal in my headphones but did not realise that it was I who had let loose that scream. I sensed my knees flexing and I thought 'you are going to live'. That urge pushed me upwards, and with the heat I had the impression that my cap was lifting off my head like a hot-air balloon. I climbed up instinctively as I had been taught, without worrying about the pain or the danger. Lifting my head I noticed the bottom of the camouflage trousers of my commander had two small burns, and it struck me that in such a grave situation I still had time to notice such details... I was then on the turret and I held my arms out in front of me ; they were just two red and black lumps and my face felt that it was covered with skin that was too tight. My overall was smoking all over. A huge cloud of smoke emerged from the turret and beside me the engine was on fire. The loader, Gerhard Kaub, an East Prussian, who had alse been severely affected, climbed up beside me and went out through the hatch in the back of the turret ; I then realised that I had to get

down and when I reached the ground, I noticed *Ustuf.* Mathis and Alisch, the driver, seemingly safe and sound, busying themselves with the wounded grenadiers. I went up to them and said '*Untersturmfuhrer,* I await your orders !'"

Heinz-Hermann Lammers, the driver of Hermani's tank, witnessed the death throes of Panther "335". He saw the flames shooting out of the turret and Gunther Gotha jump to the ground ? What to do ? He put his foot down and passed to the right of the wrecked tank as the shells had come in from the left, intending to seek cover behind the curtain of smoke pouring out of it, when he heard the order to stop. In the meanwhile Gunther Gotha had run towards the tank and recognised *Uscha.* Hermani whose head was looking out of the turret wearing his headphones. The engine of the tank was running and Hermani shouted "Panzer March !" I heard nothing, but nevertheless Gotha shouted "Hermani, Hermani". But the latter had seen nothing, as as I described, the tank drove on. Gotha tried to run more quickly and at last, Heinz Korte, Hermani's loader saw him and alerted his commander, who stopped the tank. Still running, Gotha fell into the arms of Korte who helped him to scramble up the side of the turret. "Thanks !" Gotha exhausted, closed his eyes and thought : "you are alive, you are going to be safe". The two remaining 3rd Section tanks then drove off towards Caen loaded with the wounded and the burned, through the middle of the ruins, and a halt was made at a crossroads to bandage the wounded, where Lammers got out of the tank but did not recognise the wounded man laying on the rear deck. Gunther Gotha said to him : "It's me, Gunther." His face was all swollen and singed by the fire. He thought : "We had one hell of a job to repair our tank during the night, just to have it burned under us." Gunther Gotha was finally bandaged up like a mummy and had to be fed with a small spoon. He spent several months in hospital and even after the war his face still bore the scars of his terrible ordeal.

The 1st Section of 12th SS Pz.Regiment had stayed in the line and at dawn they were in a covering position facing Franqueville and Authie where they destroyed several Sherman tanks, for which the section commander, *Ustuf.* Bogensperger, was awarded the Iron Cross First Class. Then, at sunrise, the Canadians recaptured Buron and Authie. The 3rd Section took its turn in the covering position facing the two villages and regimental HQ ordered von Ribbentrop to throw in his company to recapture Buron and free the grenadiers of the III/25th who were surrounded there. A battalion of grenadiers mounted in "SPW" armoured half tracks

The progression of Hermani' tank after *Ustuf.* Mathis's tank was wrecked. The dotted line shows the direction taken by Gunther Gotha.

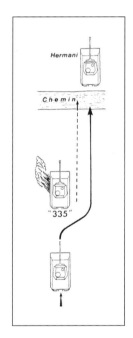

The face of Gunther Gotha will always be scarred by the terrible burns he suffered on 8 June, the terrible reality of war for the tank crews of all sides. This photo was taken in 1989.

Uscha. Heinz Freiberg was the commander of a tank in the 2nd Section of III./12th SS Pz.Regt. which was hit by a shell but could be got back to the company workshop and be repaired by the followinf gay.

were to accompany the Panthers in the counter-attack. Von Ribbentrop only had two sections available at that moment (the 1st and 2nd) as Mathis's was already engaged in the line, but he also had the support of a section of Panzer IV's on his right wing (probably *Ustuf.* Kandler's 5th Section). Unfortunately the battalion of grenadiers failed to show up and von Ribbentrop had to start his tanks off without infantry support, with Bogensperger's 1st Section on the left and Alban's 2nd plus the section of Panzer IV's on the right. The two Panther sections formed up in the orchard situated to the east of the enclosing wall around the Abbaye d'Ardenne. With their engines roaring they set off at high speed towards the north-west, passing beside the hamlet of Cussy, moving diagonally towards Buron. They made rapid progress in two leaps, as if on an exercise, with one section covering the other, to reach the edge of Buron.

What follows is the story of the *Ustuf. Rudolf* Alban's section on the right. One of his tank commanders was *Uscha.* Heinz Freiburg, a tall and sport loving German from East Prussia, who had been von Ribbentrop's gun-layer on the eastern front where he had taken part in the battles of Kharkov and Kursk, having already been wounded four times. He had still been a gun-layer at the engagement at Norrey, but as an experienced crewman, he had passed out as an nco. *Uscha.* Josef Tratnik was another of the section's tank commanders and his story was a strange one. He was born on 22 October 1922 at Maribor in Slovenia, and in 1941, that region (Marburg in German) which is a prolongation of an Austrian valley, was incorporated into the Greater Reich. The Tratnik family thus became Germans by annexation and both Josef and his elder brother were enlisted by compulsion. Josef, who was bilingual became an interpreter for the Gestapo, before joining the *Leibstandarte* and fighting at Kharkov. His three younger brothers joined Tito's partisans : the fate of a family torn apart by the war.

Thus the 2nd section advanced on the right flank but Heinz Freiberg took the wrong direction, steering initially directly north. He saw the grenadiers and the Panzer IV's, plus a small wood, and realising his mistake, swung off to the left to rejoin his section, soon finding himself directly in front of Buron, a village completely surrounded by walls, in the middle of the plain. At the same time he realised that his gun was defective, which he reported by radio, but was ordered to stay with the section and support the attack with his secondary armament of machine-guns. There were gaps in the

walls but how were they to enter Buron ? Heinz Freiburg was on the extreme right and the machine guns spat fire at anything that moved.

Up until then everything had gone well and the company had arrived rapidly at its objective. By then it was roughly **1400 hrs** and von Ribbentrop was satisfied with the initial phase but was then faced with the problem of how to get into Buron without supporting infantry, a village surrounded by ditches and hedgerows but above all by solid stone walls. The commander of the grenadiers who should have accompanied him was in his vehicle close to von Ribbentrop's tank and the latter asked him from the top of the turret, where were the SPW's and the infantry ? Their commander, an army captain, shrugged his shoulders : apparently he had not succeeded in establishing communications with his battalion.

Facing Buron was *Ustuf.* Kurt Bogensperger's 1st Section, and that young officer, only twenty years old was to lead the attack with his "315". With him as his crew were the gun-layer, Ernst Sammeth, a Bavarian, the loader, Ernst Porochnovitz, a calm but talkative Prussian, Leopold Heindl (known as Poldi), a lively Sudenten German, the radio operator, and the driver, Ferdinand Stange, a Bavarian from Blattling. The Panther on the right flank was commanded by *Uscha.* Franz Zwangsleitner, an Austrian from Styria and his gun-layer was *Sturmann* Otto Meier, also a Sudeten German ; A third Panther on the left flank, the "318", was commanded by *Uscha.* Pitsch and the fourth by *Uscha.* Walter Freier. The section commander had already opened fire on the edges of Buron and as the gun loosed off round after round, Fritz Porochnowitz let the empty cases fall into the reception container. From time to time he caught one (the container only held four "empties") and burned his hands. In the hull, Poldi Heindl blazed away with his machine gun and the empty cases let off ammonium vapours which stung his eyes although above him there was a ventilator to evacuate the fumes. In front of him, through his visor, he saw carriers disintegrating as their ammunition exploded . As the section commander's radio operator, he had two sets, placed in the middle between himself and the driver who sat on the left side of the hull. One set was used for communicating between the individual tanks in the section and the other for speaking to the company commander. His section had the code name *Ameise* (ant), that of the 3rd Section was *Haifish* (shark). *Ustuf.* Bogensperger's orders crackled in the headphones : "Watch out. Enemy tank. 11.30 o'clock.

The tank crews of the Ist Section on 8 July

● Commander : *Uscha.* Zwangsleitner
Gun-layer : Otto Meier **(1)**
Loader : ?
Radio Operator : ?
Driver : Kalipke

● Commander : *Uscha.* Walter Freier **(2)**
No identification of the rest of the crew.

● « 318 » The section commander's tank, *Ustuf.* Kurt Bogensperger. **(3)**
Gun-layer : Ernst Sammeth
Loader : Fritz Porochnowitz **(4)**
Radio operator : Leopold Heindl **(5)**
Driver : Ferdinand Stange

● Fourth tank. No crew identification

● Commander : *Uscha.* Pitsch **(6)**
No identification for rest of crew.

400 metres. Open fire." Crackling noises, acrid fumes, explosions and on top of all that, keep operating the radios !

But, while the Panthers were crossing the plain as if on exercise, the Canadians were ready to give them a warm reception. Formidable 6 pdr, anti-tank guns had been position in the breaches in the walls, and on the left, between Buron and Saint-Contest, Major Radley-Walters, who commanded "A" Squadron of the Sherbrooke Fusiliers, had positioned his four surviving tanks, three standard Shermans ond one Firefly with its 17 pdr. Gun, a veritable tank killer. At roughly **1800 hrs** Lieut. Dough Barrie, the only officer fit for action in "A" Company of the HLI, spotted eight Panthers tanks (he only observed part of the company) approaching from the south of the Abbaye d'Ardenne. He gathered together the support company of the HLI with their 6 pdr. Guns and placed them in the gaps in the wells, also obtaining the support of three M10 tank destroyers from the 3rd Antitank Regiment. The Panthers came into range and there they were. "Fire !" In ten minutes six Panthers were destroyed and two others retreated. This was how Major Radley-Walters remembered the events : "After Buron had been cleaned up, at the end of the morning, I advanced to the road situated to the south of Buron and leading to Caen (today the D126). There I turned right and moved towards our objective. It was roughly 1300 hrs." Then he positioned himself in a field between Buron and Saint-Contest. "At that moment I only had three tanks plus my own and had no accompanying infantry. We saw enemy tanks approaching our position and battle was joined. The enemy attacked in groups of between five and eleven. We confronted that counter-attack from **1500 or 1600 hrs** to **1800 hrs** and having inflicted losses on the enemy, we withdrew. The battle for Buron calmed down while the HLI winkled out the remaining enemy, house by house. I had lost 11 tanks in the battle, 7 of which were recovered and got back in fighting order. Three of my men were killed anf five wounded. The squadron claimed three Panthers destroyed and one probable."

Suddenly the anti-tank guns, the M 10's and the Canadian tanks opened fire, and von Ribbentrop noticed two explosions on the right as two of his tanks burst into flames, one of which was *Uscha.* "Sepp" Tratnik's, who had not seen Dough Barrie's 6 Pdr's. A Canadian shell burst in the turret and Tratnik was riddled with splinters, his arms and legs were broken and he received a stomach wound. He hoped to be rescued but beside him the gun-layer and loader were dead and with his last remaining energy he managed to scramble out of the turret. As Hans Freiburg noticed, whose tank was in the vicinity, the fire was quickly put out. The driver and the radio operator, Thepas, were uninjured and had already evacuated. Seeing their boss, they wanted to get him to the dressing station, but he had already lost consciousness and lost a lot of blood. Seriously wounded he was transferred to a hospital at Le Mans where his arms and legs were plastered and his stomach bandaged. He did not regain his wits until eleven days afterwards, on 20 July, the day of the attempt to assassinate Hitler. He had however, lost the use of the three languages he spoke : Slovenian, German and French of which he had a working knowledge. In hospital in Paris, a nurse retaught him German, and one could say that if the nurse had been French, then that would have been the language he reacquired. That man, terribly affected by the war which he hated always was, as he said of himself : "a bad soldier but

a good fighter. I was not an enthusiast but certainly no coward".

Heinz Freiberg saw the two explosions, Tratnik's tank being hit and then a third Panther. His crew blazed away with the machine-guns at the gaps in the walls where they saw movements, but than came a new flash. The gun mantlet was hit by a shell which penetrated the 12 cm of steel to the right of the visor and entered the turret where it came to rest, its velocity expended, a few centimetres from Freiberg's left arm. The visor was smashed, the gun-layer received a face wound and Freiberg had a small splinter in his left leg. The shell had come from the left, and thus from Buron, from one of Dough Barrie's anti-tank guns. The crew members in the turret evacuated immediately, but in the heat of the moment the driver and radio operator remained unaware of what had happened, and stayed put in the hull with the engine still running. Heinz Freiberg pulled himself up on the grill over the engine, grabbed his microphone which was hanging out of the turret and ordered the driver to go into reverse. The tank set off back towards the Abbaye d'Ardenne and after a few metres, another shell snapped the antenna off its mounting, and on looking down at his feet, Freiburg noticed that the shell had ripped off a piece of the leather from his shoe. The tank's steering was damaged and they made their way back to the abbey by a series of erratic movements, and before they got there they saw to their horror, that it was being attacked by fighter-bombers. When they finally reached the angle of the wall, they saw an 88 mm gun already destroyed which was being crushed again. *Uscha.* Freiberg's tank reported to the workshop where it was repaired by the following day.

A little further to the left, *Uscha.* Zwangsleitner's tank had had the rear turret hatch ripped off by a shell, when another went through the turret, causing a fire. Zwangsleitner was blown out through the top followed by Otto Meier who was only slightly burned and his hair singed. The crew baled out and walked back to the abbey through the corn which was high and offered good cover : there were no losses from that tank.

Seeing his Panthers destroyed one after the other and faced with the impossibility of capturing Buron, *Ostuf. v*on Ribbentrop gave the order to withdraw to the remaining tanks of his company. He was the last to retire, according to Heinz Freiberg, with his turret traversed backwards at 6 o'clock, to cover the retreat. Nevertheless, on account of its steering problems, Freiberg's tank was the last to arrive and it was decided to place them in a defensive ring around the abbey before the final withdrawal the following night. *Uscha.* Hermani's Panther had got back from Caen and had tucked itself in behind the northen wall. Hermani chose a circular gap and placed the tank behind this, slightly concealed, with some grenadiers in position in front. However, the calm did not last long and the Canadian artillery opened up a creeping barrage on the abbey and its surroundings. The firing slackened off but at that moment Heinz-Hermann Lammers heard an impact : a direct hit close to the radio to the right of the hull. The radio operator, Horst Bandow, leapt out through his escape hatch, only to discover that the damage was not serious. A shell had arrived diagonally from the right and penetrated the hull at least a metre away from Bandow's head and been stopped by the refueling can which was in the way. Horst Bandow got back into the tank just as another shell hit the gun mantlet at the front of the turret which was angled at one thirty o'clock. Heinz-Hermann Lammers, who saw thousands of small

Uscha. Josef Tratnik, a Slovene impressed into the German army : « a bad soldier but a good fighter » ; he was terribly affected by the war.

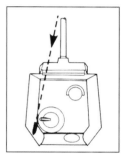

The way in which the shell entered Heinz Freiberg's Panther.

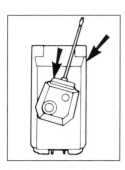

Behind the wall of the Abbaye d'Ardenne, Hermani's Panther received a hit in the hull on the right near the radio operator's seat and another on the left in the gun mantlet. (Heimdal.)

glowing splinters flying around in the tank, started the engine and reversed to escape from that dangerous area. Inside the tank it was full of smoke and Heinz Korte activiated the fire extinguisher. What had happened ? The tank did not catch fire but the turret traversing mechanism was jammed. They wanted to get it back to the workshop but were going to have problems getting through the villages with the turret angled to the right. The Panther was repaired at the workshop which was hidden under the foliage of the forest of Cinglais and H-H Lammers kept the same tank right through the Falaise Pocket and even managed to cross the Seine in it at Elbeuf when leaving Normandy.

The 3rd Company reported the loss of seven Panther tanks, which was identical and equally disastrous as in the engagement at Norrey and once again they had lost half of their tanks. The attack had taken place under very similar conditions : a headlong charge across an open plain, without infantry accompaniment and against a compact village. The infantry at Norrey were unable to keep up as they were on foot, and at Buron, they were absent from the start. Despite the losses, however, the balance was more favourable at Buron in the sense that one of the sections (Mathis's 3rd), had been engaged opposite Authie and Hermani's tank had destroyed five Canadian tanks (according to N Lorenzen) at a cost of two tanks knocked out in the section. The action opposite Buron, in its early phase, had led to the destruction of several Canadian vehicles including six tanks. Finally, the Panthers still in running order had taken part in the defence around the Abbaye d'Ardenne. It had been an engagement spread out over the entire day with three different sites. The commander, *Ostuf.* von Ribbentrop, claimed the destruction of 27 Canadian tanks, 8 carriers and 4 anti-tank guns. The human losses amounted to 7 dead, 6 seriously wounded (including Gunther Gotha and Gerhard Kaun from "335" and *Uscha.* Josef. Tratnik), and six walking wounded (including Horst Bandow from Hermani's tank and Otto Alish from "335"). According to the victories claimed by the Canadians and sifting through their reports, Lieutenant Barrie had destroyed 6 Panthers with his anti-tank guns (including Mathis's) and Major Radley-Walters had accounted for 3 Panzer IV's. The total of 27 tanks destroyed claimed by von Ribbentrop would seem to be too high, in view of the forces available to him and the losses reported by the Canadians. If they are true, however, they would indicate that the 3rd Company of the 12th SS Pz. Regt. managed to destroy four times more tanks than they lost, or five and a half times if you count everything. At any rate, this detailed study demonstrates the importance of examining the accounts of various eye-witnesses from both sides in order to arrive at accurate figures.

The withdrawal of the *12th SS Panzer Regiment* to the right bank of the Orne

The Canadian offensive continued throughout the day and at 2230 hrs. the infantry of the Regina Rifle Regiment had a foothold on the walls of the Abbaye d'Ardenne. The commander of the 12th SS Pz.Regt., *Ostubaf.* Max Wunsche, had decided to go to the abbey in order to assess the situation. *Ustuf.* Herbet Walther, liaison officer to the commander of the IInd. Battalion had a small Panzer II for his reconnaissance missions and he offered to take Max Wunsche in this vehicle. The two officers arrived at the mediaeval buildings in the middle of an artillery barrage and made their way to the

headquarters of the 25th SS Panzer Grenadier Regiment which was installed near the Saint-Norbert gate. It was there that Max Wunsche arrived at a singular decision and he ordered Walther to report back to the divisional commander, Kurt Meyer at headquarters with the following message : "Wunsche is staying at Ardenne. It will he held to the last man and the last cartridge". In spite of the fact that the regiment needed its commanding officer, Max Wunsche had decided to involve himself in this "suicide" mission. Was it fanaticism or despair ? Kurt Meyer, however, issued the following order : "All those who can march are to withdraw from the abbey in the direction of Caen. Walther returned to the abbey in his Panzer II, and *Ostubaf.* Wunsche had to obey that direct order, withdrawing in the Panther of *Stubaf.* Jurgensen, the commander of the Ist. Bn. of the tank regiment The withdrawal got underway, supported by the remaining 3rd Company tanks, and at midnight the Canadians of the Regina Rifles entered the abandoned buildings. The fight to the last round did not take place. Since landing, the 3rd Canadian Infantry Division had suffered 4,500 casualties, most of them in their confrontation with the "HJ" Division.

During the evening, Panzer Group West, confirmed the order to withdraw issued by the commander of the 12th SS and telephoned (secure from eavesdroping by Ultra) the following order to LXXXVI Corps, I SS Panzer Corps and II SS Panzer Corps : "The bulk of the heavy armaments must be withdrawn from the Caen salient during the night 8/9 July. A sufficient number of infantry reinforced by engineers and forward observers are to stay behind to form a line of resistance running from Calix/Hill 64 (north of Caen)/ northern edge of Saint-Germain/aerodrome south of the eastern limit of Carpiquet. You are not to withdraw to the line east bank of the orne/northern limit of Venoix/northern limit of Bretteville unless attacked by a numerically superior force." (War Diary Panzer Group West, chief-of-staff, Appendix 87). On 7 and 8 July, the 12th SS Pz. Regt. had suffered the following casualties : 3 nco's and 10 men killed ; 2 officers, 8 nco's and 24 men wounded ; 1 officer and 9 men were reported missing ; a toal of 58 canualties.

On **9 July** in the face of pressure from the Allies who had advanced to the centre of Caen, the withdrawal to the far bank of the Orne took place. That day the 12th SS Pz. Regt. suffered further casualties : 2 nco's and 2 men killed ; 1 nco and 5 men wounded ; 8 men listed as missing ; atotal of 18. All that was left north of the Orne were the wrecks of the 12th SS tanks which had been destroyed, and the carcasses of the Panzer IV's of 22nd Pz. Regt. which had been dug-in to the north of Caen. 12th SS Pz. Regt. could only field 32 Panzer IV's and 17 Panzer V's (Panthers), the equivalent of just three companies.

Tigers to the rescue

Even though the armoured counter-attack had been definitively,abandoned, two new battalions of heavy tanks finally arrived at the front. Too late, however, to inhibit the irresistible Allied push.

The 102nd SS Heavy Tank Battalion was allotted to the II SS Panzer Corps which was created in the spring of 1942 and received its title after having taken part in the battles of Kharkov and Kursk. After that the Corps launched two new SS Panzer divisions, the 9th *Hohenstaufen* and the 10th *Frundsberg* in December 1943. The 102nd Battalion, however, did not take part in the armoured corps' campaign in Galicia in April and May 1944. At the time of the Allied landings, the battalion was encamped at Wezep in Holland having only been formed at the beginning of 1944, under the command of *Ostubaf.* Hans Weiss, born on 28 August 1911 at Vohringen on the Iller. He was the son of a brewer and initially chose his father's trade before joining the SS VT in 1933. During the campaign in Poland he commanded the headquarters company of an SS reconnaissance battalion attached to the Kempf Panzer Division where he was wounded and received the Iron Cross Second Class. During the campaign in 1940 he served in the SS *Verfugungs* Division and was awarded the Iron Cross First Class. During the following campaign in the Balkans he commanded one of the companies of the reconnaissance battalion belonging to the *Das Reich* Divison and then went on to Russia where he was several times wounded. In February 1943 he was in command of the 2nd SS Panzer Reconnaissance Battlion , taking part at the head of his unit in the recapture of Kharkov where he surrounded between 5,000 and 6,000 Soviet troops, where, with his small unit and a battle group provided by Heinz Harmel, he completely wiped them out After that important victory which only cost him ten human casualties, the then *Hauptsturmfuhrer* Weiss was decorated with the Knights' cross on 6 April 1943. The "Brown Bomber" as he was nicknamed by his comrades was selected to command the new unit and promoted to *Obersturmbannfuhrer* (lieutenant-colonel) on I July 1944. Seriously wounded near Trun on 19 August, he was captured by the British, dying in a road accident on 2 August 1978.

The 1st Company was commanded by *Ostuf.* Kalls, the 2nd by *Hstuf.* Endemann and the 3rd by *Ostuf.* Siebenlist. By mid-May only the 1st and 3rd companies had received their Tigers, and Endemann was only able to present his company with their tanks on 6 June. The majority of the recruits to the battalion were ethnic Germans (*Volksdeutsche*) from Rumania, but instead of joining the front in Normandy on 13 June, the battalion found itself at Saint-Pol, south of Calais, where the German high command was still expecting a second landing.

Two days later, however, they were again diverted to Paris and camped in the grounds of the chateau at Versailles. From there, on **1 July,** they got underway for the front in Normandy, one section departing every hour. The drivers had to struggle not to fall asleep at the controls on account of the petrol fumes. In addition to that, they had to stop every ten to fifteen kilometres to check the tanks although theoretically the tracks of a Tiger were good for 45 km on a hard surface. The first Tigers only got as far as Rambouillet before they had to stop at 0300 hrs The following day, as night fell, they set off again : the engine temperatures climbed to 110°, the exhaust pipes trailed long jets of flame and the metal engine covers glowed red. Soon, one of the Tigers caught fire and the fire extinguishers were activated. The ventilator was changed, but after only three km it caught fire again, because the new ventilator had been fitted the wrong way round in the hurry and blew hot air back over the engine. The battalion finally reassembled on **4 July** around Cauville (to the south-west of Thury Harcourt), near the headquarters of II SS Panzer Corps which was at Hamars, six km. further to the north. from there the battalion took up holding positions at Vacognes to the south of Evrecy.

On **10 July,** the 102 nd SS Heavy Tank Battalion was at last directed towards Hilll 112 where heavy fighting was still in progress, and the Tigers took up a holding position at the northern exit of Saint-Mar-

The Tiger of the commander of the 1st Section of the 2nd Company of the 102nd SS Heavy Tank Battalion, the « 211 » en route for the Normandy front at the beginning of July. This photo comes from a series showing the battalion's tanks crossing through Falaise. One can also see « 312 » and « 231 ». (ECPA.)

tin which was two km. to the south-east of the hill. In the morning, after an artillery preparation which battered the slopes of Hill 112, seven tanks from the 2nd Company left Saint-Martin, only to encounter a thick smokescreen which blanketed everything. *Ustuf.* Schroif's section was on the left and that of *Ustuf.* Rathsack on the right, under the command of *Hstuf.* Endemann, the company commander. But as they reached

the slopes of Hill 112, the smoke suddenly dispersed. The 88 mm. guns opened fire and the eyes of the tank commanders were rivetted on the small wood located on the south-east slope, although right from the beginning of the attack, radio reception was non-existent. "213" was hit and had to do an about turn, while "212" eliminated an anti-tank gun. *Hstuf.* Endemann moved off to the right and disappeared from the view of the others who by **1000 hrs.** were occupying the slopes of the hill. There they provided fire support for the grenadiers of the 21st SS Panzer Grenadier Regiment, part of the *Frundsberg* Division, but Weiss gave the order to withdraw to the southern slope, to be replaced by artillery barrages and a smokescreen.

On the right, *Ostuf. Ke*lls Ist Company had advanced on Maltot, where English troops had been reported, the Tigers departing from Saint-Martin at high speed. When the four tanks of Baral's section reached the first houses of Maltot, the British opened fire. The following is the account of one of the section's tank commanders, *Uscha.* Willi Fey of "134" : "With determination we forced our Tigers through the hedgerows and found four Shermans in our sights. "Stop tank. The tank furthest to the left. 200 metres Fire". Two shells were enough and then the second from the left suffered the same fate. In the meanwhile, Baral, our section commander had positioned himself near us and he dispatched the third Sherman. The fourth sought safety by fleeing rapidly and was able to escape up the road leading to Eterville. The mission had been accomplished and we did not have any worries about our right flank for the next few hours. For the young

Ostubaf. Hans Weiss, the battalion commander.

Ostuf. Alois Kalls (Knights' Cross 23 Aug. 1944) the commander of the 1st Company.

Uscha. Willy Fey, who scored 88 victories in Normandy.

Above : Trautmann, the radio operator of Tiger « 134 ».

Left, fom top to bottom :
Several of the 1st Company tank commanders in front of a Type « E » Tiger. From left to right, Fey, Esser and Glagow. (Munin.)

Uscha. Willi Fey in Normandy in 1944. (W. Fey.)

were the trees to right and left and the rear of the tank in front. There was then a short halt as we arrived on the slope where the 1st Company formed a large wedge shape with its 14 tanks. Half way up the slope which ran down towards Saint-Martin there was a thick wood where we were to take up our firing positions. The Canadians (author's note – in fact British) had been observing us from the crest right down into the Orne valley where we had refuelled. Under the protection of the creeping barrage which had so impressed us in the morning, the enemy had gained the summit where they had started to dig in and showed no inclination to try conclusions with us, although we were curious about the outcome of such a trial of strength. The bitter struggle for the summit started on that 10 July and later we were to call it the Calvary Hill : there was not a single square metre of soil that had not been churned up over and over again by the shells. In that inferno of heavy weapons we sought cover from which we could entice the enemy, and soon their armour appeared on the horizon although only a half dozen of them. Part of the 1st Company advanced to observe. The tank commander darted a quick glance around the four men below him in the fighting compartment. There was the gun-layer, Albert Laumbarther, just as young as the rest of us, who had come from a motor-cycle unit of the *Das Reich* Division. The loader was Corporal Paul, who originated from Kiev ; his father, an officer, had lost a leg fighting with the *Afrika Korps.* Below us on the left was seated the driver, the 19 year old Corporal Hermann Schmidt, from Thuringia who had already driven Tigers in the East, was an experienced crewman and was counted among the veterans of the company. The same applied to the radio operator, Heinz Trautmann, a brown – haired Bavarian, whose responsibilities included refuelling and firing the machine-gun. He had also fought in Russia in Panzer III's, Panzerr IV's and all the way up to the Tiger. Those were the young lads who in Holland had asked : "What will the war in the West be like ?" Our company commander, Kalls, was in his command tank and gave us our orders by radion, unemotionally but reflectively. The crew did not notice that the temperature inside the tank was climbing. The pilot held the controls, his eyes glancing over the instruments ; speedometer, oil pressure gauge and engine temperature. We advanced and the Shermans opened fire."(1) Three Shermans were rapidly put of action and the other two on the left were finished off with five shells. But then infantry with hand-held weapons surged out and attacked the Tigers which were ordered to retire until the following morning.

At dawn on **11 July** the Tigers resumed the attack to capture the high ground to the north, setting out from the slope that turned towards Aunay, camouflaged in a sunken lane. However, an observation aircraft was circling overhead and ten minutes later, the enemy artillery loosedd of a veritable hurricane of shells on them. The grenadiers kept their heads down and many of them never raised them again. Several Churchill tanks fell victim to the Tigers' guns and then the British brought up anti-tank guns, suffering several losses before getting them in position. For their own protection the British laid down a smokescreen and through that "milk soup", *Uscha.* Fey's Tiger received several hits on

crew of our Tiger, their first engagement in the West had been a great success, and on our way back to Saint-Martin we saw the Shermans buring like torches against a twilight sky. But then it was back into the attack again as we had received orders to attack Hill 112 on a broad front at 2000 hrs, accompanied by grenadiers of the *Hohenstaufen* Division. Everyone scrambled into their places as they had been taught, because our company was going in to the attack in a few minutes. Radio ready ! The operator switched on the two ultra short wave sets which were to his left and put on his headphones and throat mike. The numbers of the frequencies glowed dimly and there was a crackling in the headphones. 2010 hrs. With a click the turret hatch closed, shutting us in on ourselves. The driver set the tank in motion with a slight jerk and we saw through our visors the camouflage branches falling off in front of us. With a grinding noise from the tracks we made a quarter turn to the right, and we set off in a long file as our company climbed the road up the slope littered with branches as thick as a man's arm. All we could see the front and the turret. The company commander gave the order to advance : "Forwards. Full speed ahead !" and when the Tigers got through the smokescreen : "Stop tanks". There they were presented with an ideal spectacle : the British were in front of them only 100 metres away, in the process of evacuating their positions with their carriers laden with men and stores. Two Churchills went up in flames, while shells and machine-gun rounds searched out other targets, but then the company commander ordered the unit to disengage. *Hstuf.* Endemann and his crew were killed during that engagement, but that evening, 11 July, Hill 112 was held by the Tigers who were to guard it during a period of twenty days and twenty nights : they remained entrenched on that strategic position until 2 August, after having received orders to withdraw southwards, having been placed under the *Hohenstaufen* Division the previous evening. The Tigers of the 102nd SS Heavy Tank Battalion were going to be engaged in the area of Vire. On 7 August, near Chenedollé, *Uscha.* Willi Fey destroyed in half an hours, fourteen out of the fifteen British tanks which appeared in front of him. Between 10 July and 20 August, the battalion's score was most impressive, managing to eliminate 227 tanks, 28 anti-tank guns, 19 half-tracks, 4 carriers and 35 lorries, successes due to the power and strength of the Tiger as well as the quality of their crews' training. The highest individual score was attributed to *Uscha.* Willi Fey, born on 25 September 1918 at Lollar in Hesse who had a cold and calculating nature, leavened with dash and dynamism out of the ordinary. As we have seen, he gained his first victories on 10 July and together with his crew and "134" on Hill 112, he accounted for 23 tanks (17 Churchill, 3 Cromwell and 3 Sherman), 3 anti-tank guns and several carriers. At Chenedollé on 7 August he knocked out 14 Shermans in half an hour and made it fifteen by the end of the day. By the end of the battle of Normany his score totalled 88 victories (73 tanks and <15 half-tracks) which made him the most successful tank commander of that campaign. He was decorated with the Knights' Cross on 29 April 1945 and he finished the war in Berlin where he eliminated 8 T 34's with a *Panzerfaust,* before later joining the post-war German army.

Another heavy tank battalion arrived at the front at about the same time. The 503rd Heavy Tank Battalion which had been formed at Neuruppin with a cadre of personnel from the 5th and 6th Panzer Regiments, although it was not fully equipped with Tigers and had several Panzer III's. It was transferred to the southern sector of the Russian front in December 1942 and received its missing Tigers in April 1943. It was involved in the Battle of Kursk and in September, it totted up its victories : 501 tanks destroyed, 388 anti-aircraft guns and 8 aircraft. In the spring of 1944 it was withdrawn to a camp at Ohrdruf in Thuringia to be reconstituted but did not receive its complement of new Tigers until the 11 to 17 June, when the 1st Company was privileged to receive Type "B's", known as *Koenigstiger* (King Tigers). The unit commander was Captain Fromme who succeeded Count Klemens von Kageneck. The 1st Company was commanded by Lieutenant Oemler, the 2nd by Baon von Eichel-Streiber and the 3rd by Captain Walther Scherf who received his Knights' Cross on 23 February 1944. The Headquarters Company was under Captain Wiegand. The battalion received orders to depart for the invasion front at tne end of June and eight convoys transported the unit from

(1) Extract from W Fey's book : *Panzerkampfe im Bild.* P. 184.

The 503rd Heavy Tank Battalion in a village to the east of Caen. Although only a few kilometres from the front line, the scene is illuminated, as the Allied aviation did not intervene at night, picking out the brown and green camouflage. The Tiger « 301 » seen from the back and the front, has its numbers painted in black with a white border was Captain Scherf's tank. The crewmen have the overalls with large pockets and are mixed here with *Luftwaffe* troops. (Photo BA.)

Germany to Paris in five days. They halted at Dreux on 2 July with the front still 200 km away, and in four night stages, the battalion reached the village of Rupierre, between Troarn and Moult, to the east of Caen.

On **7 July,** the battalion was in reserve and experienced the bombardment of Caen, and on **11 July,** it was placed on alert at 5 o'clock in the morning and attached tactically to the 22nd Pz.Regt. Half an hour later, the 3rd Company drove towards Colombelles, and when the lead tank had reached a hamlet 3 km from the objective (Cuverville ?) ; British tanks opened fire. Lieutenant Koppe who commanded one of the Tigers echelloned his section off to the right and the 1st commanded by Sergeant-major (*Feldwebel*) Sachs slanted off to the left, while Baron von Rosen remained on the road with his 3rd Section. One section fired while the other advanced. Thick dust and smoke billowed up between the houses and the British infantry withdrew. The Tigers were not more than 200 metres away from the small settlement where the Shermans were burning, while the rest fled. Two of the latter collided and their crews surrendered, their hands in the air. The British lost a dozen Shermans, and the

Captain Walter Scherf commanded the 3rd Company. His Knights' Cross was awarded on 23 February 1944.

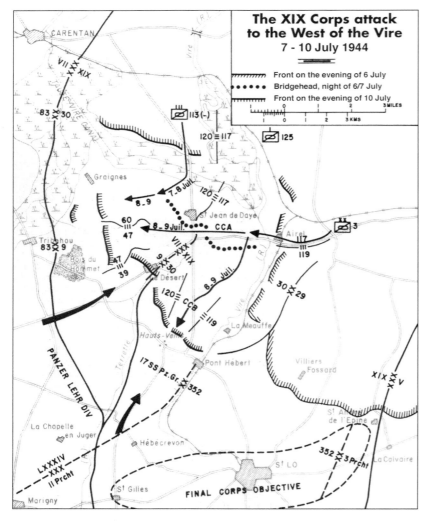

The XIX Corps attack
to the West of the Vire
7 - 10 July 1944

Front on the evening of 6 July
Bridgehead, night of 6/7 July
Front on the evening of 10 July

rienced drivers with him and was able to take the two tanks back under the rockets and salvoes from the machine-guns of the Allied fighter-bombers.

... and to the west, towards the Vire-Taute Canal

While the Panzers were pinned down in the Caen sector by the British Second Army, the First US Army had not had to content with the German armour, with the exception of the few assault guns of the 17th SS Panzer Grenadier Division, *Gotz von Berlichingen*. That unit alone had to withstand the American offensive with their 40 odd *Sturmgeschutze*, but then the 2nd SS Panzer Division *Das Reich* arrived as reinforcements, minus its tank regiment. Only the 2nd SS Assault-Gun Battalion was engaged from the **5 July** in the La-Haye du-Puits area as a part of the *Der Fuhrer* Battle Group, while the assault-guns of the 17th SS Panzer Battalion supported their division's grenadiers to the south of Carentan. From **6 July** the 6/2nd SS Pz.Regt. was at last engaged with the Ist Bn. of the SS Panzer Grenadier Regt ; *Deutschland,* to the side of the 17th SS Pz.Div. The 5th and the 7th Companies of 2nd SS Pz.Regt. were placed under the command of the *Götz von Berlichingen* Division and spread out on the defensive right across the base of the Cotentin peninsular. On **7 July** the front held thanks to the 5th Company which counter-attacked to the north of Sainteny, and that evening the *Das Reich* tanks were spread out as follows : the 2nd SS Assault-Gun Battalion was engaged with the *Der Fuhrer* Regiment battle group (*Kampfgruppe Weidinger*). The 6th Company of the 2nd SS Pz.Regt. with the Ist. Bn. of the *Deutshland* Regiment was placed under the command of 17th SS Pz.Div. to the north-west of St-Lo. The IInd. Bn. of the *Das Reich* tank regiment was placed in reserve behind the positions of the II Parachute Corps. Thus the elements of *Das Reich* were still in the south-west.

On 7 July the Americans launched an offensive with the 9th and 30th Infantry Divisions followed by the 3rd Armoured. The latter unit bumped into the tanks of *Das Reich*, mainly the Ist Bn. of the tank regiment which had started an attack on the axis Périers-Carentan, between Saint-Sébastien-de-Raids and Sainteny with the 4th Company in the lead. *Uscha.* Ernst Barkmann, a 24 years old tank commander, had been in the company for a year, from the time when the first Panthers were received. On **8 July** he destroyed his first Sherman in the thick hedgerow country broken up into small fields (*bocage),* such a difference from the wide plains of the East. On **9 July** the Panthers recommenced their counter-attack at the same time as the 3rd Armoured attempted to force a passage with its CCA towards Tribehou, which was stopped by the German armour at Hill 32 between Pont-Hébert and Saint-Jean-de-Daye.

In the meanwhile the Panzer Lehr Division had arrived to reinforce the sector, and counter-attacked on **II July** towards the Vire-Taute Canal at 0530 hrs The battle group on the right flank was commanded by Major Welsch and consisted of the 902nd Panzer Grenadier Lehr Regiment supported by 20 Panthers from the I/30th Pz. Lehr Regt., aimed at the 3rd Armoured Div. The right flank battle group came under Colonel Scholze and was made up of his 901st Grenadier Regiment assisted by a company of tank destroyers and a dozen Panzer IV's from the IInd. Battalion tasked with attacking the 9th Infantry Div. By 0630 hrs, the American lines had been broken through to a depth of three kilometres,

On 7 July, the Panzer Lehr Division arrived in the sector to be positioned on the left flank of the 17th SS Pz. Gren. Div.

Tigers camouflaged themselves to wait for infantry to arrive. Baron von Rosen got down from his tank to examine the two Shermans and from the papers he found in them, discovered they were from the Royal Armoured Corps. . But suddenly the naval artillery opened up on the small hamlet, and when the bombardment stopped, Captain Scherf reported to the battalion commander on arriving back from hospital. Captain Fromme recovered the two Shermans which had collided but were still in running order. Thus, while the Tigers of the 3rd Company withdrew, Baron von Rosen took two expe-

but after the losses suffered in the battles around Tilly, the division no longer had sufficient resources to maintain the attack. The Panzer IV of Lieutenant Stohr who had been transferred from the 7th to the 8th Company was hit by a phosphorous shell, killing him outright by a splinter in the forehead, and burning the crew alive, whose terrified screams could be heard. Towards midday the skies cleared and fighter-bombers joined in, pinning the grenadiers to the ground and picking off the isolated tanks one by one. Out of the 32 that had set off at dawn, 12 were still advancing and reached the Vire-Taute Canal, although that semi-victory was at the same time a defeat. It had cost too much and the Panzer Lehr Division was too weakened to be able to continue further. In addition to the loss of twenty tanks, 500 grenadiers had been either killed or wounded. The division was placed on the defensive to the west of St-Lo where, two weeks later on 25 July, it was to be more or less anihilated under a carpet of bombs.

As for *Uscha.* Barkmann of the 4th Company of the 2nd SS Pz.Regt., he destroyed two more Shermans on 12 July and immobilised another one with his "424", and went on to make his name during the days to come. At the beginning of August he was recommended for the Knights' Cross.

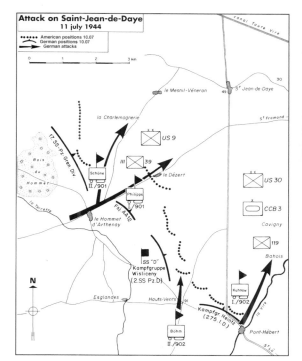

Oscha. Ernst Barkmann, who was born on 25 August 1919 at Kisdorf in Holstein, became well known as a tank commander in the 4/2nd SS Pz. Regt. during July and August 1944, in the rank of *Unterscharfuhrer.* His Knights' cross was awarded on 25 August 1944.

Left : This photo taken on 13 July show two panthers destroyed on either side of a road during the 11 July counter-attack. They belonged to the 1st Company of the 130th Pz. Lehr Regt. which attacked out of Hauts Vents against CCB of the 3rd Armoured Div. (DAVA/coll. Heimdal.)

Preceeding page at bottom : In the centre, Lieutenant Meyer, commander of the 6th Company of the 130th Pz. Lehr Regt. On the right, Lieutenant Peter who replaced Captain Reche at the head of the 8th Company. Peter was killed on 11 July near Babhois. (Coll. H. Ritgen.)

Panzer-Regiment 22

1 and **2**. After their failure on 6 June, some of the tanks of the 22nd Pz.Div. were dug-in. These photos were taken on 13 July along to road leading from Caen to Lebisey, to the north-east of the city on the banks of the Orne. « 134 », a Type « H » Panzer IV of the 1st Company had received a hit which had punched through the plate at the front of the turret in spite of the thickness of 50 mm. A large round hole is visible below the gunner's visor. Note the camouflage.

3. A different tank dug-in in the same area.

4 and **5**. « 612 » a Panzer IV of the 6th Company was recovered intact on 3 July by the Royal Electrical and Mechanical Engineers (REME) who are preparing to tow it away behind a Sherman. It was used for training replacement tank crews arriving from England. Note that the turret numbers were stencilled in white as was the case with the 1st Company tank. (IWM.)

4

5

13

Goodwood
18 to 20 July

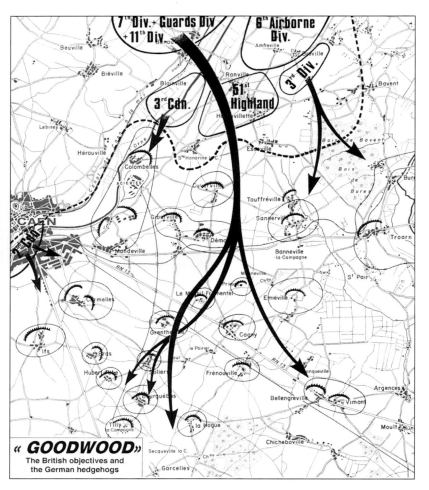

« GOODWOOD »
The British objectives and
the German hedgehogs

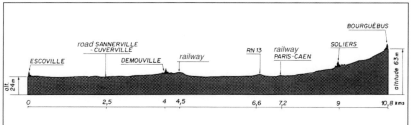

North-south cross section showing the physical obstacles which the British offensive would encounter.

A well prepared defence

After the capture of Caen an important bolt in the front had snapped., and the Germans expected a further operation by Montgomery in that sector, but would it be to the east or west of the city ? On the evening of **17 July,** the commander of Panzer Group West, General Eberbach, was summoned by Field Marshal von Kluge who had arrived to replace Rommel, wounded on that day in a Spitfire attack. Eberbach told him : "We are expecting tomorrow a large-scale attack to be launched from Caen in three directions. Two divisions and two armoured brigades are ready in the bridgehead, there are two divisions and two armoured brigades in

Caen, and in the front line to the east of the city, there are three divisions and an armoured brigade, and in the second line two divisions and two armoured brigades." Von Kluge then asked him which possibility of attack would be the most feasible for the enemy – west of Caen or in the airborne bridgehead to the east of the city ? "Which terrain do you think best for developing the attack ?" Eberbach replied : "The sector facing II Corps between Bretteville-sur-Odon and Juvigny-sur-Seulles." It is true that the battle for Hill 112 was still raging and had intensified since the 15 July, but the Germans were well informed about the threat to the second sector. During the night of 16/17 July, their aircraft had taken flash photos pof the assembly area of the 11th Armoured Division, and on top of that, the interrogation of prisoners had supplied much interesting information. As General Eberbach confirmed, the German command expected that a grand offensive would take place on 18 July.

In effect, General Montgomery had assembled more than 1000 tanks for the new offensive which came to be called Goodwood, and those resources had been gathered together, placed under the command of VIII Corps (General O'Connor) who had three armoured divisions at his disposal :

– The Guards' Armoured Division (General Adair)
– 11th Armoured Division (General "Pip" Roberts)
– 7th Armoured Division – the Desert Rats. (General Erskine)

At that time, each British armoured division had 343 tanks and both the 7th and 11th had been brought up to strength after their losses during Perch and Epsom. Hence the 1000 tanks available for the new offensive.

On their side the Germans were prepared. Thanks to their observation posts , and in particular the one positioned on top of the steel works at Colombelles, as well as their aerial reconnaissance, they were expecting an attack in the area to the northeast of Caen, east of the Orne. Field Marshal Rommel had reinforced that front with two army corps : the LXXXVI commanded by General Obstfelder (346th Inf.Div., 16th Luftwaffe Field Div. 21st Pz.Div.) and the I SS Panzer Corps (272nd Inf.Div., Ist. SS Pz.Div) in a staggered defensive pattern in three lines and a depth of ten kilometres.

The **first line** of defence was a short one between Cuverville and Démouville inclusive, facing north towards the British airborne bridgehead., was held by division of mediocre quality which had been greatly weakened by the fighting of the previous weeks, the 16th Luftwaffe Field Division. Behind them were two battalions of grenadiers from the 21st Panzer Division formed into defensive boxes (hedgehogs) – the I/125th to the west around Giberville, Démouville and Le-Mesnil-Frémental. The grenadier companies were positioned in the villages already mentioned and were supported by Major Alfred Becker's assault-guns : the 1/200 at Démouville, the 2/200 at Giberville, and the 4/200 at Prieuré. The 3/300 was slightly further to the rear, at Grentheville, south of the RN 13. The other

138

grenadier battalion, the II/125 (Captain Wilhelm Kurz) was in position to the east around the villages of (from north to south) Sannerville, Banneville-la-Campagne and Emiéville, where the companies were reinforced by Panzer IV's of the I/22nd at Banneville and the Tigers of the 503rd Heavy Tank Battalion (Captain Fromme). The Tiger I's of 2/503rd (Captain Baron von Eichel-Streiber), the 3/503rd (Captain Walter Scherf) and the formidable Tiger II's of 1/503rd (Lt. Oemler) in the grounds of the Chateau de Manneville.

The **second line** ran from Démouville and was attached to the Caen-Paris railway line. The strongpoint of Mesnil-Frémentel (3/125 and the assault-guns of 4/200) acted as a breakwater in the centre with Cagny where Major Hand von Luck had his headquarters. Behind Mesniland south of the railway, the strongpoint of Grentheville formed yet another breakwater.

The **third line** was in the form of an arc of a circle along the Bourguebus Ridge which with an altitude of 63 metres was 40 metres higher than Démouville. Positioned there were men of the 21st Panzer Reconnaissance Battalion, the 200th Panzer Engineer Battalion, plus the guns of 21st Pz.Div. and 16th Luftwaffe and most importantly the 88 mm. guns of the III Flak Corps.

To sum up, the chosen battlefield was a vast plain of open fields rising gently from the start line in the north (23 Metres altitude) to the crest of Bourguebus Ridge in the south (63 metres). It was ideal country for an armoured attack but the defense had numerous cards up its sleeve. The villages formed strongpoints, the railway cut across the line of advance, forming an obstacle that slowed it down, and finally, Bourguebus Ridge dominated the countryside. Those two obstacles were used by the Germans to advantage as they planted their second and third lines of defence along them, and moreover, they were grouped into a unified command structure. The 16th Luftwaffe Field Division, a mediocre unit was virtually sacrificed in the first line, but behind it, the diverse units in the second line were welded together into *Kampfgruppe Luck,* under the command of Hans von Luck (**Note : he is not a baron – just an ordinary "von"**). In addition to his own regiment, the 125th Grenadiers, he had at his disposal one of the batteries of *Werfer-Brigade 9* (multiple rocket launchers) ? Major Becker's assault-gun battalion (*StuG Abt. 200),* the Panzer IV's of 1/22nd Panzer, around fifty tanks, and most important of all, the Tigers of the 503rd Heavy Tank Battalion. In the third line there were the guns of the 21st Panzer divisional artillery which dominated the battlefield and the formidable 88's of the III Flak Corps which formed the ultimate anti-tank defence, plus the reserves, the most important of which was the I SS Panzer Corps.

But, on 17 July, Squadron Leader Charles Leroux, commander of 602 Fighter Squadron "City of Glasgow", managed to seriously wound Erwin Rommel, near to Vimoutiers, putting the man responsible for the conception of the defence out of action. However, the Luftwaffe had not been idle and had bombed the British assembly areas.

18 July. The start of the attack

Finally it was time for Montgomery to go over to the offensive, he who had been the subject of so much criticism from the Americans. Even the British Air Marshall Tedder, had remarked to Eisenhower, how incompetent Monty was, unable to break through the German lines with its armour, without the Air Force having to mount a huge bombard-

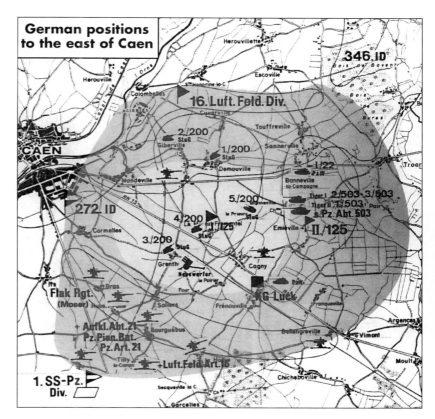

German positions to the east of Caen

ment before the attack at the risk of hitting the Allied front lines.

Curtain up was at **0535 hrs** 1035 Lancasters and Halifaxes of the RAF dropped 5938 tons of bombs between 250 and 1000 kilos. At **0615** 100 heavy bombers of the RAF attacked Cagny. Then, at **0700 hrs** ten "boses" each of Marauders and Bostons of the 9th USAAF attacked the corridor along which the armoured divisions were to roll. However, of the 415 twin-engined bombers involved, only 318 dropped their load on the targets. At **0720 hrs** a bombardment by the 8th USAAF started which lasted until 0930 hrs. Towards midday the sky clouded over which reduced the effectiveness of the Allied air arm.

The bombardment had a devastating effect on the German lines and the Ist. Bn. of 22nd Panzer, attached to the Luck battle group, was right underneath. According to eyewitness statements collected by Paul Carell, the 4th Company suffered particularly, and as they heard the throbbing note of

A 10.5 cm. Field Howitzer 18 mounted on a *Sfl 39 H (f)* chassis of the 200th Assault-Gun Battalion.. 48 of thes self-propelled guns were produced utilising the chassis of French Hotchkiss H-39 tanks married with a 10.5 cm. 18/40 howitzer. That type of gun was particularly powerful with a range of a dozen km. and a rate of fire of between 6 and 8 rounds per minute, protected by an armoured cockpit. Note the geometric pattern of the camouflage in green on a sand-coloured background. (BA.)

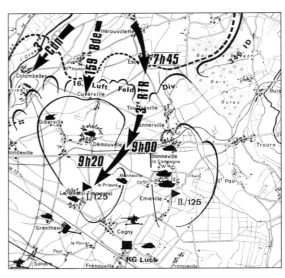

Operation Goodwood. The situation at 0900 hrs.

1. This side view of an assault-gun of the 200th Battalion shows the typical camouflage of such vehicles. (BA.)

2. One of them, a gun from the 2nd Battery was destroyed at Giberville. (IWM.)

Lieutenant Baron von Rosen was the commander of the 3rd section of 3/503. In the absence of his company commander, Captain Scherf, he led the unit into battle at midday on 18 July. Two of his Tigers were mistakenly destroyed by the Flak guns at Cagny. (DR.)

the bomber squadrons, the young crewmen bolted their hatches shut and sought shelter inside the hulls. But they heard the whistling descent of the bombs all around, their tanks were shaken like toys, in some cases overturned and the explosions resounded on the armour plate. Some crew members are said to have committed suicide while others lost their reason. The tanks that were hit, caught fire, and some were simply buried. The damage was also severe for the heavy tank battalion, the 3rd Company of which, commanded by Lieutenant Baron von Rosen, was in position in the grounds of the Chateau de Manneville during the bombardment, and was the most severely effected. His own tank was damaged, that of Sergeant Westernhausen was wrecked by a direct hit, caught fire, and the crew who were sheltering underneath, were killed. The Tiger of Sergeant Major Sachs was overturned by the blast of an explosion, landed up on its turret in a bomb crater and two crewmen were killed on the spot. The blast was terrible and von Rosen himself was unconscious for two hours, before coming to his senses again and reporting to the battalion headquarters which was in the chateau. To get there he had to pick his way through a lunar landscape of bomb craters, to discover that the chateau had been wrecked and that the battalion staff had sought refuge at the top of the staircase tower which had remained intact. Captain Fromme ordered that the surviving tanks should be got in running order, and it was necessary to dig out the tanks and scrape away the earth blocking the engine ventilation apertures. After immense effort, the 3rd Company had eight Tigers available which were sent to counter-attack westwards into the flank of the British armoured columns. The Ist. and 2nd Companies had suffered less damage and were sent a dozen kilometres towards the rear before later being engaged at Cagny. Some of the bomb craters had diameters of between eight and twelve metres. At the end of 1944 the RAF sent an investigation team which discovered the wrecks of fifteen German tanks on the battlefield including the two Tigers of Westernhagen and Sachs.

At **0700 hrs** the artillery barrage which had supported the air bombardment ceased, and at **0745 hrs** the land battle got underway. Eight km of devastated fields and orchards stretched out in front of the 11th Armoured Division, the Shermans of the 3rd RTR crushed a path through an ocean of golden corn and the 16th Luftwaffe had been annihilated by the bombardment. Those who survived were in a state of total shock and unable to fight – more than 430 prisoners were escorted to the rear.

After about an hours, at around **0900 hrs**. the tanks of the 3rd RTR which had been making slow progress against feeble opposition, found themselves faced with the first obstacle, a single-track railway line, which took them ten or fifteen minutes to cross

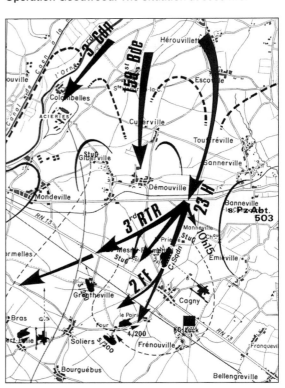

The situation at 1015 hrs.

over, and the main railway line was still further on.

Major Hans von Luck, who had been on leave in Paris had just arrived back at his headquarters, and took immediate steps to deal with the situation. He positioned a Flak battery to the west of Cagny which opened fire at the British armoured columns which were trying to cross the main railway line. By then it was **1015 hrs,** and the tanks of C Squadron of the 2nd Fife and Forfar (11th Armoured Division) were burning on the plain.

At the same time, Major Becker arrived to report to von Luck that he had lost one of his batteries of self-propelled guns (1/200) at Démouville as a result of the bombing, but two were intact and supporting I/125. The other two were supporting the II/125, Major Kurz's battalion. Major Becker's assault-guns were to intervene against the vanguard of the British armoured spearhead and cross the fire of their 7.5 and 10.5 cm guns with that of the an-

ti-aircraft battery at Cagny. It was **1015 hrs** and the 5/200, based at Prieuré had hardly started to engage the tanks of the 23rd Hussars when they had to withdraw to Four, south of the main railway line.

From Grentheville, some anti-tank guns and a dozen assault-guns (3/200) tangled violently with the lead Shermans of the 3rd RTR. Suddenly three of Major-becker's assault-guns emerged from a small wood on the left and in a few minutes, most of the tanks of Sergeant Cresswell's troop were destroyed, and to escape from that threat, the British tanks slanted off to the right. By then it was **1100 hrs** and the infantry was not following behind the tanks as they were held up by the villages were the German defenders had formed their hedgehog strongpoints – Cuverville, Démouville.

Von Rosen's Tigers attacked by anti-aircrft guns

The 3rd RTR was making good progress and its lead elements, in spite of the losses, were already in sight of Hubert-Folie at the foot of Bourguebus Ridge. Montgomery felt exultant and began to prepare his victory announcement. But as the tanks were advancing down "Tank Alley" the infantry was still making slow progress through the village strongpoints and the Germans launched counter-attacks against the flanks of the British advance.

In the meanwhile, after several hours of effort under the command of Lieutenant von Rosen, the men of the 3/503 had succeeded in clearing the earth out of the engine compartments and getting the eight remaining tanks in fighting order, ready to leave the gounds of the Chateau de Mannerville and attack westwards into the flank of the enemy armoured columns. This was von Rosens account of what happened : "We were to form a new defensive line to the south-west of Mannerville. We were surrounded by bomb craters, some of which were ten metres in diameter and the tank drivers could only move with difficulty through that lunar landscape, which had once been a labyrinth of hedgerows. I was preparing to advance in the direction of Prieuré". But to do so the Tigers had to defile past the Flak battery at Cagny and its crews, who were experts in aircraft recognition but did not know the difference between the various models of tank. They opened up with everything they had and destroyed two of von Rosen's tanks : Sergeant Major Schonrock's was hit and set on fire by an anti-tank

Near Emiéville, the I/22 Pz.Regt. was to a large extent annihilated under the hail of bombs at dawn on 18 July. Above are two of their tanks, one of which was completely overturned. The left hand track was blown off and one can see the suspension of the pairs of running wheels.

tank commanders saw below them the Shermans of the 23rd Hussars, apparently halted. They drove down from the ridge in fighting formation, catching their enemy by surprise, managing within a few seconds to knock out four Shermans which caught fire. Captain Balckman and Sergeant Barteman of the 23rd each accounted for a Panther, but seconds later their own tanks were in turn destroyed. The remainder selected reverse gear, refused battle, fired away with everything they could and sought refuge behind the nearest hedgerows, which proved to be precarious boltholes. Almost every five minutes, a Panther fired an armour piercing shell, which with a piercing whistle, hit a Sherman, creating a sharp crack as it went through the armour plate, followed by a shower of sparks and a jet of flame from the crippled tank. The blackened survivors baled out as fast as possible from the wrecks which continued to shudder with dull thuds as the ammunition exploded inside from the effects of the heat. Nevertheless, B Squadron of the 23rd Hussars exchanged blow for blow, supported by A Squadron which had come up on the right, and to the left, C Squardon which had managed to get to within 300 metres of Four thanks to a dip in the ground. The latter squadron's tanks had seen the Panthers heading towards Cagny and managed to knock out two of them, but by opening fire, revealed their position to the defenders of Four who opened up at point blank range. In less than a minute sixteen Shermans had been knocked out without the British being able to reply, and the survivors departed back to their own lines on foot. The 1st SS Pz. Div's. Panther battalion claimed 40 victories over the 23rd Hussars and its attached units, of which the 2nd Company of Hstuf. Malkomes alone had accounted for 20 of them. On the other hand, a British eye-witness, John Thorpe, spoke of Tiger II's (King Tigers) which could well have been those of 1/503, which were to the south-east of Cagny, towards Vimont, and could have engaged the flank of the 23rd Hussars column. General Eberbach had given them the task of mounting an attack in conjunction with the 1st SS Pz. Regt. and thus the company could have intervened in the battle. Anyway, in spite of its successes, the Panther battalion of 1st SS failed to push home its advantage, contenting itself with advancing as far as Soliers, having broken the assault of the 23rd Hussars, but hesitating to advance as far as the railway line which would have brought it within range of the British artillery. There was no longer any chance of throwing the British back into the sea and all that could be done was to go over to the defensive along Bourguebus Ridge. However, the balance was totally in favour of the Germans who had managed to halt the British advance, and that battle between the tanks of the LAH and the 23rd Hussars effectively marked the end of fighting to the south of the offensive on that 18 July.

shell, and Sergeant Major Muller's received a hit that went straight through. Other tanks simply caught fire on account of the damage to their engines caused by the bombing, although von Rosen thought at the time that he had come up against British anti-tank defences. The effect on the morale of his men, however, was disastrous, and they withdrew back to Manneville to form a defensive front : of the eight tanks of the 3rd Company that had set out only one returned intact.

Peiper's counter-attack

The leading tanks of the 3rd RTR arrived at Hubert-Folie at **midday**, and a little more than half an hour later, the well camouflaged 88 mm Flak guns posted on Bourguebus Ridge opened up on them. From **1400 hrs** the tanks of the 3rd RTR and G Company of the RB were forced to retire back to the railway line. The guns of the III Flak Corps had stopped Montgomery's offensive dead.

A few hours later, German reinforcements counter-attacked into the mass of British tanks, and the 1st Battalion of the tank regiment of the 1st SS Pz.Div., the Leibstandarte, became engaged from Bourguebus Ridge, when the Panther battalion entrered the fray under the direct command of the regimental commander, Ostubaf. Jochen Peiper. It was by then **1830 hrs** and the battalion had been on the road since midday, coming from the south-west. After crossing the crest of the ridge, Peiper and his

The Guards take on a Tiger II

Elsewhere in "Tank Alley" the 11th Armoured Division had been followed by the Guards Armoured. Division which was in view of Cagny at 1000 Hrs. before deploying further to the east, but it was held up there for more than six hours, faced by the resistance of elements of the II/125th and the threat posed by the Tigers of the 503rd Heavy Tank Battalion. The 2nd Irish Guards lost 9 Shermans as they advanced towards Vimont, while the Coldstream Guards in trying to get round Cagny to the west, were caught by the fire of assault-guns positioned at the Prieuré farm. Lieutenant Liddle's Sherman was set on fire, Sergeant ferguson's MW was hit and brewed up, and then it was the turn of the Firefly of Sergeant Mcnally. The rockets from the *Nebelwerfer* had hailed down on them sowing confusion, which stopped the Guards Division in its tracks, unable to advance further south-east. The Luck Battle Group had halted that elite formation with the support of the assault-guns, the Panzer IV's and the Tigers of the 2nd and 3rd Companies of the 503rd.

But the Irish Guards resumed their advance and at around **2100 hrs** saw in the distance a King Tiger, a Tiger I and two old model Panzer IV's, the crews of which were sitting under the apple trees around their commander. Lieutenant Gorman was at the head of the 2nd Squadron of the Irish Guards and viewed the scene – the Germans were taken completely by surprise and raced for their tanks which were facing in the opposite direction. "Gun jammed, sir" came the sad voice of Guardsman Schole, Gorman's gun-layer. The Tiger II turned its heavy turret slowly towards Gorman and the two M4's which were accompanying him. "Driver, go right. Ram it. Shouted Gorman, and his tank burst through the hedge, raced over the field, slipped in under the barrel of the 88 mm gun and crashed to a stop against the rear right sprocket wheel of the Tiger II. Revolvers in hand and armed with grenades, the Irish crew leaped out and took the German crew prisoner. At that moment the other Tiger got sergeant harbison's Sherman in its sights and up it went in flames, the crew baling out with some losses. Profiting from the diversion, Gorman's crew decided to make themselves scarce, but then he took over a Firefly and began to chase the Tiger I, hitting the turret with his sixth round. His second target was the Tiger II together with his own Sherman which he had abandoned, and the latter caught fire rapidly, spreading the fire to the Tiger. Gorman was decorated with the Military Cross and his Tiger II, the first to be destroyed in Normandy was one of five tanks knocked out by the Guards, for the loss of 32 of their own.

The 11th Armoured Division had lost 129 tanks during the day. The 2nd FFY was more or less annihilated, as only 16 of its tanks escaped, but it had accounted for six Panthers, two Panzer IV's, five assault guns and three 88's. The 3rd RTR had suffered serious losses at Grentheville and then Hubert-Folie. Those balances demonstrated the scale of Montgomery's defeat and his armoured offensive had exhausted itself at the foot of Bourguebus Ridge. The following two days of fighting were nothing more than local adjustments to territory captured during the early hours of 18 July.

In total, VIII Corps had had lost 197 tanks to the German defence : 126 for the 11th Armoured Division, 60 for the Guards and 11 for 7th Armoured. On the German side 30 Panzers had been destroyed in combat.

19 and 20 July

The Germans had achieved a significant success but did not have any reserves to throw into the battle. The units of the 1st SS Panzer Corps relieved the men of the 21st Pz.Div. who were exhausted and tactical groups from the Ist. and 12th SS were fitted into the line. Shortly after midnight on 18 July, Ju. 88's bombed the Allied tank concentrations, causing further losses.

On **19 July,** the British wore themselves out in various struggles. At 1600hrs they were unable to take Bourguebus in the face of the grenadiers of the LAH supported by several Tigers of the 503rd At

1840, an armoured force composed of Tigers and Panthers counter-attacked, but the Typhoons called up were able to rescue the men of the 5th RTR, and forced the panzers to withdraw to the shelter of the Bois de la Hogue from where they kept up their interdicting fire in a north-easterly direction.

Towards the east, the *Kampfgruppe* Waldmuller from the 12th SS began to take up positions at 0530hrs on either side of the Cagny-Vimont road, finalising the deployment towards midday. The "Krause battalion took up a position tothe right of KG Waldmuller while those grenadiers from the 12th SS were supported by the 8/12th SS Pz.Regt. under the command of Ostuf. Herbert Hofler, on the right of the road between the avenue leading to the Chateau Saint-Pierre and the hamlet of Franqueville, as well as the 1st Company of tank destroyers of the 12th SS Anti-Tank Battalion, commanded by *Ostuf.* Hurdebrink. The latter unit was equipped with the formidable Mark IV tank-des-

The fighting on 28 July 1944

1. From 1100 hrs to 1500 hrs.

2. From 1500 hrs to 1900 hrs.

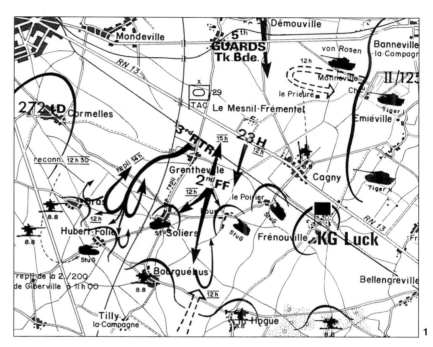

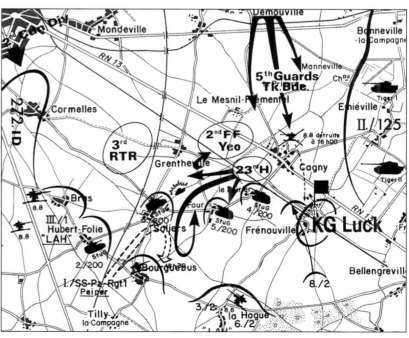

A prisoner, an artillery-man of a Major Becker 4 Stud, still distressed by the Air Raid. (IWM.)

Another prisoner. The face covered with dust, this young tankist is wearing a Feldnütze - Model 42. He is also wearing a grey under-shirt as protection treillis in reed-green linencloth. His look is still distresed by the Air Raid he just lived, through witness of the unrelenting power of the Allies' equipment. (IWM.)

Hereunder : The day of July 19. (Heimdal map.)

with the 75 mm. Pak 39/L48. The Panthers of the mixed armoured battalion of the 'HJ' Division were in offensive reserve around Argences and Vimont. In spite of the threat of a carpet of bombs, they were unable to place themselves further to the rear because of a shortage of crossings over the Muance and in an emergency, the tanks risked being cut off.

In that sector at **0900 hrs** the Cromwell tanks of the reconnaissance regiment of the Guards Armoured Division went over to the offensive, and Lieutenant Peel, commanding the Firefly of the 5th Section, immobilised a Tiger which was then set on fire by the Cromwells. That division began its offensive at 1700hrs and captured Frénouville although the tank destroyers of the 12th SS knocked out two of the Guards' tanks on the RN13. During the afternoon the Luftwaffe made a rare appearance when some Me109's strafed the battlefield.

On **20 July** thundery rain fell all over the battlefield sinking any further hopes for the Allied offensive. A severe thunder storm even burst out at teatime, transforming the whole area into a bog, impassable even for the tanks. Bourguebus fell into the hands of the 5th RTR at **0800 hrs** where they destroyed a Tiger. Allied air reconnaissance, however, showed that the German defensive positions had even been further strengthened, the 88's being based along two ridgelines to the south of Bourguebus. During the morning the 4th CLY of the 7th Armoured Division succeeded in penetrating as far as the Beauvoir farm, south of It. At 1000hrs the "Desert Rats" took on a unit of Panzer IV's, and having called for an artillery strike, all the panzers were destroyed. Such a concentration of artillery, 216 guns, on such a small surface enabled the elimination of two Tigers and seven Panzer IV's. At Bras, a counter-attack by seven Tigers, while the 159th Brigade was in process of being relieved by the 2nd Canadian Brigade, caused a lot of confusion, but the M10's of the 3rd RCA/AT restored the situation, destroying two of the Tigers. During the evening at 2000hrs. General Dempsey issued orders to all units to disengage. On **21 July**, VIII Corps was relieved by the II Canadian Corps, thus ending Operation Goodwood.

On 20 July while the thunder rumbled in the skies over Normandy, news arrived of the attempt to assassinate Hitler. In spite of the fact, however, that several generals from Army Group B were implicated in the conspiracy, the news had little impact on the men in the frontline. "Goodwood" had started with the news of Rommel having been put out of action and ended with the plot against Hitler.

Balance

The offensive represented a defeat for Montgomery which cost the Allies a total of 314 tanks lost. For 18 July, 197 tanks and on 19 July, 99 more. The attack was brought to a halt and the result was a certain defensive victory for the Germans, who, however, had lost more than a hundred tanks in the battle. What is important is that even if the British had lost 314 tanks, only 140 of those were definitively written off, whereas the Germans had no more reinforcements of men or material. Seen from that angle, the operation was an Allied success in that it had written down the Germans' defensive capability and mobilised their last reserves, rendering them incapable of putting up such a spirited defence against the next offensive when it came.

That defenitive success has always been held up as an example, and even today, several armies which follow a defensive strategy, such as Sweden, send their officer cadets to the Goodwood battlefield to learn how to conduct an anti-tank defence. Above all it was the 88 mm. guns of III Flak Corps which played the decisive role, and as far as armoured vehicles were concerned, it was Major Becker's home-made assault-guns that proved themselves in the field. Peiper's Panthers achieved a remarkable surprise whereas on the other hand, the Panzer IV's of the 22nd Pz.Regt. played an unobtrusive role, whereas the Tigers suffered heavy losses. The 3rd Company in effect left the front, to be reequipped with Tiger II's, under the orders of Captain Scherf, but did not reappear in Normandy.

The defeat of the Panzers

On the evening of 20 July, even though the front had been held once again the north-east of Caen, there had been a significant loss of ground and the final defeat of the Panzers had become obvious. There was no longer any question of counter-attacking and even if the American troops stymied in the "bocage" country by an aggressive defence, could say "we could see the war lasting for twenty years", the German front had been used up. The only reserves were the divisions that were being thrown in one after the other, but there were no replacements for the losses : on 17 July, those losses had amounted to 100,000 men, while at the same time the Allies continued their build-up. To the West, the Americans could bring three armoured divisions into the line ready to take the offensive, due to take place on 25 July. That was the great stampede, hardly inconvenienced by the German counter-attack at Mortain, and a month later, the Panzers which had escaped destruction, retreated to the Seine, together with those of the divisions which had arrived too late, the 116th and the 9th Pz. Divs. The real course of the battle was determined during the few days following the initial landings.

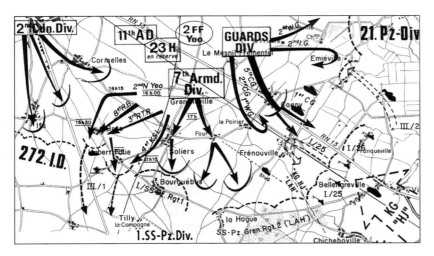

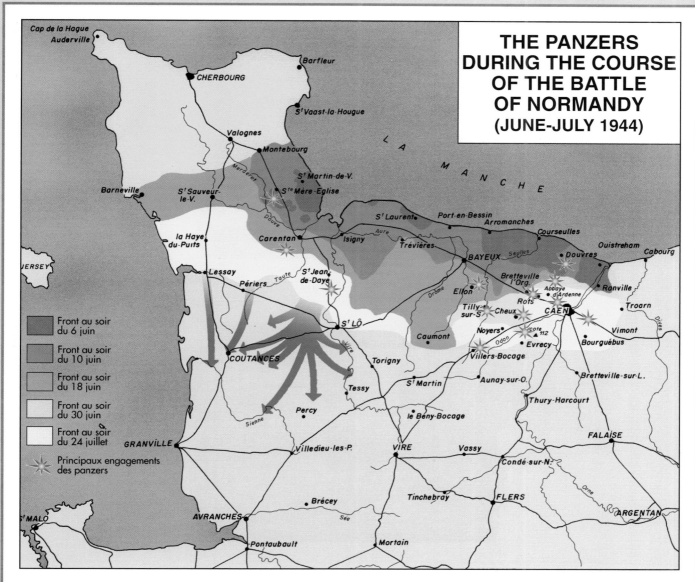

THE PANZERS DURING THE COURSE OF THE BATTLE OF NORMANDY
(JUNE-JULY 1944)

Front au soir du 6 juin

Front au soir du 10 juin

Front au soir du 18 juin

Front au soir du 30 juin

Front au soir du 24 juillet

Principaux engagements des panzers

Mid-July 1944. A Panther tank covered with camouflage branches advancing through the middle of a ruined village. From the large size of the numbers painted on the turret which were habitually seen on vehicles of the I/6th Pz. Lehr Regt. (Panzer Lehr Division) one can assume that the tank belonged to that unit. The number « 200 » indicated that it was the 2nd company commander's tank.

(Archives départementales du Calvados.)

145

Schwere SS-Panzer-Abteilung 101

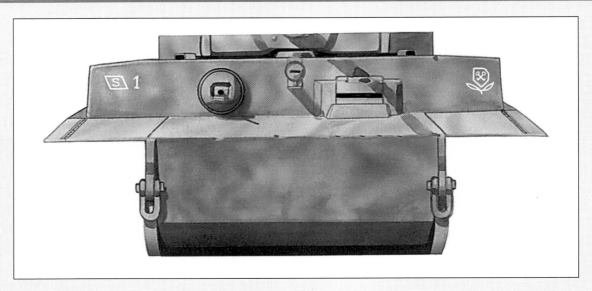

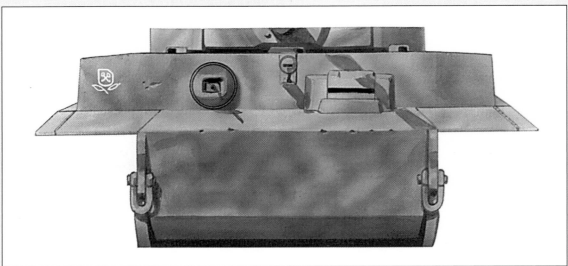

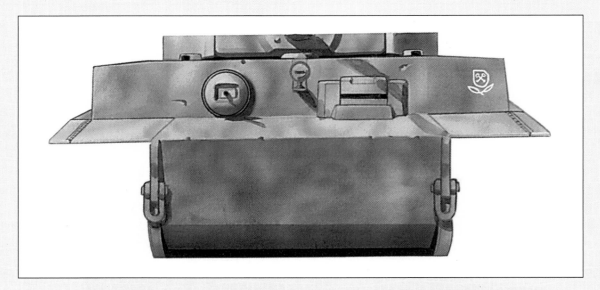

Specific markings on the tanks of the 101st. SS Heavy Tank Battalion, of which each company had its own way of marking the tactical identifications on the front of its Tigers. The 1st Company had on the left a rhombus shape with an « S » for *Schwere* (=heavy) followed by a « 1 ». On the right was the insignia of the corps slightly pointed at the base. For the 2nd Company the corps insignia was on the left, rounded at the base. The 3rd Company had the same insignia, but placed on the right.

Rear identification markings of the Tiger I's of the 101st SS Heavy Tank Battalion. Left above : the pointed corps insignia on the left and the rhombus with the « S » on the right. The numbers were painted in red outlined in white. Tiger « 122 » was *Uscha*. Arno. Salamon's tank, and « 223 » was commanded by *Oscha*. Jurgen Brandt, who destroyed three Shermans at Villers-Bocage on 13 June.

(Paintings Heimdal.)

When the 101st SS Heavy Tank Battalion was on the way to the front line in June 1944, a column of army vehicles passed the Tigers which were parked beside the road to hide them from the view of Allied aircraft. The tanks and vehicles were covered with branches to confuse the fighter-bombers which were particularly active over the German rear areas in Normandy. (BA.)

The 301st Remote-controlled Panzer Battalion

When formed on 9 September 1942, the 301st Battalion originated out of the first unit to put remote-controlled tanks (*Funklenk*) tanks into service, the Panzer-Abteilung (Fkl)) 300, which was formed on 9 February 1942 and in its turn had originated from the 1st. Mine Clearance Battalion. IN 1944 one of its companies, the fourth, was detached to the Western front while the rest of the battalion remained in Russia. That company was attached to the 2nd Pz. Div. from June to September 1944, after which time it returned to its parent unit in the East. During its engagement in Normandy, the company fielded 10 assault-guns and 36 explosive charge carriers (*Ladungstrager B IV Sd. Kfz. 301*).

The photographs on these two pages show two assault-guns of the 4th Company moving up to the front and the tactical insignia of the remote-controlled tank units is clearly visible : a white painted rectangle in the centre of another rectangle symbolising the German armoured units. The letter « 4 » which can be seen at the side indicated a 4th Company vehicle as did the first number of « 421 », on which at least 27 men have found room to perch. That vehicle, represented in the painting, was a Type « G » Mark III assault-gun, based on a Type « M » Panzer III chassis, of which 242 examples were built and can be easily identified by their prominent exhaust pipes.

(ECPA/Peinture : E. Groult.)

17th SS Panzer Battalion

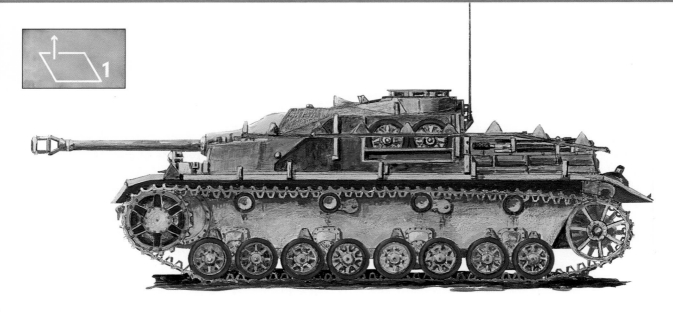

The 17 SS Pz.Div. *Gotz von Berlichingen* was the only unit of German motorised infantry engaged in Normandy, created on 3 November 1944, and formed up around Angoulême in France. Like all the units of its type, it was not equipped with tanks, and instead fielded a battalion of assault-guns, the 17th SS Pz.Bn. This was engaged on 13 June in support of the 6th Parachute Regiment and other elements, thrown in to counter-attack and recapture Carentan.

Left. This assault-gun (StuG) IV from the 1st Company of the 17th Bn. (one can see the figure « 1 » on the tactical insignia) was destroyed on the road between Carentan and Périers, near the crossroads with the D223 leading to Baupte and La Haye-du-Puits, Carentan itself lying about 3.5 km to the north. The scene was photographed on the 19 June, a week after the defeat of the German counter-attack. In the foreground, American parachutists from the 101st Airborne Division are manning a 57 mm anti-tank gun, positioned to repel any further attempt by German armour. (DAVA.)

Below. The same place as it appears today, as well as a running wheel from a StuG found nearby. (Photos et peintures : E. Groult/Heimdal.)

The *Das Reich* Division had been based in the south-west of France since February 1944 and its leading elements started to arrive in Normandy on 16 June, having become entangled with the resistance during its march to the front line. The public hangings at Tulle (99 dead) and the horrific massacre at Oradour-sur-Glane (642 dead) will for ever remain associated with name of the division. Even though the tank regiment was not involved in those reprisals, only 60 % of its effective combat strength was available when it arrived in Normandy. Held in reserve in the St-Lo area, the entire division did not fight together until July and in the meanwhile only small battle groups were thrown into sectors of the front in crisis.

Above. The Sd. Kfz. 7/1 was an 8 ton half-track tractor fitted with an armoured cab and on which was mounted a quadruple-barrelled 20 mm. anti-aircraft gun (*Flakvierling 38*). The tactical insignia painted on the left hand side at the rear of the vehicle identifies it as belonging to the anti-aircraft section of the 9th (headquarters) Company of 2nd SS Pz. Regt., and was captured intact by the Americans during their advance. (Peinture : E. Groult/Heimdal.)

Below. On 9 July 1944, a column of Sherman tanks drove past two Type « J » Panzer IV's belonging to the 6/2nd SS Pz. Regt. near Saint-Fromond, during the time when the Germans were attempting to block the American advance towards St-Lo. The two tanks had been put out of action by the men of the 117th Infantry Regiment (30th Inf.Div.). The insignia of the 2nd SS, the « runes of combat » can clearly be seen on the left of the rear hulls of the two tanks. (DAVA.)

12th SS Panzer Division

First engaged on 7 June, the 12th SS fought bitterly in an attempt to force the Allies back into the sea and then to hinder the capture of Caen. From 25 June, the division fought to stop Operation Epsom, the object of which was to outflank Caen from the west, during which time it suffered severe losses. Cheux, Fonteney-le-Pesnil and Rauray were some of the villages which were bitterly fought over and around which the German resistance was organised.

Photo right. During the fighting a group of SS grenadiers assembling in Fonteney-le-Pesnil before counter-attacking with the support of the Panthers of I/12th SS Pz.Regt. (Coll. Heimdal.)

Below left. The same view today, taken looking west along the road which leads to Caumont-l'Eventé, level with the intersection with the D139 which goes off to the left, running south towards Rauray, 2 km distant.

Above right. A recent view of the Chateau de Rauray, which between 9 and 26 June, housed the headquarters of the divisional tank regiment. During that period, the regimental commander, *Ostubaf.* Max Wunsche pinned medals on men from his unit, and on the left is his deputy, *Hstuf.* Georg Iseke. This event took place in front of one of the outbuildings situated just to the south of the chateau. One can recognise the windows in spite of the fact that the roof has since been raised. During the fighting the headquarters had to retire to Grainville-sur-Odon, two kilometres away.

(Photos actuelles : E. Groult/Heimdal.)

After the loss of Caen on 9 July, the *Hitlerjugend* Division was pulled out of the front line to be reconstituted. Only one battalion of infantry and the artillery regiment remained in the line, attached to the 1st SS Pz.Div. Following the severe losses incurred during four weeks of fighting, the other units were refitted in the Potigny area, half way between Falaise and Caen . On the evening of 16 July, a battle group from the division was moved to the Lisieux area to form a mobile reserve behind the 711th Infantry Division, engaged to the east of the Orne. Put on alert during the afternoon of 18 July, the various elements of the division were finally engaged on the following day as and when they arrived on the scene, to oppose the Goodwood offensive to the south-east of Caen.

These photos were taken in Soumont-St-Quentin, a neighbouring village to Potigny on the other side of the N158, show two Panthers probably belonging to 12th SS Pz. Regt. As an indication that they were distant from the front, the muzzle brakes of their guns had their covers on. On the other hand, the electricity pole seems to have suffered battle damage. One of the tanks is a command version, easily recognised by its multi-branch antenna. In the upper photograph one can see a sign on the ground indicating the headquarters of *Brigadefuhrer* Walkter Staudinger, who commanded the Panzer Group West's artillery component after the staff of that armoured group was reconstituted after the bombing on the evening of 10 June. (ECPA.)

Right. The church at Soumont-St-Quentin in 1990. The site has altered greatly as a result of the rebuilding of the village in the 1950's. The small cemetery around the church was transferred to the entrance to the village and the small surrounding wall was demolished. (Photo S. Varin.)

503rd Heavy Tank Battalion

(BA.)

Formed at Neuruppin on 16 April 1942 around a cadre of troops from the 5th and 6th Panzer Regiments, the 503rd Battalion was sent to the Eastern front in December, where it remained until May 1944. Brought back to Ohrdruf in Germany it was completely re-equipped in mid-June with 45 Tigers, including 12 Tiger II's (King Tigers) for the 1st Company. Shortly afterwards it was moved to the West to reinforce the German units which were trying to repel the Allied landings. The transfer by rail got underway on 26 June and the trains went via Mayence, Sarrebourg, Nancy, Paris and Versailles to finish up at Houdan and Dreux which were reached by the last convoys on 5 July. From there the tanks proceeded by road and reassembled on 7 July around Rupierre, a hamlet situated between Troarn and Canteloup, fifteen km. to the east of Caen. During the move the battalion lost Sergeant Major Seidel's tank, the « 323 » which broke through a bridge between Mezidon and Canon. After having been briefly attached to the 16th Luftwaffe Field Division , passed under the command of the 22nd Pz. Regt. and on 18 July it formed one of the supports of the German defence in the sector attacked by the british in Operation Goodwood. In the course of that day the battalion accounted for 40 Allied tanks against 13 own losses. Captain Walter Scherf's 3rd Company suffered the most damage, having been subjected to the full force of the preliminary air bombardment. The company had two days later to hand over its remaining four tanks to the 2nd Company, before being sent to Mailly-le-Camp in Champagne where it received 14 new Tiger II's.

A Tiger I of the 3rd Company of the 503rd Battalion, bearing the number « 301 » which theoretically was that of the company commander, Captain Walter Scherf. In the photo above he can be seen in the turret of his Tiger II after the company had been re-equipped with those 69 ton tanks at the end of July. The rounded outline of the turret of the King Tiger identifies it as having been made by Henschel. (Peintures : E. Groult/Heimdal.)

Tiger II
of *1./ s.Pz.Abt. 503*, the first
company in the German army to have received this type of tank. This one, seen in July in the
park of Canteloup castle, east of Caen is disposing
of a Porsche turret which equipped the first fifty
units, the following units having then received the
Henschel turret. With an armor made of inclined
plates up to 150 mm (5,1") thick on front chassis
and 180 mm (7") on turret mask, Tiger II was a
practically invulnerable vehicle on battlefields while
its 88 mm/71 calibre gun made it redoutably mur-
drous. Its weight and measurement have however
always widely encumbered qualities of this
panzer.

Hereunder : Panzer IV of Panzer-Regiment 22 guetting over the railway between Caen and Troarn some time before « Goodwood » operation.

Opposite : Same place in 1991.

1st SS Panzer Regiment

The tank regiment of the 1st SS Panzer Division *Leibstandarte Adolf Hitler,* the unit was commanded during the Battle of Normandy by *Obersturmbannfuhrer* Jochen Peiper (photo left). When it arrived at the front, the regiment fielded 98 Panzer IV's and 79 Panzer V's Panther. The latter which formed the 1st Battalion played a decisive role in defeating Operation Goodwood, launched to the east of Caen in 18 July. The tank pictured below is a Type « G » Panther as seen on the Champs Elysée when the regiment paraded through Paris on its way to the front. The camouflage consisted of large green blotches and it carried no markings other then the German cross (*Balkenkreux*) roughly painted on the front. The small measurements of the latter are explained by the easily identified silhouette of the tank which could thus dispense with highly visible national markings. Note the wire netting rolled around the gun barrel which served to fix camouflage branches.

(Photo : DR./Peintures : E. Groult/Heimdal.)

As its markings indicate, this Panther « RO2 » seen below in profile belonged to the regimental staff, and to be precise, the deputy commander. It was photographed while the crew were busily camouflaging it with branches to blend in with the hedge alongside which it was positioned. Quite uncommonly, this tank carried a superb personal insignia which represented a panther spring through a circle traversed by a lighting flask. Incised in the *Zimmerit*, the letters LSSAH leave no room for doubt as to which unit the vehicle belonged.(BA/Peinture : E. Groult.)

Insignia of the German armoured units engaged in Normandy

Army Divisions

2. Panzer-Division

9. Panzer-Division

21. Panzer-Division

116. Panzer-Division

Panzer-Lehr-Division

Panzer-Lehr-Division
(variante)

**Panzer-Lehr
Regiment 130**

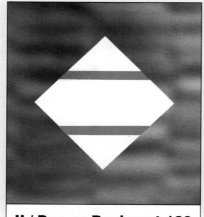

II./ Panzer-Regiment 130

II./ Panzer-Regiment 130

Waffen SS Divisions

1. SS-Panzer-Division
« Leibstandarte SS Adolf Hitler »

2. SS-Panzer-Division
« Das Reich »

9. SS-Panzer-Division
« Hohenstaufen »

10. SS-Panzer-Division
« Frundsberg »

12. SS-Panzer-Division
« Hitlerjugend »

17. SS-Panzergrenadier-Division
« Götz von Berlichingen »

Two Mark IV assault-guns in the Normandy « bocage » country in July 1944, one apparently towing the other. These two vehicles probably belonged to the 17th SS Panzer Grenadier Division. (Ullstein.)

Brigades and Independent Units

Sturmgeschütz-Brigaden

Sturmgeschütz-Brigade 341

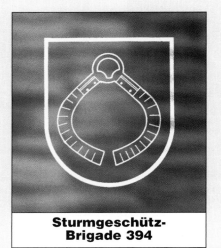

Sturmgeschütz-Brigade 394

Sturmgeschütz-Brigade XII (LL)

Heavy Tank Units

s. Panzer-Abteilung 503

s. SS-Panzer-Abteilung 101

s. SS-Panzer-Abteilung 102

Report on the situation of the German armoured force in Normandy, presented to Hitler on 28 June 1944, by Colonel-General Guderian, General Inspector of Panzer Troops.

Der Generalinspekteur der
    Panzertruppen

Nr. 052/44 g.K.

The 28.6.44

Report presented to the Führer on 28.6.44

1.) Combat fitness of the armoured formations involved

The panzer divisions have been considerably battered, but after 21 days in action, the troops are extraordinarily fresh and inclined to take the offensive.

2.) The following measures are both urgent and indispensable for conserving this attack force :

    a). reducing the wastage of manpower

    b). Increasing the tonnage of re-supply

As far as a), is concerned, up until the evening of 24 June, Panzer Lehr Division, the *Hitlerjugend* and 21st Panzer Division have each lost 2.600 men. The daily losses - without particularly heavy fighting - are running at 100 men per Division. The setting up of replacement infantry battalions has been ordered by the General Inspector, one of which is already in transit, two will arrive on 2 July and six others probably by 15 July. This reinforcement is destined to build up the strength of the divisions, as otherwise, no matter how valorously they fight, they will simply be consumed by attrition.

The losses of manpower and vehicles are caused by the total air superiority of the enemy, and the human casualties are greater than the loss of tanks. The numbers of burned-out vehicles along the roadsides are the visible evidence of the American air supremacy. The lack of vehicles would be compensated by replacements from the *Luftwaffe* and other organisations which are not bearing the brunt of the fighting as are the land forces.

3.) Engagement of armoured forces in Normandy

The broken up nature of the terrain in Normandy, divided up by hedgerows, favours the use of infantry, and an immediate reinforcement of infantry divisions would guarantee success in the concentrated actions planned in co-operation with armoured forces. Where armour is engaged on the invasion front, the "armoured troops combat tactic" is employed, which involves the close association of small tank detachments with motorised grenadiers or normal infantry. This differs from the tactic of mass hithertoo employed and which can continue to be used in the majority of cases. This tactic is valuable insofar as the tank detachments are held in close proximity to the motorised infantry battalions mounted on half-tracks so that they can quickly assemble and reach their objectives at full speed. In that way the effect of mines and enemy anti-tank weapons are reduced to a minimum. Attacks can only be mounted at night although bad weather is another factor that reduces enemy air superiority.

This account of conditions favourable to small-scale operations is equally valid as a general rule, that is to say when the panzer divisions can be held in readiness to attack immediately when the occasion arises using the previously tried mass armoured assault tactic. It is unthinkable to go into an attack without a general reserve.

In conclusion, the decision to allot powerful infantry forces coming from other sectors of the front in the West, should be taken with a view to mounting a victorious offensive. In addition, the support of our air forces must be assured at the moment of attack.

4). The newly arrived armoured divisions and detachments must be trained in the conditions pertaining to the engagement of tanks against the enemy as well as in anti-aircraft defence.

5). Enemy fighting strength

The morale and leadership shown by the adversary up until now has been good. All the enemy successes have been achieved by a crushing abundance of materiel, in particular in aviation and artillery including naval gunfire.

The following new weapons have been encountered : 1.) The Cromwell tank with a 9.2 or 7.62 cm gun.
                                              2.) M4A4 medium tank (General Sherman)
                                              3.) Tank fitted with a 12cm rocket-launcher
                                              4.) 5.7 cm anti-tank gun firing a fused shell
                                              5.) 9.2cm anti-tank gun.

These weapons were not a surprise and can be combated with our available weapons.

6.) <u>Re-supply</u>

To improve the situation, the following measures have been decided upon.

a) The stockage points and the re-supply routes will be guarded by a security battalion which will be set up by the General Inspector of Armoured Troops.

b) Energetic commanders for the re-supply columns will be put in place by the General Inspector to ensure the rapid achievement of re-supply.

c) The maintenance situation will be improved by the setting up of advanced spare parts depots.

d) The transfer of an army repair battalion from the East to the West is necessary.

e) The losses of vehicles caused by enemy aircraft can be compensated by aggressive requisitioning in France.

f) The diversion routes around places completely ruined by bombing are well sign-posted, but nevertheless need to be constantly controlled.

7.) <u>The evacuation</u> of the civilian population needs to be undertaken energetically.

8.) The following suggestion has been made by the troops, that they be supplied with devices to simulate a fire and a cloud of black smoke. The idea came from our tank crews after an attack on a vehicle by a fighter-bomber, the destruction of which was thus simulated.

9.) <u>Technical details</u>

a.) The Marks IV, V and VI tanks have performed well, but the Panther catches fire very quickly and in an astonishing way. The engine life of the Panther (1.400 - 1.500 km) is far higher than that of their transmissions. A speedy solution is necessary.

b.) The fixing of the side protection plates (skirts) needs to be done in a more solid manner on account of the *bocage* terrain.

c.). An extra plate of armour has been asked for rapidly by the crews because of attack by enemy aircraft. This is not considered to be a good idea as it would increase tank weight which in the case of the German models, is too high already.

d) In the compartmentalised Normandy countryside the rate of fire of the light tank-destroyers and assault guns is considered to be too feeble (commander of the Panzer Lehr Tank-Destroyer Battalion).

Bibliography

The battle of Normandy

BELFIELD, Eversley ; ESSAME, Hubert. *Normandie, été 1944*. Paris, Presses de la Cité, 1966.

BEDARIDA, François (sous la direction de). *Normandie 44*. Paris, Albin Michel, 1987.

BENAMOU, Jean-Pierre. *La bataille de Caen*. Bayeux, Heimdal, 1988.

BENAMOU, Jean-Pierre; BERNAGE, Georges ; GRENNEVILLE, Régis. *Normandie, album mémorial*. Bayeux, Heimdal, 1991.

BENAMOU, Jean-Pierre ; BERNAGE, Georges. *Goodwood : bombardement géant brise-panzers*. Bayeux, Heimdal, 1994.

BENAMOU, Jean-Pierre ; BERNAGE, Georges ; MARI, Laurent *et al*. *Bataille de Normandie*. Bayeux, Heimdal, 1993.

BERNAGE, Georges. *Les Canadiens face à la Hitlerjugend : 7 au 9 juin 1944*. Bayeux, Heimdal, 1991.

- *Mourir pour l'Abbaye d'Ardenne. Buron la sanglante : 7 juin au 8 juillet 1944*. Bayeux, Heimdal, 1992.

BLUMENSON, Martin. *Libération*. Condé-sur-Noireau, Charles Corlet éditeur, 1993.

BUFFETAUX, Yves. *Les blindés alliés en Normandie*. Paris, Hors-série Militaria-magazine, 1991.

CARELL, Paul. *Ils arrivent !* Paris, Robert Laffont, 1994.

COMPAGNON, Jean. *Le débarquement en Normandie, victoire stratégique de la guerre*. Rennes, Ouest France, 1984.

ELLIS, L.F. *Victory in the West : the battle of Normandy*. Londres, Her Majesty's Stationery Office, 1962.

ESTE, Carlo d'. *Decision in Normandy*. New-York, Harper Perennial, 1991.

GRANDAIS, Albert. *La bataille du Calvados*. Paris, Presses de la Cité, 1973.

KEEGAN, John. *Six armées en Normandie*. Paris, Albin Michel, 1992.

LE CACHEUX, Geneviève ; QUELLIEN, Jean. *Dictionnaire de la Libération du Nord-Ouest*. Condé-sur-Noireau, Charles Corlet éditeur, 1994.

LIDDELL HART, Sir Basil. *Histoire militaire de la Seconde Guerre mondiale*. Paris, Fayard, 1970.

MAC KEE, Alexandre. *La bataille de Caen*. Paris, Presses de la Cité, 1965.

MASSON, Philippe. *Une guerre totale, 1939-1945 : stratégies, moyens, controverses*. Paris, Tallandier, 1990.

- (sous la direction de). *La Seconde Guerre mondiale : campagnes et batailles*. Paris, Larousse, 1992.

- (sous la direction de). *La Seconde Guerre mondiale : les acteurs*. Paris, Larousse, 1992.

MORDAL, Jacques. *La bataille de France*. Paris, Arthaud, 1964.

OSE, Dieter. *Entscheidung im Westen, 1944 : der Oberbefehlshaber West und die Abwehr der alliierter Invasion*. Stuttgart, DVA, 1982.

PIPET, Albert. *D'Omaha à Saint-Lô : la bataille des haies*. Bayeux, Heimdal, 1980.

- *Mourir à Caen*. Paris, Presses de la Cité, 1974.

QUELLIEN, Jean. *La Normandie au coeur de la guerre*. Rennes, Ouest France, 1992.

RUGE, Friedrich. *Rommel face au débarquement : 1944*. Paris, Presses de la Cité, 1960.

SHULMAN, Milton. *La défaite allemande à l'Ouest*. Paris, Payot, 1948.

STACEY, C.P. *La campagne de la victoire*. Ottawa, Ottawa King's Printer, 1966.

WILMOT, Chester. *La lutte pour l'Europe*. Paris, Fayard, 1953.

The German armoured units

AGTE, Patrick. *Tiger : le bataillon de chars lourds de la Leibstandarte*. Bayeux, Heimdal, 1996.

BENDER, R.J. ; TAYLOR, H.P. *Uniforms, organization and history of the Waffen-SS*. San Jose, R.J. Bender Publishing, 5 volumes.

BERNAGE, Georges ; MEYER, Hubert. *12. SS-Panzer-Division « Hitlerjugend »*. Bayeux, Heimdal, 1991.

BERNAGE, Georges ; LANNOY, François de. *Dictionnaire historique. Les divisions de l'Armée de Terre allemande*. Bayeux, Heimdal, 1997.

BERNAGE, Georges ; LANNOY, François de. *Dictionnaire historique. La Luftwaffe, la Waffen-SS*. Bayeux, Heimdal, 1998.

BERNAGE, Georges ; PERRIGAULT, Jean-Claude ; MAC NAIR, Ronald *et al*. *Leibstandarte SS : la garde personnelle d'Adolf Hitler au combat*. Bayeux, Heimdal, 1996.

BUFFETAUX, Yves. *Les Panzer en Normandie*. Paris, Hors-série Militaria-magazine, 1991.

COLLECTIF. *3. Kompanie*. Amicale de la 3./SS-Pz.Rgt. 12.

FÜRBRINGER, Herbert. *9. SS-Panzer-Division « Hohenstaufen »*. Bayeux, Heimdal, 1984.

HASTINGS, Max. *La division « Das Reich » et la Résistance, 8 juin-20 juin 1944*. Paris, Pygmalion, 1983.

JENTZ, Thomas. *Panzer-Truppen : the complete guide to the creation and combat employment of germany's tank force, 1933-1945*. 2 vol. Atglen, Schiffer Military History, 1996.

KLEINE, Egon ; KÜHN, Volkmar. *Tiger : die Geschichte einer legendären Waffe, 1942-1945*. Stuttgart, Motorbuch Verlag, 1976.

KORTENHAUS, Werner. *Die Geschichte der 21. Panzer-Division, 1943-1945*. Forthcoming.

KUROWSKI, Franz. *Die Panzer-Lehr-Division*. Bad Nauheim, Podzun-verlag, 1964.

LEFEVRE, Eric. *Les panzers, Normandie 1944*. Bayeux, Heimdal, 1978.

LEHMANN, Rudolf ; TIEMANN, Ralf. *Die Leibstandarte.* 6 vol. Osnabrück, Munin Verlag, 1977-1987.

LELEU, Jean-Luc. *10. SS-Panzer-Division « Frundsberg ».* Bayeux, Heimdal, 1999.

LUCK, Hans von. *Panzer commander.* New York, Praeger Publishers, 1989.

MAC NAIR, Ronald. *1944. Les panzers : les divisions de panzers du Heer.* Bayeux, Heimdal, 1991.

- *1944. Les panzers : les divisons de panzers SS et les bataillons indépendants.* Bayeux, Heimdal, 1992.

MEYER, Kurt. *Soldats du Reich.* Bayeux, Heimdal, 1996.

PERRIGAULT, Jean-Claude. *La Panzer-Lehr-Division.* Bayeux, Heimdal, 1995.

SCHNEIDER, Wolfgang. *Tigers in combat.* Manitoba, J.J. Fedorowicz Publishing Inc., 1994.

STEINZER, Franz. *Die 2. Panzer-Division, 1935-1945.* Friedberg, Podzun-Pallas-Verlag.

STÖBER, Hans. *Die Sturmflut und das Ende : Geschichte der 17. SS-Pz.Gren.Div. « Götz von Berlichingen ».* 2 vol. Osnabrück, Munin Verlag, 1976.

TIEKE, Wilhelm. *Im Feuersturm letzer Kriegsjahre.* Osnabrück, Munin Verlag, 1975.

VERWICHT, Alain. *La 21. Panzer-Division, 1.6.1944.* Panzer Voran, Hors-série n°1. Saint-Boes, à compte d'auteur.

WEIDINGER, Otto. *Division « Das Reich ».* 6 vol. Osnabrück, Munin Verlag, 1967-1982.

WEINGARTNER, James. *Hitler's guard : the story of the Leibstandarte SS Adolf Hitler, 1933-1945.* Nashville, Battery Classics.

Eye-witness accounts

The author received accounts from the following participants in the battle. An asterix indicates that the interview was carried out on the actual site of the particular engagement described :

Willi Fey, Willi Fischer, Heinz Freiberg, Otto Funk (*), Reinhold Fuss (*), Günther Gotha, Leopold Heindl, Georg Isecke, Heinz-Hermann Lammers, Hans von Luck (*), Otto Meier (*), Hubert Meyer (*), Fritz Porochnowitz, Rudolf von Ribbentrop, Hans Siegel (*), Heinz Schiemann, Willi Schwarz, Manfred Stephan, Herbert Walther (*).

Photo Credits

Federal German Archive - Koblenz

76/100/9 (54) ; 297/1722/28 (1); 297/1725/11 (31) ; 297/1725/16 (32) ; 297/1725/17 (33) ; 297/1725/19 (31) ; 297/1725/20(33) ; 297/1725/22 (30) ; 297/1725/37 (31) ; 297/1726/5 (33) ; 297/1726/6 (32) ; 297/1726/9 (33) ; 297/1726/13 (32) ; 297/1726/20 (30) ; 297/1726/25 (30) ; 297/1740/19a (26) ; 298/1759/25 (104) ; 298/ 1761/19 (105) ; 298/1761/25 (105) ; 298/1761/32 (104) ; 299/1802/20a (95) ; 299/1804/4 (83) ; 299/1804/12 (83) ; 299/1804/15 (83) ; 299/1805/9 (82) ; 299/1805/23 (82) ; 299/1818/5 (95) ; 299/1818/6 (95) ; 299/1818/7 (95) ; 300/1876/2a (125) ; 300/1876/3a (125) ; 300/1876/7a (125) ; 493/3354/2a (23) ; 493/3355/10 (23) ; 493/3355/24 (6) ; 493/3356/5(7) ; 493/3356/7 (7) ; 493/3358/34a (139) ; 493/3359/27 (140) ; 493/3365/27 (4) ; 721/364/6 (141) ; 721/378/24 (3) ; 721/378/28 (3) ; 721/378/33 (3) ; 721/395/3 (122) ; 721/395/21 (122) ; 721/395/22 (123) ; 738/267/18a (94) ; 738/ 271/8 (108) ; 738/275/9a (94) ; 738/275/10a (94) ; 738/287/36a (157) ; R82/III/31a (11).

Imperial War Museum - London

B5375 (57) ; B5376 (57) ; B5525 (96) ; B5441 (57) ; B5446 (57) ; B5768 (98) ; B5769 (98) ; B5770 (98) ; B5780 (96) ; B5783 (96) ; B5784 (97) ; B6043 (108) ; B6045 (120) ; B6046 (120) ; B6047 (121) ; B6050 (121) ; B6053 (47) ; B6055 (113) ; B6226 (120) ; B6343 (137) ; B6348 (137) ; B7598 (114) ; B7054 (136) ; B7056 (136) ; B7057 (136) ; B7666 (144) ; B7675 (144) ; B7752 (140) ; B8028 (142) ; B8029 (142) ; B8030 (141) ; B8032 (141) ; B8377 (81).

Calvados Departmental Archive

10Fi 138 (147) ; 10Fi 368 (99) ; 10Fi 447 (145).

Glossary of abbreviations

A.A.   Aufklärungs-Abteilung *(reconnaissance battalion)*

Abt.   Abteilung *(battalion or similar sized detachment)*

A.K.   Armee-Korps *(Army Corps)*

AOK   Armeeoberkommando *(état-major d'armée)*

Art.   Artillerie *(artillery)*

Aufkl.   Aufklärung *(reconnaissance)*

Ausb.   Ausbildung *(training)*

Brig.   Brigade *(brigade)*

Btl.   Bataillon *(battalion)*

Div.   Division *(division)*

Fallsch.   Fallschirm *(airborne or parachutist)*

F.H.   Feldhaubitze *(field howitzer)*

Flak   Fliegerabwehrkanone *(anti-aircraft defence or weapon)*

gep.   gepanzert *(armoured)*

Gren.   Grenadier *(motorised infantry)*

H.Gr. B   Heeresgruppe B *(Army Group B)*

HJ   Hitlerjugend *(Hitler Youth)*

Ia   1.Generalstabsoffizier *(Operations officer)*

I.D.   Infanterie-Division *(infantry division)*

I.G.   Infanterie-Geschütz *(infantry field gun)*

Inf.   Infanterie *(infantry)*

Inst.   Instandsetzung *(repair and maintenance)*

K.   Kanone *(canon or gun)*

Kgr.   Kampfgruppe *(battle group)*

Kp.   Kompanie *(compagny)*

Kradsch.   Kradschütze *(motorcycle dispatch-rider)*

KWK   Kampfwagenkanone *(tank gun)*

l.   leicht *(light)*

LSSAH   Leibstandarte SS Adolf Hitler *(1st SS Pz.Div. Hitlers guard unit)*

Lw.Feld-Div.   Luftwaffen-Feld-Division *(Luftwaffe field division)*

M.G.   Maschinengewehr *(machine-gun)*

mot.   motorisiert *(motorised)*

O.B.   Oberbefehlshaber *(supreme commander)*

Ob.West   Oberbefehlshaber West *(Supreme Commander West)*

OKH   Oberkommando des Heeres *(Army High Command)*

OKW   Oberkommando der Wehrmacht *(Wehrmacht High Command)*

Pak   Panzerabwehrkanone *(anti-tank gun)*

Pi.   Pionier *(pioneer or engineer)*

Pz.   Panzer *(tank or armoured)*

Pz.Gren.Rgt.   Panzergrenadierregiment *(motorised infantry regiment)*

Pz.Jäg.   Panzer-Jäger *(tank-destroyer unit or vehicle)*

Pz.Kpfw.   Panzerkampfwagen *(armoured fighting vehicle)*

RAF   Royal Air Force *(Royal Air Force)*

Rgt.   Regiment *(régiment)*

s.   schwer *(heavy)*

Sd.Kfz.   Sonderkraftfahrzeug *(armoured car)*

Sfl.   Selbstfahrlafette *(self propelled gun chassis)*

SPW   Schützenpanzerwagen *(armoured personnel carrier)*

SS   Schutzstaffel *(Nazi guard unit)*

Stu.Gesch.
(ou StuG.)   Sturmgeschütz *(assault-gun)*

WFSt   Wehrmachtsführungsstab *(Wehrmacht operational staff)*

Index of places mentioned in the text *

* Incidentally numbers corresponds to the French department numbers.

TABLE OF COMPARTIVE RANKS

Armée allemande	Abréviation	Waffen-SS	Abréviation	British Army
Grenadier	Sch.	SS-Grenadier	SS-Gren.	Private
Obergrenadier	Osch.	SS-Obergrenadier	SS-Ob.Gren.	Private
Gefreiter	Gefr.	SS-Sturmmann	SS-Strmm.	Lance Corporal
Obergefreiter	Ogfr.	SS-Rottenführer	SS-Rttf.	Corporal
Unteroffizier	Uffz.	SS-Unterscharführer	SS-Uscha.	Sergeant
Unterfeldwebel	Ufw.	SS-Scharführer	SS-Scharf.	Staff Sergeant
Feldwebel	Fw.	SS-Oberscharführer	SS-Oscha.	Warrant Officer 2
Oberfeldwebel	Ofw.	SS-Hauptscharführer	SS-Hscha.	Warrant Officer 2
Stabsfeldwebel	Stfw.	SS-Sturmscharführer	SS-Stuscha.	Warrant Officer 1
Oberfähnrich	Ofhn.	SS-Standarten-Oberjunker	SS-Std.Ob.Ju.	Officer Cadet
Leutnant	Lt.	SS-Untersturmführer	SS-Ustuf.	Second Lieutenant
Oberleutnant	Oblt.	SS-Obersturmführer	SS-Ostuf.	Lieutenant
Hauptmann	Hptm.	SS-Hauptsturmführer	SS-Hstuf.	Captain
Major	Maj.	SS-Sturmbannführer	SS-Stubaf.	Major
Oberstleutnant	Obslt.	SS-Obersturmbannführer	SS-Ostubaf.	Lieutenant Colonel
Oberst		SS-Standartenführer	SS-Staf.	Colonel
-	-	SS-Oberführer	SS-Obf.	(no equivalent)
Generalmajor	Gen.Maj.	SS-Brigadeführer	SS-Brigf.	Brigadier
Generalleutnant	Gen.Lt.	SS-Gruppenführer	SS-Gruf.	Major General
General der Inf., der Art., ...	Ge.d.Inf., d.Art., ...	SS-Obergruppenführer	SS-Ogruf.	Lieutenant General
Generaloberst	Gen.Oberst	SS-Oberstgruppenführer	SS-Oberstgruf.	General
General-Feldmarschall	GFM			Field Marshal

Note : In the German army, the branch of the service was often attached to a soldier's rank, but the generic term *grenadier* was applied to the ordinary infantryman from November 1942. Within the armoured troops, a 2nd class private was known as a *Panzerschuetze* and a 1st class private was a *Panzerroberschuetze*.